DataCAD for Architects & Designers

DataCAD for Architects & Designers

Carol Buehrens

McGraw-Hill, Inc.

New York San Francisco Washington, D.C. Auckland Bogotá
Caracas Lisbon London Madrid Mexico City Milan
Montreal New Delhi San Juan Singapore
Sydney Tokyo Toronto

pbk   1 2 3 4 5 6 7 8 9 BBC/BBC 9 9 8 7 6 5

Library of Congress Cataloging-in-Publication Data
Buehrens, Carol.
    DataCAD for architects & designers / by Carol Buehrens.
      p.   cm.
    Includes index.
    ISBN 0-07-008914-0 (pbk.)
    1. DataCAD.   2. Architectural design—Data processing.
  3. Architectural drawing—Data processing.   I. Title.   II. Title:
  DataCAD for architects and designers.
  NA2728.B83   1995
  720'.28'402855369—dc20   95-3073
                                                              CIP

Acquisitions editor: Brad J. Schepp
Editorial team: Robert E. Ostrander, Executive Editor
                    Sally A. Glover, Book Editor

Contents

Chapter 2: Beginning DataCAD   25

Chapter 3: Basic floor plans   49

Chapter 4: Adding symbols   73

Chapter 5: Viewing your drawing in 3D 95

Chapter 6: Adding dimensions and notes 115

Chapter 7: Plotting and printing your drawing   137

Chapter 8: Setting up a site plan default drawing   155

Chapter 9: Site Plans   171

Chapter 10: Copying techniques   193

Chapter 11: Setting up detail default drawings   225

Chapter 12: Drawing Details   255

Chapter 13: Creating templates and symbols   295

Chapter 14: Modeling walls, openings and roofs 317

Chapter 15: Modeling windows and doors 349

Answers to exercises   363

Index   367

About the author   379

Acknowledgments

This book was designed and produced entirely in desktop publishing using Adobe PageMaker 5.0, for both text editing and layout. All illustrations were drawn with DataCAD and transferred into PageMaker using plot files in HPGL format.

I wish to thank Bob and Claudia Martin, owners of *Key Solutions Magazine*, for testing the projects in this book.

A special thanks to my husband, Karl, who puts up with his writer-wife (who sometimes doesn't leave her computers for days, sitting transfixed at the keyboard, wearing her *writer's uniform*; a bathrobe, sweatshirt and sweatpants). Honey, I swear I'll brush my hair and put makeup on today.

And to my children, Adam and Lora, who didn't argue as much as they would have liked to while I was in my office, - hugs and kisses.

Introduction

DataCAD is a highly sophisticated software program that, through the help of expert programmers and architects, is easy to learn and use. This means that, as a beginning user, you can draw your project with ease after only limited experience. And, as an expert user, you'll want to explore advanced options and techniques, also available to you in an easy-to-use format.

DataCAD provides everything you need to complete your production drawings. You can also model design studies and create three-dimensional client presentations. And there are macros that allow you to gain productivity and efficiency. For example, one macro allows you to easily create three dimensional framed windows. Another automatically creates a complete three-dimensional framing model for cut lists and material cost estimating.

DataCAD for Architects & Designers is an easy-to-follow guide for the beginning user. Each chapter contains fully illustrated, step-by-step procedures to complete a series of architectural projects. You'll learn production drafting techniques, symbol creation, site planning, and three-dimensional modeling. Along the way, you'll acquire the skills needed to become a proficient and expert user of the Data-CAD program.

Each chapter (except for the installation chapter), closes with a multiple choice, reinforcement exercise. This is a tool for your use, reminding you of what you've learned and important facts to remember. The answers are found in the appendix, but don't cheat!

Good luck with DataCAD! I'm sure you'll agree with me that it's a great product for today's architect.

CHAPTER 1

Installing and configuring DataCAD

The DataCAD software

This chapter explains how to successfully install the DataCAD software, and how to configure it for your computer. If you've already installed it but still have a few questions concerning the configuration process, this chapter will be helpful.

Here are some of the things you'll learn in this chapter:

- Minimum computer system requirements.
- Installing DataCAD.
- How much hard disk space DataCAD requires.
- Use of the configuration software.
- Installing the plotter and printer drivers.
- Selecting the graphics card drivers.
- Setting up display list processing.

The DataCAD installation manual

When you purchased DataCAD, you received a complete set of reference manuals. One of these manuals, *Up and Running* (previously called *Getting Started*), contains valuable information pertaining to the installation of your system. It's recommended you read this before continuing.

DataCAD software description

The DataCAD installation disks have six main software parts. These are: the DataCAD basic software, online help documentation, DCAL programming language, RenderStar, DC Print (DataCAD's printer utility program), and a complete bundle of symbol libraries.

Each one of these parts requires a certain amount of hard disk space, so you'll want to make sure you have not only enough space to load them, but also extra room to run your software and create drawings. (If you also use Windows, you'll want to keep at least 10KB free to run it.) The hard disk space requirements are displayed with each option during the installation program, and are also listed here.

You must, of course, load the *basic DataCAD software* to get started, along with the driver for your graphics card. The other parts of DataCAD are options. You could load them now or later. The installation disks allow you to add on the options when you want, by simply selecting a menu choice. When loading the basic software, you should have at least 15MB (megabytes) of hard disk space available. This number gives you a little space for a few drawings.

The *online help documentation* is very useful to the beginning user. It is also helpful to the experienced user who is upgrading to a new version of DataCAD, since it helps to explain the new features of the software. It takes 4.4MB to load on the hard disk.

The *DCAL* programming language is only used by individuals that want to program additional software for DataCAD. It is not necessary to load DCAL in order to run these programs. This book will not teach you how to program in DCAL. DCAL requires 3.2MB of hard disk space available.

RenderStar is an optional model rendering program. It requires 16.7MB of hard disk space available.

DC Print is a program that allows you to use your printer to create a plot of your drawing. It requires about 1/2MB of hard disk space to load. If you own a printer that has HPGL (Hewlett Packard Graphics Language) or PostScript, you don't have to use this software. DataCAD has special drivers that will allow you to run your HPGL/PostScript printer as if it were a plotter. DC Print is basically for any printer that doesn't have this capability. This book will explain how to use DC Print in Chapter 7, Plotting and Printing Your Drawing.

The *symbol libraries* (templates and symbols) require about 18MB of hard disk space to load. They are very extensive and include kitchens, bathroom plumbing, electrical symbols, etc. If you have more than one computer you're installing Data-CAD on, it would be wise to only load the symbols on one. Then, after checking the templates, either proceed with loading them on your other computers, or create your own templates, selecting any existing symbols you need from these templates and making new ones as necessary.

Other features

Display list

DataCAD also has a unique feature that allows you to operate a *graphics display list*. A "graphics display list," or just "display list," is a term used to describe a method of storing the graphics displayed on the screen (your drawing), in memory (computer chips) to make the computer operate faster. This means you'll be able to move your drawing on the screen quickly.

In other words, if you need to zoom into a part of your drawing (magnify an area) in order to see it better, the amount of time it takes to perform this operation is greatly reduced. For example, it could take 40 seconds to "zoom in" to a particular piece of your drawing. With a display list, this same zoom might take 5 seconds. Since you zoom in and out of a drawing constantly while working on it (perhaps once a minute), the display list saves a great amount of time. Display list processing requires a minimum 1MB of RAM (random access memory).

Quick Shader

DataCAD comes with a simple surface rendering package called *Quick Shader*. It appears as an option in DataCAD. It's quick and easy to use and will shade your drawing with 15 different colors using a light source. If you plan to later use the more powerful RenderStar software, the Quick Shader is a good tool to preview your model for correctness prior to using RenderStar. Quick Shader processing requires 1MB of RAM.

Computer system requirements

There is a certain set of requirements for DataCAD to run properly:

- 386 or 486 DOS (disk operating system) type computer (referred to as IBM compatible).

- Hard disk drive with at least 50MB free.

- High-density floppy disk drive.

- Serial port for a mouse, or a special mouse port.

- Pointing device, preferably a three-button mouse (track ball and *some* digitizer tablets will work.)

- If you own a 386 or 486SX, a math coprocessor is required.

- At least 4MB expanded memory.

- 640KB RAM with 530KB free.

- DOS 5.0 or greater.

- A VESA-type or other supported graphics card and a color monitor.

Optional:

- One parallel port for printer.

- One parallel or serial port for plotter.

- Printer.

- Plotter.

- Tape backup unit, internal or external.

Computer

The type of computer you own must be DOS or IBM compatible. Most generic DOS-type computers will work, as long as they're either a 386 or 486SX with a math coprocessor, or a 486DX or higher (math coprocessor is built in).

DataCAD won't run without the math coprocessor, not even slowly. But most computers in this category can be easily fitted with a math chip. This is called *upgrading*. Other upgrading options work well with DataCAD, such as changing out the motherboard to upgrade to a 486.

DOS

DataCAD is a DOS-driven software. Your computer must have DOS version 5 or greater.

Hard disk drive

The bigger the hard drive, the better. CAD uses a lot of hard drive space. You need about 50MB to install the complete

DataCAD software package. An average-size two-story residential set of drawings, with about 1800 square feet, might take 8 to 12MB of file space. Detail sheets can take more. Even if you're planning to off-load your projects (back them up and clean them off the hard drive), you'll want more than one on your computer at the same time, either for simultaneous working, showing clients, or to share design data.

You'll probably want to run Windows software, also. Windows itself requires around 20MB to install, and at least 10MB free to run. Adding a good writing software with fonts might take another 15MB. In summary, the biggest drive you can afford is the best drive. 300 to 500MB is a good start with today's software.

Memory

The amount of available RAM you have is very important. The amount of free conventional memory recommended is a minimum of 530KB. The more conventional memory you have (memory below the 640KB barrier), the faster DataCAD will run.

Expanded memory is used for both the Quick Shader rendering software and the display list feature. Quick Shader uses 2MB of expanded memory. The display list uses a minimum 1MB of expanded memory. However, both of these features are options that can be turned on and off as necessary.

Graphics card

It's important to get a good graphics card. Some are tremendously faster displaying graphics than others, which is essential since DataCAD is graphics intensive. However, you can buy a good card for a reasonable price.

Don't worry about spending extra for cards that have memory for display list graphics. DataCAD provides its own software for that. Don't spend extra for a graphics card that allows you to get multiple windows or bird's-eye-view windows. DataCAD doesn't support multiple windows.

If you do want to spend a little more to get a high-quality card, you might call CADKEY Inc. first. The support staff might be able to advise you on which high-priced cards are worth the money and which ones they're running.

Your CONFIG.SYS startup file

Before you run DataCAD, you'll want to set up some statements in your config.sys startup file. These settings control the way your system handles files and TSR drivers to optimize the operation of DataCAD. If you don't know how to set up your files using the DOS editor, have someone who is knowledgeable help you.

The minimum statement required in your config.sys file to run DataCAD is:

```
files=40
buffers=15
```

The following example uses the extended memory manager supplied with DOS 6.0, 8MB RAM, and a VESA-type graphics card. This is for your guidelines only and is not intended to be the only way a config.sys file can be structured or work in all circumstances:

```
device=c:\dos\himem.sys
dos=high,umb
device=c:\dos\emm386.exe 3072 ram
files=40
buffers=15
c:\dos\ramdrive.sys 3072 /e
```

First, this installs DOS 6 extended memory manager. Then it loads DOS into high memory and allows high-memory access. It sets up 3072K extended memory as expanded memory. The files and buffers are defined. Finally, a 3MB RAM disk is created in extended memory.

Your AUTOEXEC.BAT startup file

You'll also want to modify your autoexec.bat file. Again, if you don't know how to set up your files, have someone who is knowledgeable help you.

The minimum requirement is to add your mouse driver statement, as shown as an example below:

```
c:\mouse\mouse
```

The following example shows use of the smart drive disk-caching software supplied with DOS 6.0, 8MB RAM installed, and a VESA-type graphics card. Again, this is an example and not meant to work in all instances. Use an a guideline only:

```
path c:\dos
```

```
prompt $p$g
c:\dos\smartdrv 1024
c:\mouse\mouse
c:\vesa\vesa
```

This file creates a path statement to the DOS directory. Your path statement may have additional requirements. It instructs the DOS prompt to displays path and greater-than sign. For example, c:\dcad6>. Next, it installs 1MB disk cache using Smart Drive. Then it loads a typical mouse driver. Finally, it installs a VESA-type graphics card driver.

Getting ready to install DataCAD

If you have a working knowledge of computers and DOS, it would be extremely helpful. If this is the first time you ever used computers, you might want to ask someone to sit with you that has these qualifications. Then, follow these steps:

1. Write down the name of the graphics card in your computer. You'll need this name during the installation and to configure the driver.

2. Sit down at your computer. Turn it on and let it run through the boot-up process.

3. Organize the stack of DataCAD diskettes by you. Arrange them in order.

4. At the DOS prompt (C:), check the available hard drive space. You can do this by typing: **chkdsk** and pressing ENTER . This stands for Check Disk. Don't add any spaces to your command or it won't work. You can use either upper or lowercase letters.

5. If you're on a network, chkdsk won't work. Type in: **mem** and press ENTER .

6. Check that you have at least 15 to 20MB of available space (more if you run Windows, about 30). Fifteen will allow you to load the basic software. Fifty will allow you to load everything.

7. If you don't have that much free space, you might try checking if you have another partition that has more space. Type in **d:** and press ENTER .

8. If you have a D drive, your prompt will change from C to D. Try the **chkdsk** or **mem** commands again.

9. Make sure your mouse or other pointing device is connected to your computer.

10. DataCAD uses the mouse driver software that comes with the mouse. Follow the steps included with the mouse diskettes to install the mouse driver. If you don't know how to do this, have someone help you.

11. Run the mouse driver now. Make sure you add the mouse statement to your autoexec.bat program so that the driver is installed automatically next time you start your computer. If you don't know how to do this, have someone help you. The mouse driver *must* be loaded to work with DataCAD.

Installing DataCAD

Once you have the name of your graphics card, have checked your hard disk for space, and have installed the mouse, you're ready to go.

1. Place the first diskette, labeled 1, in the diskette drive. Close the drive door, if applicable.

2. If you put the diskette in the A: drive, type in **a:** and press [ENTER] .

3. If you put the diskette in the B: drive, type in **b:** and press [ENTER] .

4. Now type in **install** and press [ENTER] .

5. A CADKEY title screen appears, as shown in Figure 1.1. Press [ENTER] to continue.

```
Cadkey - Installation Utility


Cadkey, Inc.
Windsor, Connecticut (USA)
Copyright (c) 1984-1994
All rights reserved




Press any key to continue, or press the [Esc] key to abort...
```

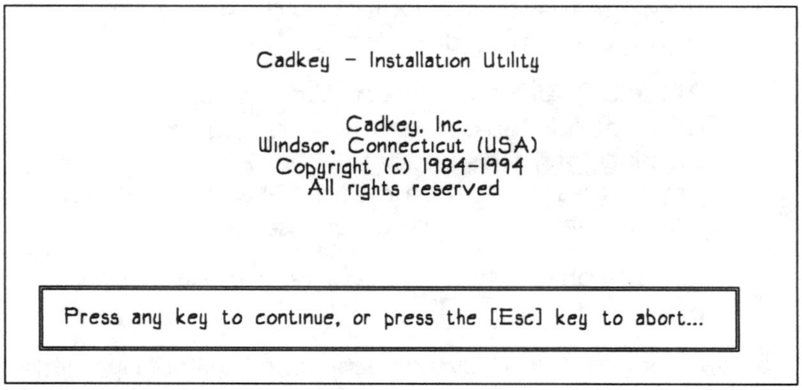

Figure 1.1: The installation title screen.

Note: *The installation procedure can be halted at any time by pressing the* [ESC] *key.*

---

6. A screen is displayed that further explains the installation procedure, as shown in Figure 1.2. Press [ENTER] to continue.

```
┌─────────────────────────────────────────────────────────────────┐
│                                                                   │
│  This program installs DataCAD Version 6.00 on your computer      │
│  system and verifies the integrity of the distribution files.     │
│  It asks you several questions about your computer hardware and   │
│  then gives you the option of installing only selected parts of   │
│  DataCAD (such as the DataCAD Program).                           │
│                                                                   │
│                                                                   │
│   ┌───────────────────────────────────────────────────────────┐  │
│   │ Press any key to continue, or press the [Esc] key to abort...│  │
│   └───────────────────────────────────────────────────────────┘  │
└───────────────────────────────────────────────────────────────────┘
```

Figure 1.2: The installation procedure is explained.

7. A installation choice menu appears, as shown in Figure 1.3. You can install the basic DataCAD software only, or some of the modules, which includes DCAL, DC Print, all templates and symbols, and RenderStar. You can also elect to install ALL.

```
┌─────────────────────────────────────────────────────────────────┐
│                                                                   │
│  Now you need to select the parts of DataCAD you want to install. │
│                                                                   │
│   ┌───────────────────────────────────────────────────────────┐  │
│   │ Install All files - 49.1M Bytes                      YES   │  │
│   │ Install DataCAD - 11.3M Bytes                        NO    │  │
│   │ Install DataCAD Online Documentation - 4.4M Bytes    NO    │  │
│   │ Install DCAL - 3.2M Bytes                            NO    │  │
│   │ Install RenderStar 2 - 16.7M Bytes                   NO    │  │
│   │ Install DataCAD Printer Utility - 393K Bytes         NO    │  │
│   │ Install Symbol Libraries - 17.7M Bytes               NO    │  │
│   │ Install DataCAD Graphics Driver(s)                   NO    │  │
│   └───────────────────────────────────────────────────────────┘  │
│                                                                   │
│  Use the [Up Arrow], [Down Arrow], [PgUp], & [PgDn] keys to move  │
│  the bar to the group(s) you wish to install and then press the   │
│  [Space] key to toggle the option from "No" to "Yes". Press       │
│  <Enter> when you have selected the option(s) you want to install.│
└───────────────────────────────────────────────────────────────────┘
```

Figure 1.3: The installation choice menu.

8. Listed with each choice is how much space the software will consume on your hard drive.

9. Pick one of the choice(s) you desire. As an example, you can choose to load:

    DataCAD
    Online Documentation
    Printer Utility
    Symbol Libraries
    Graphic Drivers

    To make these choices, move the highlight bar with the ⬆ and ⬇ keys. When the choice is highlighted, press the SPACE to toggle the **NO** to a **YES**. Remember, if you're not installing everything, toggle the "*Install All files*" choice to **NO**.

Your screen might look like Figure 1.4. You can always come back to this installation program and add something later.

```
Now you need to select the parts of DataCAD you want to install.

    ┌─────────────────────────────────────────────────────────────┐
    │ Install All files - 49.1M Btytes                         NO  │
    │ Install DataCAD - 11.3M Bytes                            YES │
    │ Install DataCAD Online Documentation - 4.4M Bytes        YES │
    │ Install DCAL - 3.2M Bytes                                NO  │
    │ Install RenderStar 2 - 16.7M Bytes                       NO  │
    │ Install DataCAD Printer Utility - 393K Bytes             YES │
    │ Install Symbol Libraries - 17.7M Bytes                   YES │
    │ Install DataCAD Graphics Driver(s)                       YES │
    └─────────────────────────────────────────────────────────────┘

Use the [Up Arrow], [Down Arrow], [PgUp], & [PgDn] keys to move the
bar to the group(s) you wish to install and then press the [Space] key
to toggle the option from "No" to "Yes". Press <Enter> when you
have selected the option(s) you want to install.
```

Figure 1.4: Selections made in the choice menu.

10. Once you've made your selections, press ENTER to continue.

11. A screen is displayed that shows the selections you've made for your confirmation, as in Figure 1.5. If it is correct, press ENTER to accept **YES**.

    If this screen reveals an error in your selections, press the SPACE to toggle the **YES** to **NO**, then press ENTER and change your selections.

```
            You will be installing:

                DataCAD Program files
                DataCAD Online Documentation
                DataCAD Printer Utility
                DataCAD Symbol Libraries
                DataCAD Graphics Driver


        Use the space bar to toggle between "Yes" and "No".


                ┌──────────────────────────┐
                │  Is this correct?   YES  │
                └──────────────────────────┘
```

Figure 1.5: Your selections are presented to you for confirmation.

If you're installing RenderStar:

12. If you chose RenderStar, the next screen asks you to indicate which parts of the RenderStar program you wish to install, as shown in Figure 1.6. Highlight your choice using the ↑ ↓ keys. Press the SPACE to toggle

the **NO** to **YES**. When you're through with your selections, press ⌜ENTER⌟ to continue.

```
You elected to install RenderStar, now please indicate which
part(s) of RenderStar you want to install.

If you are familiar with RenderStar 2 eXtension-24 you may
choose to install the Executable & Support files only.

Use the cursor up/down keys to move the lightbar and then
press the (Enter) key.

┌─────────────────────────────────────────────────────┐
│ Complete RenderStar installation - 16.7M bytes   YES │
│ Executable & Support files only - ??.?M bytes    NO  │
│ Sample & Tutorial files only - ??.?M bytes       NO  │
│ Texture files only - ??.?M bytes                 NO  │
│ RenderShell Screen Driver                        NO  │
│ Image Display Driver only                        NO  │
└─────────────────────────────────────────────────────┘
```

Figure 1.6: The RenderStar choice menu.

13.   The next screen displays the current drives and allows you to choose where you want DataCAD installed, as shown in Figure 1.7. If you want **C**, press ⌜ENTER⌟. If you want another drive, move the highlight bar using the ⌜↓⌟ key. Once the proper drive is highlighted, press ⌜ENTER⌟ to continue.

```
Choose the drive on which you want to install DataCAD.

                    ┌──────────────┐
                    │ Drive C:     │
                    │ Drive D:     │
                    │ Drive E:     │
                    └──────────────┘

Use the [Up Arrow], [Down Arrow], [PgUp], & [PgDn] to move the light-
bar to the disk drive on which you want to install and then press the
(Enter) key.
```

Figure 1.7: Select the drive for DataCAD.

14.   Now you're asked for the name of the directory for your DataCAD software, as in Figure 1.8. The default is **\DCAD6**. To accept this, press ⌜ENTER⌟.

Note: \DCAD6 is the recommended path name and it appears throughout this book. However, if you desire a different name, type in the name you wish and press ⌜ENTER⌟. Make a note of the name change for your later reference.

```
Enter the name you want for your DataCAD subdirectory. This
subdirectory is the location on your disk where DataCAD will reside.



Which subdirectory ((Enter) = \DCAD6)?

  \DCAD6
```

Figure 1.8: The DataCAD directory path screen.

15. The program now displays where the software will be installed. For the most part, this will be **\dcad6** or the name you indicated, as shown in Figure 1.9. Press `ENTER` to accept **YES**. Or, if you've changed your mind or there is an error, press the `SPACE` to toggle the answer to **NO**, press `ENTER` and make your changes in the previous screen.

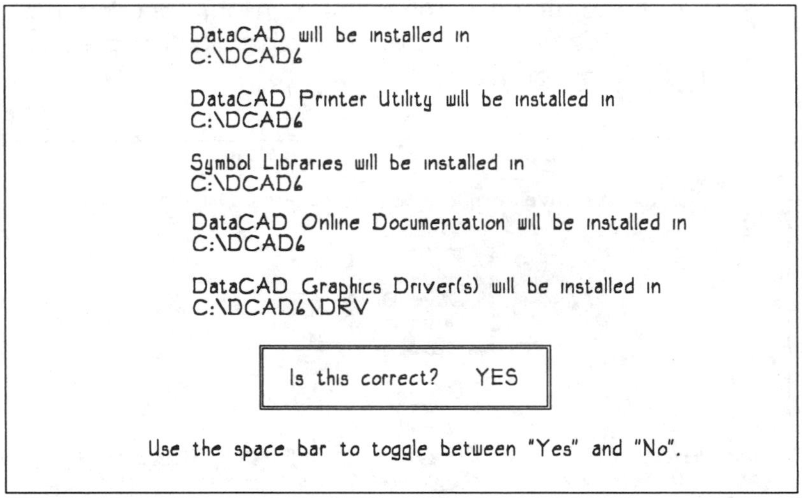

```
DataCAD will be installed in
C:\DCAD6

DataCAD Printer Utility will be installed in
C:\DCAD6

Symbol Libraries will be installed in
C:\DCAD6

DataCAD Online Documentation will be installed in
C:\DCAD6

DataCAD Graphics Driver(s) will be installed in
C:\DCAD6\DRV

        ┌─────────────────────────────┐
        │  Is this correct?    YES    │
        └─────────────────────────────┘

Use the space bar to toggle between "Yes" and "No".
```

Figure 1.9: The directory paths.

16. At this point, the program asks you to identify the graphics driver you want to install, as shown in Figure 1.10. If your selection is shown here, press the `↓` key to highlight it, then press `ENTER`.

17. If your selection is not shown here, highlight the **Other (Advanced Options)** choice, and press `ENTER`. A list of other graphics cards are displayed. Press `PG DN` to scroll forward through the list. When you find the correct driver, press `↑` or `↓` key to highlight, then press `ENTER`.

```
Please select one of the following displays to use as your initial
DataCAD and RenderStar configuration. Selecting "Other" will allow
you to select from a list of supported graphics adapters for both
DataCAD and RenderStar and run DataCAD's Configuration Utility at
the end of this installation to allow fine tuning of your system's
configuration.

        IBM VGA Compatible should work in 90% of all systems.

    ┌────────────────────────────────────────────────────────┐
    │  IBM VGA Compatible - 640x480 - 16 Colors               │
    │  VESA Compatible - 800x600 - 16 Colors                  │
    │  VESA Compatible - 800x600 - 256 Colors                 │
    │  VESA Compatible - 1024x768 - 256 Colors                │
    │  Tseng Labs ET4000 - 256 Colors                         │
    │  Tseng Labs ET4000 Sierra Hi-Color - 256 Colors         │
    │  Other (Advanced Options)                               │
    └────────────────────────────────────────────────────────┘

        Use the (Up Arrow) and (Down Arrow) keys to move the
        lightbar to the graphics driver you want to select.
```

Figure 1.10: Selection your graphics card.

18. Now a picture is displayed, requesting that you take the time to fill out the software registration card. Press `ENTER` to continue.

Note: *Sending in your registration card is important. You'll receive timely information about your software and a free subscription to Key Solutions magazine.*

---

19. If you choose to install DataCAD, there will be some files loaded at this point, as shown in Figure 1.11.

```
Installing DataCAD - Please wait ...

Decompressing: CONFIG.EXE

Verifying: C:\DCAD6\CONFIG.EXE

Decompressing: EMMSTAT.EXE

Verifying: C:\DCAD6\EMMSTAT.EXE

Decompressing: HPGLIII.DAT

Verifying: C:\DCAD6\HPGLIII.DAT

Reading: Library File --) RUNDCAD.BAT

Verifying: RUNDCAD.BAT
```

Figure 1.11: Files loading from the installation diskette.

20. You'll be instructed to insert the diskettes required to install the software you selected, as shown in Figure 1.12. Follow the instructions, putting in the proper diskettes requested and pressing `ENTER` to continue.

```
Installing DataCAD - Please wait ...

Decompressing: CONFIG.EXE

Verifying: C:\DCAD6\CONFIG.EXE

Decompressing: EMMSTAT.EXE

Ve  ┌────────────────────────────────────────────────────────┐
    │ Please place the disk labeled 'DISK 2 OF 12' in drive B: │
De  │ Press any key to continue, or press the [Esc] key to abort ... │
    └────────────────────────────────────────────────────────┘

Verifying: C:\DCAD6\HPGLIII.DAT

Reading: Library File --> RUNDCAD.BAT

Verifying: RUNDCAD.BAT
```

Figure 1.12: Requesting the next diskette.

21. You could halt the installation program by pressing [ESC] when you're prompted for a new diskette. This would result in an incomplete installation and you would only do this if you wanted to start over.

Configuring DataCAD

If you selected *Other* when choosing the graphics card, the configuration program will begin automatically. Otherwise, you'll receive the "Thank-you" screen and you'll exit at the DOS prompt. Either way, you should configure your Data-CAD system now.

1. If the DOS prompt is displayed (c:\dcad6>), type in: **config** and press [ENTER]. The DataCAD Configuration Utility's main menu is displayed, as in Figure 1.13.

```
┌─────────────────────────────────┐
│ Select item to change           │
│                                 │
│    1. Display device options    │      ┌──────────────────────┐
│    2. Digitizer options         │      │                      │
│    3. Plotter/printer options   │      │  Quick Shader Settings │
│    4. Path names                │      │                      │
│    5. Character set             │      │  Quick Shader is off. │
│    6. Default drawing name      │      │                      │
│    7. Screen colors             │      └──────────────────────┘
│                                 │
│ Esc: Exit                       │
│                                 │
│ Choice: 1_                      │
└─────────────────────────────────┘

┌── DataCAD Configuration Utility v6.00 ──┐
│                                          │
│  Current Settings                        │
│                                          │
│  IBM Personal Systems/2 - VGA Small Font │
│    640x480, 16 colors.                   │
│    New Menus (Left), No Display List, Single Monitor. │
│                                          │
│  #1 Hewlett Packard HP-GL. (Large "D" or "E" size) │
│  COM1:   9600 baud. No parity. 8 bits. Xon/Xoff │
└──────────────────────────────────────────┘
```

Figure 1.13: The main menu in the Configuration utility program.

2.	The upper-left box displays the menu options, as shown as 1 in Figure 1.14.

3.	The small middle box to the right is the status of the Quick Shader setting, as shown as 2 in Figure 1.14.

4.	The current default settings appear in the lower box, shown as 3 in Figure 1.14.

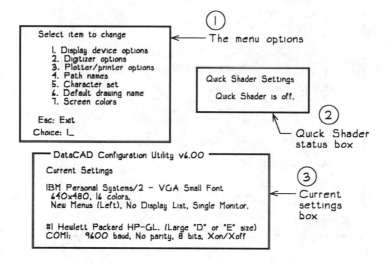

Figure 1.14: The main menu boxes explained.

5.	To highlight an option, move the highlight bar by pressing the ⬆ and ⬇ keys.

6.	To select the option, highlight it, then press ENTER .

7.	To exit a menu, press ESC .

Setting the graphics display options

1.	To select the display options, move the highlight bar to **Display device options**, using the ⬆ and ⬇ keys and press ENTER .

2.	The display device options appear, as in Figure 1.15.

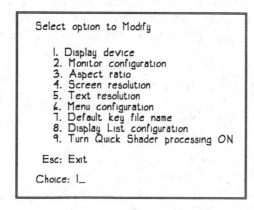

Figure 1.15: The display device options menu.

3. Select **Display device** by highlighting it and pressing [ENTER] .

4. The graphics card driver list is displayed, as in Figure 1.16.

```
Select display device   Page 1 of 2

      1. ATI VGA Wonder 256 color
      2. Compaq Portable Plasma Display
      3. DGIS compatibles
      4. IBM 8514/A - Register Direct
      5. IBM 8514/A - Requires HDILOAD
      6. IBM Color Graphics Adapter
      7. IBM Personal Systems/2 - MCGA
      8. IBM Personal Systems/2 - VGA
      9. IBM Personal Systems/2 - VGA Small Font
     10. Orchid ProDesigner VGA 16 color
     11. Orchid ProDesigner VGA 256 Color
     12. Paradise VGA Professional 16 Col
     14. Paradise VGA Professional 256 Col
     15. S3 86C911
     16. STB VGA EM 16 color

  PgDn: Next Page

   Esc: Exit

  Choice: 9_
```

Figure 1.16: The graphics card list.

5. Find your graphics card on the list. If you need to scroll forward through the list, press [PG DN] .

6. Once you find your driver, move the highlight bar to it and press [ENTER] . As an example, I chose **VESA compatible 16 color**.

7. If you don't find your graphics card on the list, try selecting the **IBM Personal Systems/2 - VGA**.

8. Now select the **Screen resolution option**.

9. The choices you're given are dependent on the graphics driver you selected, as shown in Figure 1.17 as an example. Select the choice that will give you the best resolution your graphics and monitor can display. As an example, I chose **800x600, 16 colors**.

```
Select graphics mode

      1. 800 x 600, 16 colors
      2. 1024 x 768, 16 colors

   Esc: Exit

  Choice: 1_
```

Figure 1.17: Some resolution choices.

Note: *If you are working in a particularly bright office, you might want to lower your resolution so that the lines are brighter and easier to see. Or your monitor might flicker at a high resolution (interlacing). If you pick a high resolution, and the lines are too dim to see (tiny pixel width results in skinnier lines) or you get flickering, refer back to this section to lower your resolution.*

To turn on the display list

1. Select the **Display List configuration** option.

2. With the display list turned off (the default), the menu appears as shown in Figure 1.18.

```
Select Display List Option

    I. Turn display list processing ON

  Esc: Exit

  Choice: I_
```

Figure 1.18: The display list menu when display list is turned off.

3. Select the **Turn display list processing ON** option. Now the menu appears as shown in Figure 1.19.

```
Select Display List Option

    I. Turn display list processing OFF
    2. Amount of EMS space to leave free (in kilobytes)
    3. Amount of disk space to leave free (in kilobytes)

  Esc: Exit

  Choice: I_
```

Figure 1.19: The display list menu when display list is turned on.

4. Select **Amount of EMS space to leave free**.

5. A menu appears with three choices, as shown in Figure 1.20. Select the correct choice for your setup of extended memory. For example, I selected **Use all available EMS**.

```
┌──────────────────────────────────────────────────┐
│                                                    │
│   Amount of EMS space to leave free (in kilobytes) │
│                                                    │
│      I. Do not use EMS at all                      │
│      2. Use all available EMS                      │
│      3. Enter amount of EMS to leave free (in kilobytes)│
│                                                    │
│   Esc: Exit                                        │
│                                                    │
│   Choice: 2_                                       │
│                                                    │
└──────────────────────────────────────────────────┘
```

Figure 1.20: The display list EMS menu.

6. Now select the **Amount of disk space to leave free**
    option.

7. A menu appears with three more choices, as shown in
    Figure 1.21. Select the correct choice for your set up.
    For example, I selected **Use all available disk**.

```
┌──────────────────────────────────────────────────┐
│                                                    │
│   Amount of disk space to leave free (in kilobytes)│
│                                                    │
│      I. Do not use disk at all                     │
│      2. Use all available disk                     │
│      3. Enter amount of disk to leave free (in kilobytes)│
│                                                    │
│   Esc: Exit                                        │
│                                                    │
│   Choice: 2_                                       │
│                                                    │
└──────────────────────────────────────────────────┘
```

Figure 1.21: The display list disk space menu.

8. Press [ESC] to exit the Display list options and return to
    the Display device options.

Turning Quick Shader on

If you have enough expanded memory to run Quick Shader
with display list processing (3MB), follow these steps. If you
don't, you can always turn off the display list before turning
on Quick Shader. If you turn it on, a TSR (terminate and stay
Resident) program, which grabs EMS space, is turned on
when you start DataCAD.

1. Select the **Turn Quick Shader processing ON** option
    in the Display options menu.

Setting up a printer and plotter

You can configure three different printer/plotter connections
at one time. This section will walk you through setting up a
printer (maybe you use it most often for check prints), a
plotter (for final output), and a "To File" setting (to send a file
to a plotting service, to use with DC Print, or to create an

HPGL file for desktop publishing). Of course, you can configure any combination you wish, but these three examples
should cover most situations.

The example will illustrate the following settings:

Plotter #1 = Printer
Plotter #2 = Plotter
Plotter# 3 = To File

1.   Select **Plotter/print options**. The three plotter choices
     are displayed, as in Figure 1.22.

```
Select plotter/printer to configure

   I. Plotter #I
   2. Plotter #2
   3. Plotter #3

   Esc: Exit

   Choice: 2_
```

Figure 1.22: The menu lists 3 plotter choices.

2.   Select the **Plotter #1** option. The Plotter parameter
     menu is displayed, as in Figure 1.23.

```
Select plotter #I parameter to change

   I. Select plotter
   2. Port
   3. Baud Rate
   4. Word size
   5. Parity
   6. Handshaking

   Esc: Exit

   Choice: 2_
```

Figure 1.23: The Plotter parameter menu.

3.   Select the **Select plotter** option.

4.   A list of plotters appears, as shown in Figure 1.24. Since
     this example is setting up a printer that is supported by
     a plotter driver, I chose **Hewlett Packard HP-GL.
     (LaserJet III version)**. You can scroll to the next page
     of this list by pressing [PG DN] .

```
┌─────────────────────────────────────────────────────┐
│  Select plotter   Page 1 of 2                         │
│                                                       │
│     1. CADKEY Uniplot Format. (Inches)                │
│     2. Calcomp 104x Alternative                       │
│     3. Calcomp 104x.                                  │
│     4. Calcomp 104x. Big Block Size                   │
│     5. Calcomp Electrostatic.                         │
│     6. Encapsulated Postscript (EPS)                  │
│     7. Enter SPI000.                                  │
│     8. Hewlett Packard HP-GL. (Large "D" or "E" size) │
│     9. Hewlett Packard HP-GL. (LaserJet III version)  │
│    10. Hewlett Packard HP-GL. (Small "A" thru "C" size)│
│    11. Hewlett Packard HP-GL. Large, RollFeed         │
│    12. Hewlett Packard HP-GL/2 (HPGL Command Set)     │
│    13. Hewlett Packard HP-GL/2 (HPGL/2 Command Set)   │
│    14. Houston Instruments (DMP), multi pen.          │
│    15. Houston Instruments (DMP), single pen.         │
│    16. Numonics.                                      │
│                                                       │
│   PgDn: Next Page                                     │
│                                                       │
│    Esc: Exit                                          │
│                                                       │
│   Choice: 9_                                          │
└─────────────────────────────────────────────────────┘
```

Figure 1.24: The list of plotters.

5.   Once you've made your selection, the setting is
       displayed in the **Current Settings box**, as shown in
       Figure 1.25.

```
┌─── DataCAD Configuration Utility v6.00 ──────────┐
│                                                   │
│  Current Settings                                 │
│                                                   │
│  VESA compatible 16 color                         │
│   800x600, 16 colors.                             │
│   New Menus (Left), Display List, Single Monitor. │
│                                                   │
│                                                   │
│  #1 Hewlett Packard HP-GL. (Large "D" or "E" size)│
│  COM1:   9600 baud, No parity, 8 bits, Xon/Xoff   │
└───────────────────────────────────────────────────┘
```

Figure 1.25: The Current Settings box updates to show choice.

6.   You'll notice the **Current Settings box** shows the baud
       rate, parity, bit, Xon/Xoff handshake default settings,
       and the port for this particular plotter. You'll want to
       set the correct port connection for your plotter/printer.

***

Note: If the port is defined as **COM1:**, in most likelihood your
mouse is also set to that port. You MUST change it, because
this conflict in settings would result in problems when running
DataCAD, especially if you tried to plot!

***

7.   Select the **Port** option.

8.   Choose the appropriate option for your plotter/printer.
       As an example, I chose **LPT1:** for my LaserJet connec-
       tion.

9. If your plotter/printer needs other adjustment to these settings, change them now.

10. Press [ESC] to go back to the three-plotter choice menu.

11. Select **Plotter #2**.

12. Select the **Select plotter option** again.

13. Set the second plotter choice you'll use. For example, I chose **Hewlett Packard HP-GL. (Large "D" or "E" size)**.

14. Pick **Port** and set the port to the appropriate connection for this plotter. As an example, I chose **COM1:**.

15. Check the other settings in the **Current Settings box**.

16. Press [ESC] to go back to the three-plotter choice menu.

17. This time, select **Plotter #3**.

18. Select the **Select plotter option** one more time.

19. Set the third plotter choice you'll use. For this example, I chose **CADKEY Uniplot Format. (Inches)** to plot with the DC Print utility.

Note: *If you're planning to use the DC Print utility, you MUST configure to CADKEY Uniplot Format. If you're planning to use a plotting service, you should configure to the Hewlett Packard HP-GL. (Large "D" or "E" size) or whatever your service requires. This last setting also works to create .plt files for desktop publishing.*

---

20. Select the **Port** option.

21. Select **FILE:**. This will automatically force you to create a file of your plot when you have plotter #3 selected.

Exiting the configuration program

1. Press [ESC] until the save menu is displayed, as in Figure 1.26.

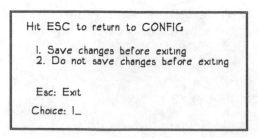

```
Hit ESC to return to CONFIG

    1. Save changes before exiting
    2. Do not save changes before exiting


    Esc: Exit

    Choice: 1_
```

Figure 1.26: The Save configuration menu.

2.   Press ENTER to accept the default **1** to **Save changes before exiting**.

3.   You'll return to the DOS prompt, C:\dcad6>.

Running DataCAD

You'll want to try running DataCAD to make sure everything works.

1.   Type in at the DOS prompt: **rundcad** and press ENTER .

2.   The DataCAD software should start, and the opening menu and drawing list should be displayed, as in Figure 1.27.

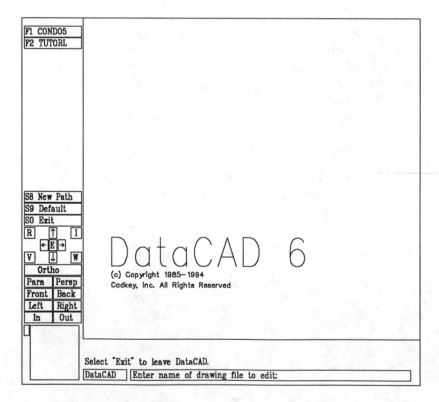

Figure 1.27: The DataCAD opening menu.

If DataCAD doesn't run

There might be many different reasons DataCAD doesn't run. Some common causes are listed here.

1. The mouse is not connected - If your mouse becomes loose at the connection, DataCAD cannot load. It looks for the mouse to start properly.

2. Mouse software isn't installed - You must run the mouse software prior to running DataCAD.

3. The VESA driver is not installed - If you have an older VESA card, a program must be copied onto the hard drive, from the original diskettes that came with the card when you purchased it. Once this software is loaded, you must run a statement prior to running DataCAD. For example, if the driver is loaded into a VESA directory, the statement might be **\vesa\vesa**. You can add this to your *autoexec.bat* file.

4. The wrong graphic card is installed - Sometimes the symptoms of this problem allow DataCAD to start, but as soon as you move the mouse, the program terminates. Check the driver you selected in the DataCAD Configuration Utility.

5. You turned on EMS memory, but didn't install EMS - You must have extended memory properly installed in order to use it.

6. DataCAD can't find the default character set to load - DataCAD must be able to find the default font (typeface) to display on the screen. If not, it won't load at all. If you've changed the character path names or the character set when using the Configuration Utility, you'll need to reset the character path to **CHR** and the default character set to **ROMAN**.

Installing and configuring DataCAD

Beginning DataCAD

Welcome to DataCAD

DataCAD is an easy-to-use software that is designed just for you: architect, facilities manager, space planner, or other architectural professional. This book will guide you through the use of many of the functions of DataCAD while you complete small projects. By the time you have finished this book, you'll be well on the road to becoming an expert user!

Here are some of the things you'll learn in this chapter:

- The basic operations of DataCAD.
- Starting a new drawing.
- Use of the two- and three-button mouse.
- Use of the menus.
- Drawing lines.
- Changing colors.
- Object snapping onto lines.
- Erasing items by entity, area, and fence.
- Zooming in and out of your drawing.
- Refreshing the display.
- Using the tool bar.
- Creating a pictogram image of your drawing.

Opening DataCAD screen

When you start the DataCAD software, the opening screen will be displayed. This screen consists of three active areas, as shown in Figure 2.1. They are:

1. **Existing drawing list** - The existing drawing list displays names of drawings that appear in the current directory. To change directories, you would use the New Path option.

2. **Preview box** - When you highlight an existing drawing name with your cursor, information about the drawing will be displayed, such as the size of the drawing file and the last time it was edited. If an image of the drawing was saved, it would be displayed in the preview box window. CADKEY calls this a POF (pixel out file). You'll learn how to make one.

3. **Message area** - The message area prompts you to type in a name for your new drawing. Messages will always appear in this area while you use DataCAD.

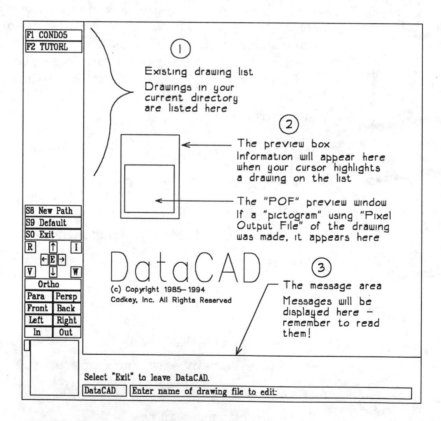

Figure 2.1: The opening screen.

Checking your drawing directory

You'll want to check the project directory you're in prior to creating a drawing. If you've just installed DataCAD, you'll probably be in the DWG directory. This is a good directory for your training drawings. However, if someone has used DataCAD already, another directory might be set. You'll want to check this before continuing.

1.   Pick the **New Path** option by moving your cursor over to highlight it and pressing mouse button 1 (the leftmost button).

2.   Check the *message area* of your screen.

3.   It should say: **dwg** or, it might say: **\dcad6\dwg**.

4.   If it reads something other than these two choices, type in: **dwg** and the other path should go away. If it doesn't, press ⌑DEL .

5.   Press ⌑ENTER .

Beginning a new drawing

To begin a new drawing, all you have to do is type in a new drawing name. Drawing names can only be eight characters long. Because of this, you'll want to develop special naming conventions for your drawings. For practice drawings, you can use a simple naming convention.

1.   Type in the name of your new drawing: **practic1** and press ⌑ENTER .

Note: *If someone has already created a PRACTIC1 drawing, it will appear on the drawing list. Use PRACTIC2 or another unique name. Also, certain characters are illegal in names of files. These characters include: .,?:;\ / and spaces. The characters that are legal include: A thru Z , 0 thru 9, dash (-) and underline (_). Other characters are legal but not recommended.*

The main menu screen

Once you name your drawing and press ⌑ENTER , the DataCAD main drawing screen will be displayed. There are six major areas that make up this screen, as indicated in Figure 2.2. They are:

1. *Drawing Area* - Your drawing will be displayed here.

2. *Menu Options* - Your menu options will always appear in this column.

3. *Control Panel* - "Buttons" are displayed here that can be picked with your cursor. You'll use these buttons soon.

4. *Status Area* - This area informs you of your present set-tings: the active layer, the present viewing scale, the selection set, and the SWOTHLUD status.

5. *Message Area* - Your coordinate readout, system mes-sages, and user prompt appear here.

6. *Tool Bar Icons* - A tool bar appears at the top of the screen with picture icons. You can pick these with your cursor to enter into menus instantly. You'll learn how to use these tools later.

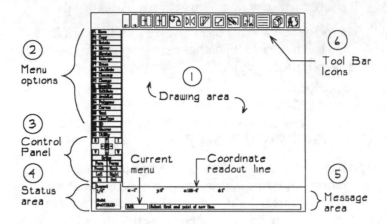

Figure 2.2: The 6 major areas of the screen.

What is SWOTHLUD?

The word SWOTHLUD, which appears at the lower left corner of the status area, represents the current setting status. Each letter stands for a particular setting. It keeps you in-formed "at a glance" of what settings you have active.

The letters "SWOTHLUD" stand for:

S   Snap - Increment snapping is on. (Press ⊠ to turn on, press ⊠ again to turn off.)

W   Walls - You're creating walls. (Press ▤ and enter wall width, press ▤ again to turn off.)

O   Ortho - Orthomode lock is on, 45-degree angle lock. (Press ⊡ .)

T   Text - Text is displayed on screen (instead of boxes only, controlled in Display menu).

H   Hatch - Hatch is displayed on screen. (Controlled in Display menu.)

L   Line weight - Thicknesses of lines are displayed. (Con-trolled in Display menu.)

U   User linetypes - Linetypes are displayed (compared to appearing as solid, controlled in Display menu).

D   Dimensions - Dimensions are displayed on screen. (Controlled in Display menu.)

When a switch is active (for example, walls are on), the letter will appear capitalized (as the w in SWOTHLUD). If the switch is off (walls are off), the letter will appear in lowercase (SwOTHLUD). You'll see how this works later in this chapter.

The screen cursor

Notice that the cursor appears as a small + on your screen. As you might have discovered earlier, if you move the cursor into the *menu option* area, the option closest to the cursor will be highlighted. The cursor is also used to pick items in the drawing area. You can try this by drawing a few lines.

Drawing lines

Look at the "W" in the status line (SWOTHLUD). Does the W appear in upper or lowercase (SwOTHLUD)? As mentioned earlier, this means that you'll either be drawing walls (a double set of lines) or single lines. First, you'll want the W to be in lowercase for your line drawing. You'll practice drawing walls later.

1.   If the W Is capitalized in SWOTHLUD, press ▣ to make it lowercase. If your W is already in lowercase, skip this step.

2.   Notice that the user prompt (bottom of screen) is asking you to pick a point to draw a line.

3.   To draw lines, all you have to do is point with the cursor in the drawing area of your screen and press mouse button 1. This is called *picking*. (If you have a digitizer tablet with a pen, see the next section, Digitizers.) You can continue drawing lines, always picking the next point with mouse number 1. To quit drawing the line, you simply press mouse button 3.

4.   Move the cursor to the desired area in the *drawing window* where you wish to begin drawing a line.

5.   Press mouse button 1. Move your cursor and you'll draw a line! Press mouse button 1 again to indicate the second point of your line.

6.   Continue making multiple lines, moving the cursor, and using mouse button 1, as shown in Figure 2.3.

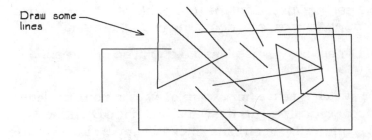

Draw some
lines

Figure 2.3: Drawing lines.

7.　To end your line, press mouse button 3 (the right-most button on your mouse).

Colors

It very easy to change colors as you draw.

1.　Try drawing some lines again.

2.　Press ⬚K and the color of your line you're dragging will change. Draw a few more lines.

3.　Press ⬚K again. Draw a few more lines.

4.　There are 15 colors to choose from: *White, red, green, blue, cyan, magenta, brown, grey, light grey, light red, light green, light blue, light cyan, light magenta* and *yellow.* You'll learn how color helps your final plots later.

Your mouse

Hopefully, you have a three-button mouse, which is the easiest drawing tool with DataCAD. DataCAD was designed to work with a mouse that has three buttons. If you have a two-button mouse, however, don't panic! You can still use it. DataCAD will support most mice.

Note: *Some older, off-brand mice don't work as well as the newer models. If your mouse seems "sticky," clean it before using. I recommend a three-button Logictech.*

You just used your mouse to pick points on the screen for your lines, and to detach the line. These are only two of the uses for your mouse. If you have a three-button mouse, its button uses are described in Figure 2.4.

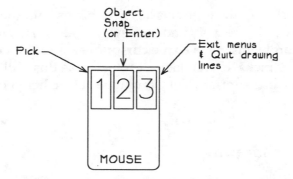

Figure 2.4: The three-button mouse.

The *first button*, as you found out, is used to "pick". You can pick a location on the screen for a line or wall, or you can pick an option from the menu.

The *second button* is used to "object snap" to an existing object, such as a line. Object snap means to "grab onto an object."

The *third button* is called the "quit button" because it's used to "quit" drawing a line or to "exit" from a menu. When you're not drawing a line, this button actually selects the option found in the S0 position of the menu window and you can see the option highlight as you press the button. In many submenus, this option is "Exit."

Two-button mouse

If you have a **two-button mouse**, note that mouse button 1 "picks" like mouse button 1 on the three-button mouse. The second button "Quits" like mouse button 3. To object snap, hold the cursor by the item you wish to grab and press the Ⓝ key on your keyboard. You can think of the N as *Need snap*.

Digitizers

Digitizers usually are packaged as a tablet and pen or a puck. If you have a pen, you can press down on the tablet with it to make it "pick." If it doesn't have any buttons, you could always use the Ⓝ key to make it object snap and the ⦂ key to stop drawing a line or exit a menu, or pick Exit. If it has a puck, which has buttons like a mouse, you'll have to experiment with it to find out which button picks and if any of the buttons will operate as the object snap and quit buttons like the mouse.

A few older digitizer models have problems with the new drivers, which are designed for newer models. This results in strange problems, such as the cursor freezing after a certain amount of picks. If you have a problem like this, call CADKEY Inc. support. They might be able to help you over the phone.

Object snapping

Now you can see how object snapping works. Remember, object snapping is "grabbing" an existing item, so there has to be some lines on your drawing already.

1.   Make sure there are a few lines in your drawing area.

2.   Quit drawing lines by pressing mouse button 3.

3.   Move the cursor close to an existing line, so that the + part of the cursor touches part of the line, as shown in Figure 2.5.

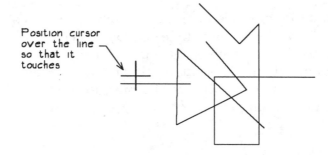

Figure 2.5: Your cursor must touch the line.

4.   Press mouse button 2. Or, if you have a two-button mouse, press ⃞N on your keyboard. When you move your cursor, you'll see that the first endpoint of the line snapped onto the endpoint of the existing line your cursor was touching, as in Figure 2.6.

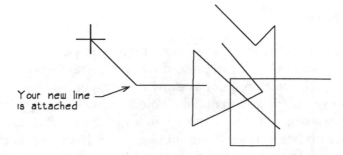

Figure 2.6: Line object snapped to endpoint.

5. Move the cursor close to another existing line, perhaps on the other side of the screen. Again, make sure the + part of the cursor touches part of this line. Press mouse button 2 (or N).

6. Press mouse button 3 to quit.

Orthomode On and Off

The orthomode tool helps you draw in straight lines. Soon, you'll learn how it can also help you move things and modify items.

1. Press the O key (oh, not zero), until the message in the bottom of the screen says: Orthomode is ON.

2. Draw some lines. They'll be in straight 45-degree angles.

3. Press the O key again. This time the message in the bottom of the screen says: Orthomode is OFF.

4. Draw some more lines. Now you can create your lines in any angle. See Figure 2.7.

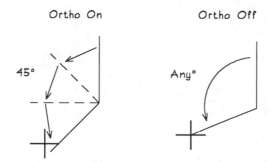

Figure 2.7: Drawing with Orthomode on and off.

Quick erasing

You can quickly erase entities you drew by using the ◁ key. To erase all the lines you drew as multiple lines during a single series (without pressing mouse button 3 to detach your line), you'd use the SHIFT and ◁ keys together. Lines drawn as a single series are called a *group* of lines.

1. Press the ◁ key. Did one of your lines disappear?

2. Press the SHIFT and ◁ keys together. How many lines disappeared? Remember, a bunch of lines drawn together without detaching (mouse button 3) are thought of as one "group." Using the SHIFT and ◁ key together will erase the last group you have drawn.

Restoring

You can restore the last entity or group you erased!

1. Press the ▷ key. Whatever you deleted last (group or single entity) will be restored. You'll learn other ways to erase items soon.

The EDIT and UTILITY menus

There are two main menus in DataCAD, as shown in Figure 2.8. They are:

Edit - This menu contains options that allow you to create or change items, such as walls, windows, doors, etc.

Utility - This menu contains menu options that allow you to define certain settings, defaults for your drawing, and other utility items such as drawing file control.

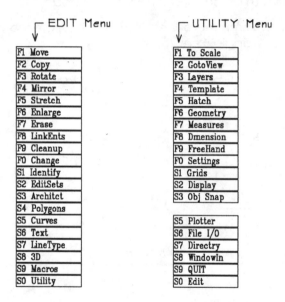

┌ EDIT Menu   ┌ UTILITY Menu

EDIT Menu		UTILITY Menu
F1 Move		F1 To Scale
F2 Copy		F2 GotoView
F3 Rotate		F3 Layers
F4 Mirror		F4 Template
F5 Stretch		F5 Hatch
F6 Enlarge		F6 Geometry
F7 Erase		F7 Measures
F8 LinkEnts		F8 Dmension
F9 Cleanup		F9 FreeHand
F0 Change		F0 Settings
S1 Identify		S1 Grids
S2 EditSets		S2 Display
S3 Architct		S3 Obj Snap
S4 Polygons		
S5 Curves		S5 Plotter
S6 Text		S6 File I/O
S7 LineType		S7 Directry
S8 3D		S8 WindowIn
S9 Macros		S9 QUIT
S0 Utility		S0 Edit

Figure 2.8: The two main DataCAD menus.

To change between the two main menus, all you have to do is press mouse button 3. (Of course, if you're drawing a line, the first time you press mouse button 3 it will detach your line. The second time you press mouse button 3, you can switch menus.) Try it.

1. Look at the message area at the bottom of the screen, where the current menu name is displayed as in Figure 2.9. Does it say *Edit* or *Utility*?

2. If the current menu says Edit, then you're in the Edit menu. Switch to the Utility menu by pressing mouse button 3.

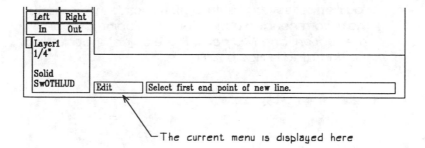

The current menu is displayed here

Figure 2.9: The message area displays current menu.

3.   Press mouse button 3 again until the main menu changes back to Edit. Notice the options that are displayed in this menu.

4.   Press button 3 until it changes to Utility. This is called toggling between menus. Notice the options that are displayed in the Utility menu.

Note: *As you press mouse button 3 to go back and forth between menus, the S0 option lights up. As mentioned earlier, pressing mouse button 3 will select S0 for you. When you're in the Edit menu, the option S0 is "Utility," and you'll change to the Utility menu. When you're in the Utility menu, the option S0 is "Edit," and you'll change to the Edit menu.*

Object snap menu

Now that you know how to change main menus, you can use a submenu. The first one you'll use is the Object Snap menu. You used object snapping earlier to grab onto existing line "ends" with your cursor. By using the menu, you can set other options for snapping, such as middle point, centerpoint, intersections of two lines, etc.

1.   Press mouse button 3 until the Utility menu is displayed (Utility name appears in the message area).

2.   Pick the option called **Obj Snap**. The Object Snap menu will be displayed. You'll see that one of the first group of options at the top is green, while the others are red.

3.   When an option is *green*, it means it's *active*. In this case, the active option is **End pt**. When you put your cursor close to a line and pressed mouse button 2, it grabbed onto the closest *end* of that line.

4.   When an option is *red*, it means it's an setting that could be active but it's presently turned off.

5. You can set several useful options active in this menu. The recommended options are: *End point*, *Center*, *Intersection*, and *Mid point*. These object snap settings are illustrated in Figure 2.10.

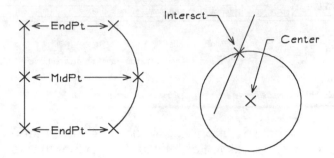

Figure 2.10: Common object snap settings illustrated.

6. Pick the **Center** option until it's green. Now it's active.

7. Pick the **Midpoint** option until it's green.

8. Pick the **Intrsect** option to make it green also.

9. If you pick an option by mistake, or wish to turn one off, just pick it again and it will turn *red*, indicating it's off.

10. When you're through, press mouse button 3 to exit the Object Snap menu.

11. Now try to object snap to the middle of a line by holding your cursor near the midpoint of a line, and pressing the object snap button, mouse button 2, or by pressing the [N] key. Remember that your cursor must touch the line you're object snapping to.

11. Did it work? If not, try again and check your settings.

Quick keys

Most of the options you can pick from menus can also be entered quickly by simply typing in a key, or a combination of keys, from the keyboard. These are called *quick keys*. You can use quick keys from within other menus in order to access the next needed function fast and easy. This saves on the time it takes to scan each menu for the correct option!

For example, you can use quick keys to enter the Object Snap menu.

1. Press the [SHIFT] [X] keys simultaneously to type a capital X. (You can hold down the [SHIFT] key, then press [X]).

2.	You'll enter the Object Snap menu! Press mouse button 3 to quit.

Note: *You can switch to the Object Snap menu, using* [SHIFT] [X] *, anytime you're drawing lines or walls, or even from another menu. Once you quit the Object Snap menu, you'll be returned to whatever you were doing and whatever menu you were in. This is called an "interrupt key."*

The tool bar

The tool bar can also work as a shortcut to menu options. The DCAD tool bar is shown in Figure 2.11.

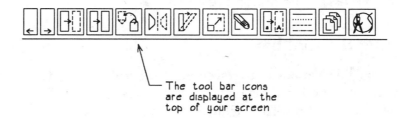

The tool bar icons are displayed at the top of your screen

Figure 2.11: The DCAD tool bar.

This icon styled bar contains tools for Move, Copy, Rotate, Mirror, Stretch, Enlarge, Erase, Change and other menu options.

If a tool bar is not displayed

Do you own DataCAD 6? Since the menu bar was first included in DataCAD 6, earlier version won't have it. If you own DataCAD 6 but the tool bar isn't displayed, you can turn it on by following these steps:

1.	Press mouse button 3 until you're in the Utility menu.

2.	Pick **Display**.

3.	Pick **Menus**.

4.	Pick **Icons** to make it active (green). This option toggles the bar on and off.

5.	Press mouse button 3 to exit.

If the wrong tool bar is displayed

There are 3 tool bars that come with DataCAD, and more can be made. Once you make a bar active, it stays active until it's changed. If a tool bar is displayed, but not the one pictured in Figure 2.11, follow these steps to make the DCAD tool bar active:

1. Press mouse button 3 until you're in the Utility menu.

2. Pick **Display**.

3. Pick **Menus**.

4. Pick **IconFile**.

5. Pick **DCAD**.

6. Press mouse button 3 several times to exit.

Using the tool bar

The tool bar is made of two sections: the Scroll Forward and Back tools, and the function tools that correspond to a Data-CAD menu option. This is illustrated in Figure 2.12.

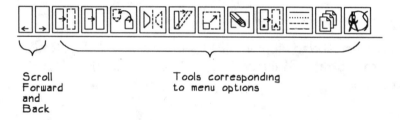

Scroll
Forward
and
Back

Tools corresponding
to menu options

Figure 2.12: The tool bar has two sections.

1. Move the cursor to an icon in the bar. Notice that the name of the tool is displayed in the message area.

2. Try using the tool bar by picking the different tools, as shown in Figure 2.13.

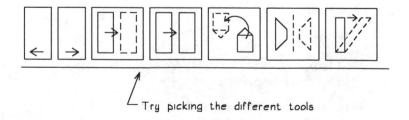

Try picking the different tools

Figure 2.13: Pick the tools to use them.

3. To show the rest of the tools in the bar (only 11 tools are shown at a time, and you can have up to 45 in the bar), pick the **Scroll Forward** tool, as in Figure 2.14. You can pick **Scroll Forward** as many times as necessary to show all the available tools. (2 or 3 times in this case.)

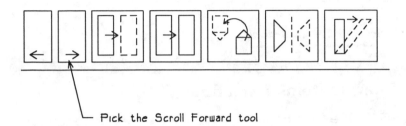

Pick the Scroll Forward tool

Figure 2.14: Pick the Scroll Forward tool.

4. To return to the main tools, pick the **Scroll Back** tool, shown in Figure 2.15, until the tools no longer scroll. (2 or 3 times again.)

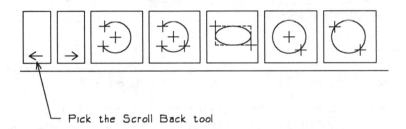

Pick the Scroll Back tool

Figure 2.15: Pick the Scroll Back tool.

The Erase menu

You already know you can "quick erase" using ⟨ as you're drawing. To erase by picking and by boxing around items, you'll use the Erase menu.

1. Press E to go to the Erase menu. This is the quick key.

2. Or, you can use the Erase tool. Press mouse button 3 to exit the Erase menu.

3. Pick the **Erase tool**, shown in Figure 2.16.

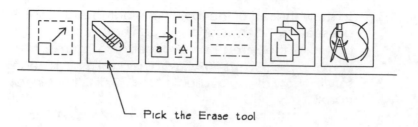

Pick the Erase tool

Figure 2.16: The Erase tool.

To erase items 1 at a time

1. The first 6 choices that appear in the Erase menu are the *item selection modes*. They are: *Entity, Group, Area,* and *Fence*.

Note: *These selection modes are your options for defining how you'll "pick" items. These same selection modes appear in almost every menu in DataCAD. You can select an Entity (single item), a Group (all drawn together), an Area (items that can be enclosed by a box), or a Fence (items enclosed by a polygon).*

---

2. Pick the **Entity** option until it's active (green).

3. Pick a line to erase by moving your cursor until it touches a line, then pressing mouse button 1. It will be deleted!

Erasing a group of items

You can also select a group of items at one time. A group is a series of items, in this case lines, that were made without pressing mouse button 3 to stop drawing.

1. Pick the **Group** option until it's active. (Notice that only one of these options can be active at a time.)

2. Pick a line to erase, again by moving your cursor until it touches a line, then pressing mouse button 1. This time, all lines that were drawn in one continuous picking session will be deleted. This might be half your drawing at this point!

3. You might want your lines back for the next step, so pick **Undo**. All of the items you erased last will come back! Try it. (You only get one Undo. Sorry!)

Erasing by area (box)

You might want to try erasing by using a rectangular box:

1. Pick the **Area** option until it's active.

2. Pick two points indicating a rectangle around the lines you wish to erase, as indicated in Figure 2.17.

3. Only the items completely enclosed in the box will be erased. You'll get used to this later with more practice. As an example, items that wouldn't erase by this area are indicated in bold in Figure 2.17.

4. Pick **Undo** to bring the erased lines back.

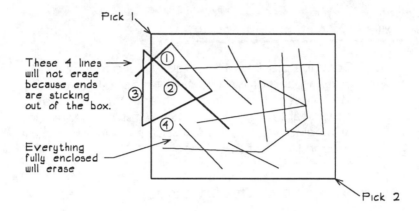

Figure 2.17: Erasing by area.

Erasing by a polygon fence

Another way to erase is to indicate a "corral" around them using a fence:

1. Pick the **Fence** option until it's active.

2. Pick the first point of your fence, shown as step 1 in Figure 2.18.

3. Pick the second point of your fence, shown as step 2 in Figure 2.18.

4. Now pick a third point. Notice that a corner of the fence is attached to your cursor. This indicates the "closing" line. Continue picking to "wrap" the polygon fence around items you want erased. This is illustrated by the steps in Figure 2.18.

5. The **Backup** option allows you to "repick" the last corner.

6. After the third point of the Fence is created, S0 becomes "**Close**." Press mouse button 3 to close the fence, erasing the items you have drawn the fence around. Again, only fully enclosed items will be erased.

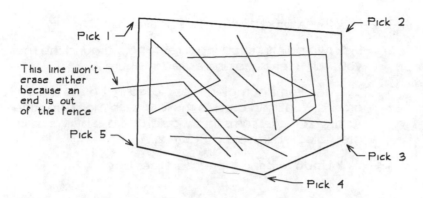

Figure 2.18: Creating an erase fence.

7. Continue playing with DataCAD for a few minutes, drawing and erasing lines. Get a good feel for using the mouse and pointing to objects. When you feel comfortable using the mouse, switching menus, and practicing what you learned during this lesson, continue to the next steps.

Refreshing your display screen

Do you have little shadows on your lines that look like they're broken? When you have erased items that partially cover another item, a little shadow will be left where the erased item crossed. Some people complain that it looks like the item "has a hole in it."

What really has happened is the "pixel" have been drawn black temporarily. All you have to do is refresh the screen by pressing the ESC key.

1. Press the ESC on your keyboard. Your screen will be refreshed.

Sometimes when you erase items, especially circles, some of the pixels will remain ON, leaving behind a "ghost." Pressing the ESC key will get rid of ghosts also.

If you're using display list processing

If you're using a display list, and have garage left on the screen even after using the ESC key, you can force a regeneration of the display list by pressing the U key. This type of regeneration will take longer in a large drawing.

1. Press U . Your display list will be regenerated. If nothing happens, maybe you're not using a display list?

Filing your drawing

You should practice saving your drawing periodically. All you have to do is press the capital F, for *File*.

1. Hold down the [SHIFT] key.

2. Press [F] on your keyboard. Your drawing will be saved under the original name you gave it: PRACTIC1

Changing the viewing window

As you draw, you'll want to view your drawing in different sizes. Some people refer to this as *zooming in* and *zooming out*. It's very easy with DataCAD.

1. To get a smaller view of your drawing, pick the **[Out]** button in the control panel of your screen. This will move you out, or away, from your drawing, making it appear smaller.

2. This button works the same as pressing the [PG UP] key on your keyboard. Try it by pressing [PG UP].

3. The **[In]** button in the control panel helps you get a larger view of your drawing. You'll zoom in, or get closer, to your drawing. Pick the **[In]** button.

4. This button works the same as pressing the [PG DN] key on your keyboard.

5. Before pressing [PG DN], you can define a center point to zoom in on. Hold the cursor over an item in your drawing and press the [HOME] key. Your drawing will center around this item. Now press [PG DN] several times. You'll zoom in to the item you centered on.

6. If you wish to move your view across the drawing, known as "panning," simply pick one of the appropriate [↓] [←] [→] [↑] arrow buttons found in the control panel.

7. These arrow buttons also correspond to the arrow keys on the keyboard. Press them to see what happens!

8. To get a full view of your drawing, pick the **[E]** button found in the middle of the arrow buttons in the control panel. This "E" stands for view *Extents*.

9. If you picked **[E]** and you didn't get a full view, the view window might need to be *Recalculated*. Pick the **[R]** button and your view will be corrected.

2

Creating a "Pictogram" of your drawing

Remember at the beginning when you learned about the preview box and the preview window? (See Figure 2.1 and Figure 2.21.) When you start DataCAD, you can hold the cursor on the drawing name, and a small picture of the drawing will appear in the preview window.

1. Press mouse button 3 until you're in the **Utility** menu.

2. Pick the **File I/O** option. (Files In and Out.)

3. Pick the **PixelOut** option.

4. Pick **Pictogram**.

5. The name of your drawing will appear at the text line in the message area. Press [ENTER] to accept it as the name of your POF file. (Pixels Out File.)

6. Move the cursor into the drawing area. Notice that a small box is attached. This is the size of the preview window. Now you'll want to make your drawing small enough to fit in this small box, as shown in Figure 2.19.

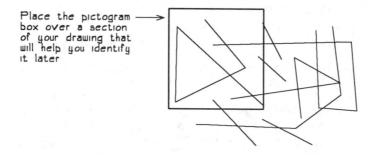

Place the pictogram box over a section of your drawing that will help you identify it later

Figure 2.19: Fitting your drawing in the preview window box.

7. Pick the **[Out]** button in the control panel until your drawing is small enough to fit. Of course, it doesn't have to fit entirely into the box, just enough so that you know what it's.

8. Place the box over your drawing and pick. The picture is now created as a POF file in the same directory as your drawing file. In other words, if your drawing was **practic1**, your picture file will be **practic1.pof**.

9. Press mouse button 3 to exit.

Exiting your drawing

Follow these next steps to exit your drawing. In order to ensure that your drawing is permanently saved, make sure that you pick the **Yes** option from the New Drawing menu.

1. Press mouse button 3 until you're in the Utility menu.

2. Select the **File I/O** option.

3. Pick **New Dwg**. The menu displayed is shown in Figure 2.20.

4. Notice that you're given three choices:

   Abort - This option allows you to leave your drawing without saving any of the current changes since your last file save (SHIFT F).

   Yes - This option allows you to leave your drawing and *file save it* at the same time.

   No - Selecting this option means you don't want to leave the drawing, and you'll be returned back into DataCAD with your current drawing displayed.

5. Pick **Yes**.

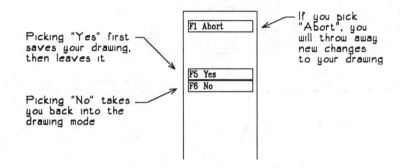

Figure 2.20: Leaving the DataCAD drawing.

Previewing your drawing

Now you can check out the image you saved to the POF file.

1. Move your cursor to the name of your drawing in the drawing list, **PRACTIC1**. Don't pick; just hold your cursor on it to highlight it.

2. Look at the preview box. Is the picture of your drawing in the window? You'll also notice the date and time are displayed, along with the file size. See Figure 2.21.

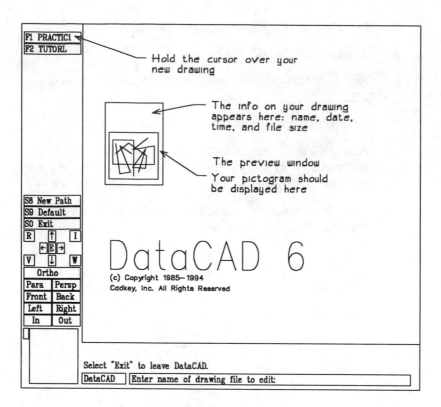

Figure 2.21: Your drawing appears in the preview window.

DataCAD exercise 1

Please complete the following exercise by reading each question carefully, then circling the letter that corresponds to the correct answer.

1. The first (left-most) button on the mouse is used to:
    a. Pick on the screen.
    b. Object snap or to enter a typed value.
    c. Quit an operation or exit a menu.

2. The second (middle) button on the mouse is used to:
    a. Pick on the screen.
    b. Object snap or to enter a typed value.
    c. Quit an operation or exit a menu.

3. The two main menus in 2D DataCAD are called:
    a. Erase and Edit.
    b. Edit and Utility.
    c. Edit and Object Snap.

4. To object snap with a two-button mouse, you press the:
    a. [X] key.
    b. [S] key.
    c. [N] key.

5. To make the selection of DataCAD options found in the different menus easy, you can use:
    a. The mouse to pick the menu options only. There is no quick way to enter menus.
    b. Either the mouse to pick options as you read them, press the correct function keys, or (preferably) use the "quick" keys, by pressing the correct key(s) on the keyboard.
    c. The mouse or function keys only. It's not recommended that you use the "Quick" keys from the keyboard.

6. The letters "SWOTHLUD" displayed on your screen:
    a. Mean nothing to you, and are only displayed for programmers.
    b. Help to let you know what your coordinates are.
    c. Are to help you know what the current status of certain settings are (e.g.; if you're drawing "W"alls or lines).

7. Object snapping means to:
    a. Grab onto an item.
    b. Pick anywhere on the screen.
    c. Snap to a grid dot.

8. To erase the last line you drew, you press the:
   a. ⊠ key.
   b. ⊠ key.
   c. ⊠ key.

9. To restore the last line you erased, you press the:
   a. ⊠ key.
   b. ⊠ key.
   c. ⊠ key.

10. To enter the Erase menu quickly, you press the:
    a. [ALT] [D] keys.
    b. [E] key.
    c. [ALT] [E] keys.

11. To erase many items at one time by indicating a box around them, you use the Erase option, then pick the:
    a. **Box** option.
    b. **Area** option.
    c. **Group** option.

12. To restore all of the items you erased by indicating a box around them, you use the:
    a. **Restore** option.
    b. [ALT] [E] keys.
    c. **Undo** option, before you leave the Erase menu.

13. To save the new changes to your drawing as you leave it, you select File I/O, New Dwg, then pick the:
    a. **Yes** option.
    b. **Save** option.
    c. **Abort** option.

14. To create a little picture of your drawing that shows up in the preview box, you use the:
    a. **File I/O, Show Image** options.
    b. **Picture, Preview** options.
    c. **File I/O, Pictogram** options.

15. If you don't see the tool bar, but you do own DataCAD 6:
    a. You probably don't have it loaded. Rerun the install program.
    b. Use **Display, Menus, Icons** to turn the bar on.
    c. Use **Tools, Tool Bar, On** to turn the bar on.

16. To see the rest of the tool bar options, pick:
    a. The **Scroll Forward** or **Back** tools.
    b. **Show Rest**. The tool bar becomes smaller so you can see it all.
    c. **Double**. The tool bar doubles to display all options.

Basic floor plans

Drawing walls, doors, and windows

DataCAD has been designed to make the drawing of
floor plans a breeze. In this chapter, you'll use DataCAD
to create walls, windows, and doors. Along the way,
you'll find yourself becoming more familiar with the
software, and techniques will become easier to you.

Here are some of the things you'll learn in this chapter:

- Using a standard drawing sheet.
- Creating walls.
- Setting the grid snap increment.
- Changing layers.
- Adding windows.
- Adding doors.
- Defining a reference point to help place items.
- Using coordinate input.

Walls

Look at the floor plan shown in Figure 3.1. This will be
your first drawing project. The first items you'll draw for
this project are the walls.

When you draw a wall with DataCAD, it's created as a
double line. The space between the line is the *wall width*.

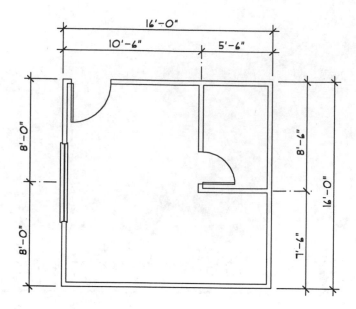

Figure 3.1: Your first project.

What you won't notice while you're drawing your wall is that there is a "height" for your wall also. Your walls can be drawn with the real floor, or "base" elevation, and the real ceiling, or "height" elevation. The default is set to 0'-0" for the floor and 8'-0" for the ceiling. You're drawing a three-dimensional wall, as shown in Figure 3.2.

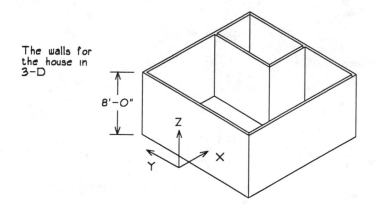

Figure 3.2: Walls in 3-D.

Layers

When you examine a drawing, you naturally look at the entities (lines, arcs, etc.) as being certain types of items. These items might be walls, doors, windows, or property lines, among other types of items that appear in your drawings. Using a computer allows you to separate certain types of items from other items in your drawing. An example of this is separating doors from walls or plumbing from electrical and HVAC. This is done by using what is called *layers*.

When items are put on layers, you can "peel them off" from one another. For instance, you'll put your walls on a layer called "Walls." When you create a different type of item, such as doors, you'll separate that item onto another layer, called "Doors." When you create windows, you'll put them on the "Windows" layer. This type of item layering helps you organize the entities in your drawing, as illustrated in Figure 3.3.

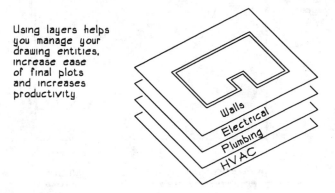

Using layers helps you manage your drawing entities, increase ease of final plots and increases productivity

Walls
Electrical
Plumbing
HVAC

Figure 3.3: Layers help you separate types of items.

The concept of layering started with the pin graphics technique used in manual drafting, often called overlaying or overlay drafting. This technique permits items pertaining to certain disciplines to be divided onto separate sheets for many different reasons. The same idea is used in your CAD drawings. When each type of entity is separated onto layers, then a series of layers can be viewed, plotted, and worked on independently or in conjunction with other entities in the drawing. During this chapter, you'll learn how easy it's to apply these techniques and to learn the essential skills for beginning drafting with DataCAD!

Picking up the drawing sheet

To start your first real drawing project, you'll want to pull up a drawing sheet in DataCAD. One drawing sheet is supplied with your software, called PLAN_1-4. This *default drawing*, as it's referred to, is set up for a 1/4" scale floor plan. Later, you'll want to create more drawing sheets, such as one for 1/8" plans.

1. If you're not in the DataCAD program, make sure you're in the DCAD6 directory, and start DataCAD by typing in **rundcad** and press ENTER .

2.   At the opening menu, pick the **Default** option.

3.   Now pick the default you'll use for this project: **PLAN_1-4**. You'll be returned to the opening menu.

4.   Type in the name for your first project: **house1** and press ENTER .

5.   Your drawing file will be created and your drawing sheet will be displayed, as shown in Figure 3.4. Now, you're ready to begin drawing!

The drawing sheet is set up for your floor plan

Figure 3.4: The drawing sheet is displayed in your drawing.

Changing Layers

Notice that in the lower-left *status area* of your screen there is a "Layer name" displayed. It might be Walls. This indicates that the current layer that is active to draw on. Only one layer at a time can be drawn on. You might want to change layers right now, just to see what other layers are set up for you!

1.   Press the Tab key once (your tab key might look like this ⇆). Did the layer name change? Did the color change also?

2.   Press the Tab key again. What layer are you on now?

3.   Continue press the Tab key until you have returned to the Walls layer. This is called "scrolling" throught the layer list.

4.   To "scroll" through the list in reverse, press SHIFT and then press Tab . This techniques takes you backwards through the list.

Drawing walls

Refer to your project shown in Figure 3.1. Notice that your project has exterior walls, interior walls, doors, and windows. First, you'll make the exterior walls. This is easily done by using the "drawing walls" mode and either picking the placement of the wall with your cursor, or by using X,Y coordinates.

1. Make sure your Walls layer is active by pressing the Tab key until the Walls layer appears as the active layer in the status area of the screen, as in Figure 3.5.

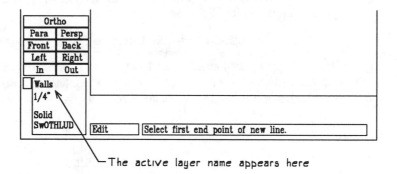

The active layer name appears here

Figure 3.5: "Walls" appears as the active layer.

2. Press the wall ▤ key. This is the quick key to turn from the "drawing lines" mode, to "drawing walls." You'll be prompted for the wall width.

Note: *If you're not prompted for a wall width, then walls mights have been on already, and pressing ▤ turned them off. Just press ▤ again!*

You'll want to define the wall width by typing in the amount. In DataCAD, it's easy to define feet, inches and fractions. For example:

1 = 1'-0"	**0.0.1/2** = 1/2"
1.6 = 1'-6"	**.16** = 1'-4"
0.6 = 6"	**..1/8** = 1/8"

So, as you can see, *periods* divide the values of *feet.inches.fractions.* As shown in the last example of *..1/8*, two periods in a row drop the value to a fraction. Also, notice that you can type in inches and it will be converted to feet/ inches when appropriate, as shown by **.16** = 1'-4".

Note: *Care must be given that an extra space doesn't get typed in by accident while typing in values! Experience has shown that these spaces are interpreted as periods, and will change the value of your input!*

---

3. Type in a width for your walls: **.4** and press ⌷ENTER⌷ . This will set the wall width to 4".

4. You'll draw the exterior walls first. Notice that these walls are dimensioned to the outside of the walls. You'll want to use an option called **Sides** to draw your walls.

5. Press ⌷A⌷ , which is the quick key to go to the Architect menu, found in the Edit menu.

6. Pick the **Sides** option to make it active (green).

7. Pick the start point of your wall with your cursor, using mouse button 1, as indicated in Figure 3.6. Make sure the start point is inside the border rectangle.

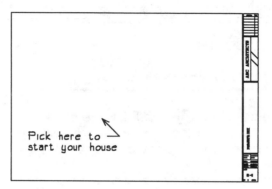

Figure 3.6: Pick the start point of your wall.

8. Notice that as you move your cursor, the coordinate readout changes to reflect the measurement of your wall, as shown in Figure 3.7. You could draw practically everything by using this coordinate readout. When you move the cursor across the screen, you'll see that the X coordinate changes. When you move the cursor up and down the screen, you'll see the Y coordinate change. Try it!

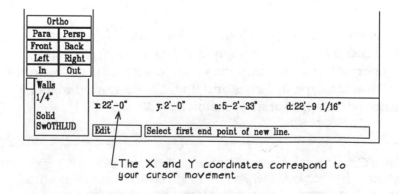

Figure 3.7: The coordinate readout.

9. Move the cursor over to the right so that the **X = 16′-0″** and the **Y = 0**.

10. Pick to place the second corner of your wall, as shown by pick 2 in Figure 3.8. Your wall is 16 feet long.

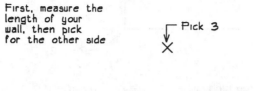

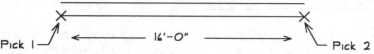

Figure 3.8: Picks for creating a wall.

11. Now a user prompt appears in the message area, asking you to enter the "other" side of the wall. This will be the undimensioned side of the wall, which in this case is the *inside* of the house.

12. Pick on the inside to create the inside wall, as shown by pick 3 in Figure 3.8.

Note: *Don't press mouse button 3 before performing the next steps.*

Zooming in while drawing

Your first wall is drawn, but it appears very small on this drawing sheet. You'll want to "zoom in," or "window in," to see the wall better, as you did in the previous chapter. You don't have to quit drawing to zoom in, so don't press mouse button 3 to let go of your wall.

1. Pick the **[W]** button in the control panel. This button puts you in the *Window-In* menu, which allows you to "zoom in" using two picks to define a new viewing window.

2. Now pick two diagonal points around the wall that you drew, as indicated as pick 1 and 2 in Figure 3.9. Did the wall get bigger on your screen?

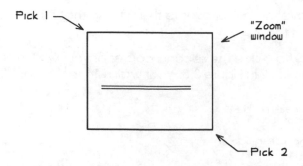

Figure 3.9: Picks for zooming in.

3. To exit the Window-In menu, press mouse button 3 only once; you'll return to drawing walls. Notice that the cursor is still connected to your wall, and you can continue drawing!

4. Move your cursor up on the screen until the **X = 0** and the **Y = 16**.

5. Pick to position the next corner of your wall.

6. Move the cursor to the inside of the house and pick again to define the "other side" of your wall.

7. Move your cursor to the left until the **X = -16** and the **Y = 0**. Notice that when you move to the left, the X is displayed as a *negative* (-) value.

8. Pick to position the next corner of your wall.

9. Move the cursor to the inside of the house and pick again to define the "other side" of your wall.

10. Hold your cursor to the first corner of the house and press mouse button 2 to object snap in order to close your walls.

11. Move the cursor to the inside of the house and pick again to define the "other side" of your wall. Look at the corners of your walls. They have automatically "cleaned up" after themselves. See Figure 3.10.

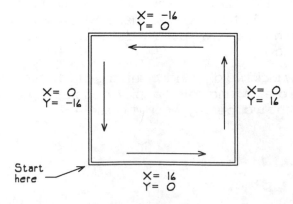

Figure 3.10: Picks for creating the exterior of your house.

Erasing

You'll erase the house and draw it again, this time using coordinate input by typing in the values.

1. Press ⌷E⌷ to enter the Erase menu.

2. Pick **Group** to make it active.

3. Pick anywhere on a wall of your house. If you drew it in one session, it will erase in one piece!

X, Y Coordinate input

Another, and usually more practical, way of indicating a length for a wall is by using coordinate input. You already used X, Y coordinates when you picked on the drawing. There are two major coordinate systems used by DataCAD. They are:

1. Cartesian   2. Polar

X, Y coordinates are called *Cartesian coordinates*, and are used for most of the simple X,Y movements. As you found out, X is the axis that is horizontal, or "across" the screen. Y is the axis that is vertical, or "up and down" the screen. This is illustrated in Figure 3.11.

Polar coordinates are typically used for defining angles. An example of polar coordinates is illustrated in Figure 3.11 also.

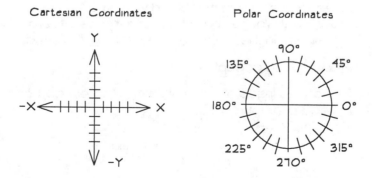

Figure 3.11: Two common coordinate systems.

This time to draw your walls, you'll use *relative Cartesian coordinates* by typing them in. You might have noticed that when you picked on the screen, your pick point became zero, and you measured from there. In other words, you measured *relative* to the last point.

In contrast, another choice would be *absolute* Cartesian coordinates. You *absolutely don't* want to use this, since this Cartesian system relies on one constant point in your drawing always remaining zero, and all movements have to be measured from it.

Setting your coordinate system

1. Press the [INS] key (Insert) 2 or 3 times until *relative Cartesian coordinates* appears as the input mode, displayed in the message area of your screen.

    You might have to press the [INS] key more, since you might scroll past it by accident. There are only four settings. That's all there is to it, you *don't* have to press [ENTER] !

Using coordinates

Since the corrdinates will be *relative from the last point,* you'll want to give the house a starting point.

1. Pick a starting point on your screen.

2. Press the [SPACE] bar to invoke the coordinate mode. Notice the prompt in the message area asks you for the relative X *distance,* which means the wall length.

3. Type in: **16** and press [ENTER] .

4. Now, you're prompted to *Enter a relative Y distance.* Any value here would send you up or down the screen, which when combined with a horizontal movement would create an angle. You want zero movement in the Y. Notice 0.0 is already displayed.

5. Press [ENTER] to accept **0**.

6. Pick on the inside of the wall, for the "other side," as indicated in Figure 3.12.

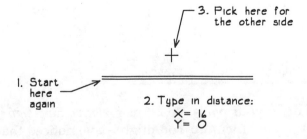

Figure 3.12: Using coordinates to create a wall.

7. Press [SPACE] again.

8.   Type in the "Y distance" for the next wall: **16**.

x = **0** [ENTER]

y = **16** [ENTER]

9.   Pick on the inside for the other side of the wall.

10.   Press the [SPACE] again.

11.   Type in the "X distance" for the next wall: **-16**. Use a minus sign (dash) to make the wall go to the left.

x = **-16** [ENTER]

y = **0** [ENTER]

12.   Pick on the inside for the other side of the wall.

13.   To finish the exterior walls, place the cursor by the beginning of the first wall, and object snap to it using mouse button 2.

14.   Remember to pick on the inside for the other side of the wall.

15.   Your drawing should look like Figure 3.13.

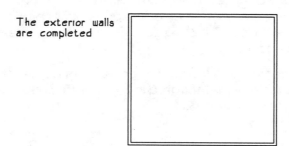

The exterior walls
are completed

Figure 3.13: The exterior walls of your house.

Drawing the interior walls

You're ready to add the interior walls for your project. Notice that the interior walls are dimensioned to the centers, unlike the exterior walls, which were dimensioned to the outside. Creating walls by center is easily accomplished by setting the Center option in the Architect menu. You'll want to make the "Center" option active (instead of the Sides option), whenever your walls are dimensioned to centerlines.

1.   Press [A] to go to the Architect option, found in the Edit menu.

2.   Pick the **Center** option until it's active.

Measuring from a reference corner point

Notice that the interior wall, as pointed out in Figure 3.14, is dimensioned from an outside corner of your exterior wall. To help you draw this wall, DataCAD allows you to measure from this point by defining the corner as a "reference point."

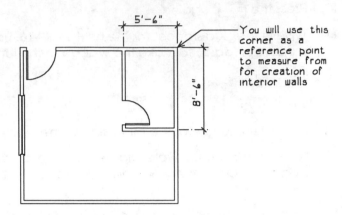

Figure 3.14: Walls are dimensioned from outside corner.

1.   Press the ⌐~⌐ key. (Don't use shift.) Some people call this key the "wave" key or squiggle, but its proper name is *tilde*. This is a quick key to establish a reference point.

2.   Object snap to the outside upper-right corner of the exterior wall, as illustrated in Figure 3.15. Be sure to use the mouse button 2!

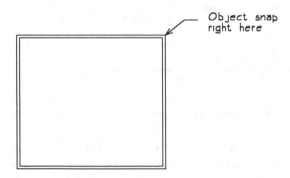

Figure 3.15: Using a reference point.

3.   You'll see that if you move your cursor back to this corner again, it now reads out as the 0,0 coordinate location! This is shown in Figure 3.16.

4.   Press the ⌐SPACE⌐ to invoke the *Relative Coordinate* mode.

5.   Type in: **-5.6** in the X direction. This will define the start point of the interior wall.

x = **-5.6** [ENTER]

y = **0** [ENTER]

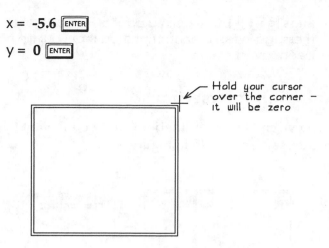

Hold your cursor
over the corner —
it will be zero

Figure 3.16: Referencing zeros out the corner.

6. Press [SPACE] again. Type in the length of your wall, -8.6 in the Y direction.

    x = **0** [ENTER]

    y = **-8.6** [ENTER]

7. Finish your wall by picking the last endpoint using mouse button 1, and using mouse button 3 to quit. Don't worry that your wall overlaps the next one. It will be easy to clean it up. Your drawing should now look similar to Figure 3.17.

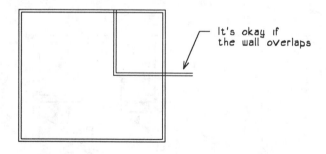

It's okay if
the wall overlaps

Figure 3.17: The interior walls are draw.

Filing your drawing

Remember that while you're working on your drawing file, it's a good idea to periodically save it to a permanent hard disk file. This way, if something happens to your drawing, or if you just goof it up entirely, you can get back a clean, saved version. It's easy to "file" your drawing and you can do it at anytime.

1. Press ⌈SHIFT⌉ ⌈F⌉ to type in a capital F. You'll get a message in the user prompt area that your file has been saved.

Cleaning up intersections

Once you've created your interior walls, you'll want to clean up the intersections noted in Figure 3.18.

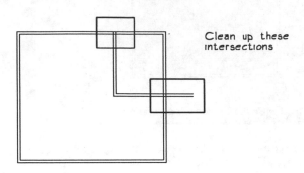

Clean up these intersections

Figure 3.18: Intersections must be cleaned.

1. Pick the **Cleanup** option from the Edit menu.

2. Pick the **T Intsct** option. (T-intersection.)

3. Pick two points indicating a rectangle around the first intersection you want to clean up, as indicated as step 1 in Figure 3.19. The rectangle must grab the two endpoints.

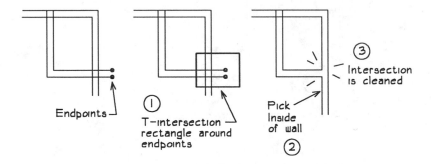

Endpoints

T-intersection rectangle around endpoints

Pick Inside of wall

③ Intersection is cleaned

Figure 3.19: Grab the two endpoints with the rectangle.

4. Pick the line of the wall you want the interior wall trimmed to, indicating the inside of your wall, as shown as step 2 in Figure 3.19.

5. Your wall will be trimmed, as in step 3, Figure 3.19.

6. Clean up the second intersection the same way.

If the intersection won't trim

If your wall is not trimmed, you might be given a message that DataCAD found *more* than two endpoints or *less* than two endpoints.

More than two endpoints - This could mean that you have a small segment of a line in this area. Sometimes this happens because you're just learning and you might have double picked as you were drawing, or you hit Enter twice or some other reason.

This is not always easy to correct, because you might have became frustrated and forgot what happened. Sometimes, it can be corrected by using the Erase option and erasing by Area, indicating a small area around the intersection you're trying to clean up. You might see a small piece of extra line disappear. Or, you might just erase the whole thing and start over again. The problem probably won't reoccur.

Less than two endpoints - Make sure you're enclosing both endpoints of the wall in your box, as shown in Figure 3.19.

Other intersection options

There are also L and X intersections that you'll eventually have to clean up. See Figure 3.20 for examples of how the intersection cleanups work.

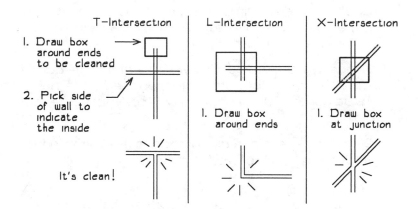

Figure 3.20: Intersection examples.

Refreshing your display screen

Remember, if your walls appear to have little holes in them after cleaning up an intersection, it's temporary. (A deleted entity "shadow.") To eliminate these shadows, all you have to do is refresh the screen. You'll find that once you get used to the shadows, you won't be inclined to refresh your screen as often.

1. Press the ESC key on your keyboard. Your screen will be refreshed.

Adding doors

When you add doors to your drawing, the walls automatically will be cut. You can set this so that they're not cut (by turning off the Cutout option), but this is usually not desired. You'll add the doors 4 inches from the inside corners of the walls. Again, this is achieved by using the "reference" key [~] and by object snapping to indicate a corner point.

Remember to make your doors on the Doors layer.

1. Press the Tab key until the layer is changed to Doors.

2. Press the A key to go to Architect.

3. Pick the **DoorSwng** option. Make **Sides** and **Single** active.

4. Pick the **LyrSrch** option twice, until the layer list is displayed. This option tells the system which layer contains the walls you want cut when you insert the doors. (You can have many different layers with different kinds of walls if you wish. This option tells the system which walls to cut.)

5. Pick **Walls**. You won't have to perform these steps again until you begin a new drawing, as DataCAD will remember that you've set the Walls layer as the layer to cut when you insert doors.

6. Notice that the prompt asks you to *"enter hinge side of door."* Because door jambs are measured off of the inside corner, you'll want this corner as your reference point.

7. Press the [~] key, and object snap to the corner in the small room, as indicated in Figure 3.21.

8. Press the SPACE .

9. Type in a Y distance of **0.4** (4"), pressing ENTER twice, once for the X, another for the Y.

   x = **0** ENTER

   y = **0.4** ENTER

10. Now the prompt asks you to *"enter strike side of door."* Press the SPACE again.

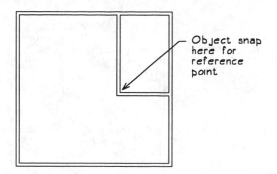

Figure 3.21: Referencing the inside corner.

11. Type in the width of the door width in the Y direction again: **2.6**.

    x = **0** [ENTER]

    y = **2.6** [ENTER]

12. Pick on the inside of the small room for the *direction of swing*, as shown as step 1 in Figure 3.22.

13. Pick in the larger room for the *outside of the wall*, as in step 2 in Figure 3.22. This pick determines where the centerpoint (for dimensioning) will be placed.

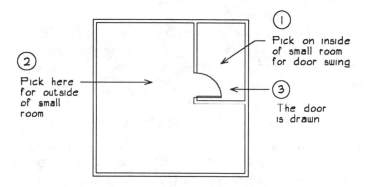

Figure 3.22: Steps for creating the first door.

14. Your door is created, as in step 3 in Figure 3.22.

15. Create the entry door 4" from the inside corner, this time using the relative **x** distance. This door is **3'-0"** wide. Follow steps in Figure 3.23.

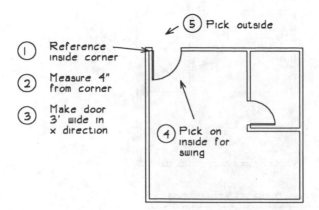

Figure 3.23: Steps for creating the second door.

Remember to use the ⌑ key, object snap for the reference corner, and use SPACE to invoke coordinate mode.

Removing a door

If you make a mistake adding a door, don't worry, it's easy to remove. You might want to try out these steps even if you made your door correctly, just to see how it works. But, beware. There's no undo!

Notice that there is a *Remove* option in the Door Swing menu. This option allows you to remove the door from the wall, and close up the wall at the same time. There is also a remove option in Windows.

1. Pick **Remove**. Make sure **Lyr Srch** is active.

2. Indicate two points to draw a box around the door you just created, being careful to enclose the entire door and just the adjoining wall, NOT the vertical wall. Don't include any other walls in your box. See Figure 3.24.

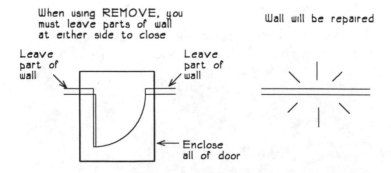

Figure 3.24: Removing a door.

3. The door is erased and the wall is "welded" close!

4.   Make sure you add the door back in correctly, follow-
      ing the previous steps, before continuing.

Turning off and on the display of layers

Now that you have completed your walls and doors on two
different layers, you might want to try turning them on and
off to see how they work.

1.   Press [L] . This is the quick key to enter the Layers
      option found in the Utility menu.

2.   Pick the **On/Off** option, to turn the layers "on and off."

3.   The layer names will be listed. Notice that most layers
      will be green. This means they are displayed.

4.   The Doors layer will be red. This means the layer is
      active. In other words, as you draw items such as
      doors, they reside and appear in this layer.

5.   Press the [Tab] key. Did the next layer become red
      instead? Notice that this layer name now appears in
      the status area of your display screen. Only one layer
      can be active at a time.

6.   Pick the **Walls** layer with your cursor. The Walls layer
      will be turned off from displaying, and the layer name
      will be gray. See Figure 3.25.

```
The walls have
been turned off
using layers

Only the doors
are displayed
```

Figure 3.25: The walls layer is turned off.

7.   Pick the **Walls** layer again. The walls will come back
      and the name will be green again.

8.   When you're done turning the layers off and on, make
      sure they are all back on before you leave this menu.
      Then press mouse button 3 to quit.

Creating windows

The window in your project is located in the center of the
wall. You'll set the center option in windows, which allows
you to create the window by the center point and one side.
Then, you can object snap to the center of this wall for window placement.

1. Make sure the Windows layer is active before you add the windows. Remember to press the [Tab] key until Windows appears as the active layer.

2. Press [A] to enter the Architect menu.

3. Pick **Windows**.

4. Pick the **Sides** option until it's turned off (red). This will allow you to create windows by defining where the center of the window is located. The message line will say: *Windows defined by center and jamb.*

5. The user prompt now asks you to: *Enter center of window.* Object snap to the middle point of the inside face of the wall, as indicated as step 1 in Figure 3.26. Remember to use mouse button 2. (Actually, you could snap to either side of the wall in this case.)

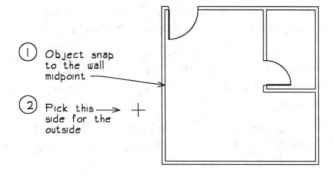

Figure 3.26: Object snap to midpoint of wall.

6. Now the prompt asks you to: *Enter one jamb of window.* You'll use coordinate input. Press [SPACE] .

7. Type in a relative y distance of 3 feet. Press [ENTER] for each direction.

   x = 0 [ENTER]

   y = 3 [ENTER]

8. Now pick a point on the outside of the wall, shown as step 2 in Figure 3.26.

9. Your window is created, as illustrated in Figure 3.27.

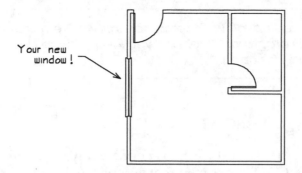

Your new window!

Figure 3.27: Your window is created.

Notice that this menu contains a "Remove" option just like Door Swing does. You can use this option to remove your window if you make a mistake or are modifying your project. You could also remove Doors with this option, and you can remove windows with the Door Swing Remove option!

Automatic save

As you worked on your drawing, you might have noticed that every few minutes it was "automatically saved." This is a process that temporarily saves your current drawing to a file that ends with an .ASV extension. This save file is *temporary*. This means it's created while you're working on your drawing, and when you quit DataCAD it's erased.

However, if you experience a problem with DataCAD (such as a power failure), then DataCAD is not exited normally and the ASV file still exists. You would be able to recover the last "Autosave" of the drawing you were working on from this temporary save file when you restart DataCAD.

Note: *The Autosave file is not a replacement for permanently saving your drawing. You can only do this using the File I/O, Save Dwg options, or by pressing (Shift) F.*

Saving your drawing

As a reminder, every hour or so that you work on DataCAD, you should permanently save your drawing. It takes one step.

1. Press [SHIFT] [F] to type in a captial F to file your drawing. Your drawing will be saved.

__Note:__ Never turn off your computer until you've quit from the DataCAD program. Otherwise, you'll leave swap files and temporary files open.

Quitting DataCAD

To assure that your drawing is permanently saved when you leave DataCAD, make sure that you pick the *Yes* option from the *Quit* menu.

1.   Press the `ALT` and `Q` keys, or pick **Quit** from the Utility menu. The Quit menu will be displayed.

2.   Pick **Yes**, and your file will be permanently saved, and you'll leave DataCAD.

__Note:__ Don't pick Abort. Remember that picking Abort will "trash" your drawing and won't save any changes or additions you made to it.

DataCAD exercise 2

Please complete the exercise by reading each question carefully, then circling the letter that corresponds to the correct answer.

1. The second (middle) button on the mouse is used to:
   a. Pick an option or pick on the screen.
   b. Object snap or to enter a typed value.
   c. Quit an operation or exit a menu.

2. To toggle to the UTILITY menu when you're in the EDIT menu, you press:
   a. Mouse button 3.
   b. Mouse button 2.
   c. ⊟ key.

3. The quickest way to turn from lines to walls, or from walls to lines, is to use the:
   a. Menu option choices.
   b. ⟨ key.
   c. ⊟ key.

4. To draw the exterior walls in your project, which were dimensioned to the outside of the walls, you used the:
   a. **Sides** option.
   b. **Centers** option.
   c. **Exterior** option.

5. To draw the interior walls, which were dimensioned to the center of the walls, you used the:
   a. **Sides** option.
   b. **Centers** option.
   c. **Interior** option.

6. In order to define a reference point, you press the:
   a. SPACE .
   b. ∼ key while pressing the SHIFT key.
   c. ∼ key.

7. The X,Y type of coordinates you used, is called:
   a. Relative polar.
   b. Absolute Cartesian.
   c. Relative Cartesian.

8. To set the coordinate input mode, you press the:
   a. INS key.
   b. Tab key.
   c. ALT key.

9. To clean up wall intersections after you create them, you use the:
    a. Cleanup menu.
    b. Edit menu.
    c. Erase menu.

10. To erase the last item you created, you use the:
    a. **Delete** option.
    b. [<] (less than) key.
    c. [>] (greater than) key.

11. To erase an entire area at one time by using a box, you use the:
    a. Erase menu, **Area** option.
    b. [SHIFT] [<] keys together.
    c. [SHIFT] [>] keys together.

12. To erase items in your drawing by picking them one at a time, you use the:
    a. Erase menu. Make sure the **Any** option is active, then pick any item to erase.
    b. Erase menu. Make sure the **Entity** option is active, then pick the items to erase.
    c. Change menu. Pick the **Delete** option, then pick the items to delete.

13. The Automatic-Save file is:
    a. Really good for permanently saving your drawing file.
    b. Only temporary. You would only retrieve it if Data-CAD was halted abnormally (such as a power failure).
    c. Retrievable even if you quit DataCAD normally.

14. To permanently save your drawing file, you:
    a. Press [SHIFT] [F] every hour or before a major change in your drawing, or pick **Yes** to save your drawing as you quit DataCAD.
    b. Let the Automatic-Save do it for you.
    c. Quit DataCAD, then pick the Abort option.

CHAPTER 4

Adding symbols

Using symbols in your drawing helps make the drawing of repeated items fast. DataCAD organizes a series of symbols into a template, much like the plastic templates used for manual drafting.

Here are some of the things you'll learn in this chapter:

- Calling up templates.
- Adding symbols to your drawing.
- Rotating, replacing, and renaming symbols.
- Exploding new and existing symbols.
- Changing the elevation height when placing symbols.
- Changing the directory paths for templates.
- Finding the size and status of your drawing.
- Pausing the screen display.
- Changing the color of existing items.

Templates and symbols

DataCAD comes bundled with many templates and symbols. In this chapter, you'll add the necessary furniture and plumbing to your floor plan, as shown in Figure 4.1. These symbols are already made for you, but you can also make your own.

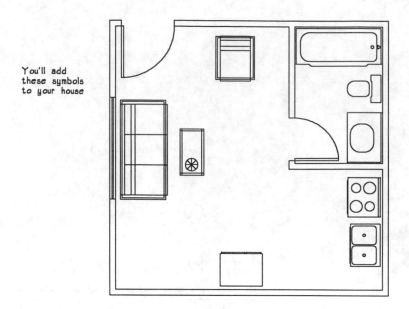

You'll add
these symbols
to your house

Figure 4.1: Added symbols to the house project.

Template directories

When you install DataCAD, the templates that are supplied with the software are organized into a series of directories. The main directory for all the DataCAD software is called DCAD and is usually accompanied by a number that identifies the version of software, such as DCAD5 or DCAD6.

The main *template subdirectory* resides in the DCAD directory and is called TPL. The different types of templates are further organized into subdirectories within TPL For example, electrical templates are put in the ELEC subdirectory (dcad\tpl\elec). Only a part of the possible directory organization is illustrated in Figure 4.2. You'll be using the FURN and PLUMB directory templates, as noted.

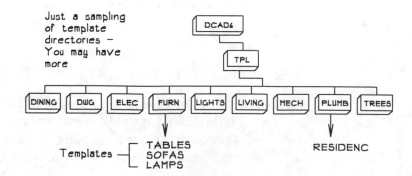

Just a sampling
of template
directories —
You may have
more

Figure 4.2: Some of the template directories.

Setting the correct template directory

As mentioned earlier, DataCAD comes with a large quantity of templates. How many you have loaded in your computer depends on the version of DataCAD you own and the choices you made when loading the software. Let's assume that you have loaded the basic templates.

However, it's hard to assume that there is a standard directory already set for your templates, especially if production work has already been performed with your software. So, please follow these few steps to assure that you have the template path needed for this exercise. Also, it's good practice and allows you to see how the New Path option works.

1. Press ☐T☐. This is the quick way to enter the Template option, found in the Utility menu.

2. Pick the **New Path** option. This option allows you to define the correct directory path for the template you wish to use.

3. The menu options probably display some directory names at this point. Or, it might only display two choices, which are **<Root>** and "**..**" (double dot). Picking the **<Root>** option will take you to the root, or top directory. The **..** (double dot) option takes you up to the root one directory at a time.

4. Look at the message at the bottom of your screen in the message area. This message can tell you what template directory you're currently in. It might say something like this: *"Enter the path for your template: tpl\plumb."*

5. The *prompt* part of the message is *"Enter the path for your template."* The *text line* part of the message is: *"tpl\plumb."* This would mean that the current direct path is set to *dcad6\tpl\plumb* (if you, of course, had DataCAD version 6)

6. You'll also notice a little text cursor blinking at the beginning of the text line. It's waiting for you to type something. You could type in a pathname of: **tpl\furn**, but you can also *pick* your path using the following steps.

7. Pick the **..** (double dot) option.

8. Look at the text line now. If it had said **tpl\plumb**, it will now say just **tpl**. If it said **tpl** before, now it won't say anything, but you'll be at the *top directory*. In both cases, there will probably be some directory names in the left column where menu options usually are.

9. Pick the **<Root>** option. Now you'll be in the top directory if you weren't before. (If you don't have <Root> as an option, perhaps you're already in the top directory.)

10. Look for your DataCAD directory. For example, this might be **DCAD6** or **DCAD5**. You might have to pick the **ScrlFwrd** option to see the rest of the directory list.

11. When you locate your **DCAD** directory, pick it.

12. Now look for the **TPL** directory choice and pick it.

13. Find the **PLUMB** directory choice and pick it.

14. You'll notice that the text line in the message area now says something like: **\dcad6\tpl\plumb**. Press ENTER .

15. Now you have the correct template directory set. The templates that reside in the FURN directory will be displayed.

Calling up the template

1. Pick the template named **SOFAS**.

2. The symbols attached to the Sofas template will be displayed, as indicated in Figure 4.3.

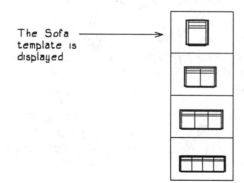

The Sofa template is displayed

Figure 4.3: The Sofas template.

Adding symbols to your drawing

1. Press the Tab key until the **Furn** layer is active, as displayed in the status area of your screen.

2. Move your cursor over to the template symbols. Notice that, as the cursor is positioned over a symbol, the name of the symbol is displayed in the message area of your screen, as in Figure 4.4.

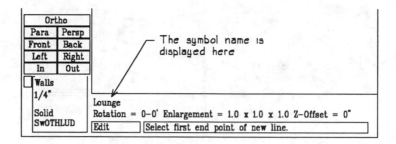

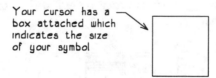
The symbol name is displayed here

Lounge
Rotation = 0-0' Enlargement = 1.0 x 1.0 x 1.0 Z-Offset = 0"
Edit   Select first end point of new line.

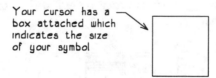

Figure 4.4: The symbol name is displayed.

3. Pick the symbol for the lounge, as indicated in Figure 4.5, by pressing mouse button 1.

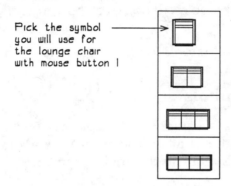
Pick the symbol
you will use for
the lounge chair
with mouse button 1

Figure 4.5: Pick the lounge symbol.

4. As you move your cursor back to the drawing area, you'll notice a box indicating that a copy of the symbol is now attached to your cursor, as in Figure 4.6.

Your cursor has a
box attached which
indicates the size
of your symbol

Figure 4.6: A box indicates the size of the symbol.

5. Place the lounge symbol in the living room, as in Figure 4.7, by moving it into position with the cursor then pressing mouse button 1.

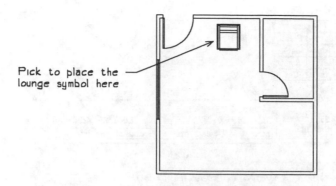

Figure 4.7: Put the lounge symbol in the living room.

6. Notice you still have a box connected to your cursor. You could place more copies of the symbol if you wanted.

7. Press mouse button 3 to quit placing the symbol.

Replacing symbols

Replacing symbols is a quick way to replace a symbol in your drawing with another symbol. The replaced symbol will have the same orientation as the original symbol.

1. Let's say you wanted to replace the lounge with a loveseat. Pick the **Replace** option.

2. Pick the Lounge symbol on your drawing.

3. Pick the Loveseat symbol in the template box.

4. Pick **All**. The lounge will turn into a loveseat, as in Figure 4.8. However, you didn't really want this. That's okay, you can do it again.

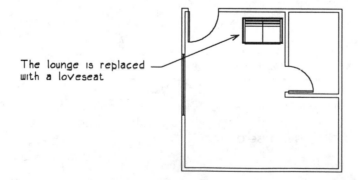

Figure 4.8: Replacing the lounge.

5. Pick the **Replace** option.

6. This time, pick the Loveseat symbol on your drawing.

7. Pick the Lounge symbol in the template box.

8.   Pick **All**. The Lounge symbol will be returned to your drawing.

This feature might be useful if you had designed an auditorium seating arrangement and the type of chair to be used was changed. They could all be switched at once. Or, if you were making a presentation to show the city what your structure would look like with new planting, the tree growth at five years, ten years, and maturity. Another example is a change of lighting types for a reflected ceiling plan or just a simple design on how you want your symbol to look. All of this can be managed quickly with replace.

A note about adding symbols in your workfile

The first time you pick a symbol from your template, you'll notice that it takes a little while before the box appears at your cursor. The second time you pick the same symbol, it appears almost instantly. Why?

Because the first time you pick the symbol, before you even add it to your drawing, the symbol was added to your drawing database, called a "workfile." After adding the symbol to your workfile, when you place the symbol, you're really just placing a "pointer." In other words, you add the symbol to your workfile, then you point to several positions and say "I want it here, and here, and here."

The advantage to this system is you can save a lot of file room in your drawing by using repeated symbols over and over. One good example of this is a large site layout of a housing tract with repeated footprints of models. The layout might have A, B, C, and D models repeated 30 times each. If you use symbols for your models, it would save you time, of course, but it also would result in a smaller file. Your drawing file might be only 120,000 bytes, versus 1,480,000 bytes if your models were not symbols.

Another advantage is the immediate updating of symbols. If the B footprint changes in our example, you could easily use the Redefine option to update all of the 30 B symbols in one step. If you wanted to replace all of the C footprints with the D, you could simply use the Replace option to update them, again in one step.

Rotating symbols

The other furniture symbols in your living room will have to be rotated 90 degrees. You can set the rotation value once, then all symbols you bring in will be rotated until you reset the value back to 0.

1. Pick **DymnRot** from the Template menu twice or until the Angle menu is displayed, to specify a rotation angle. (The first time you pick DymnRot, it will become active. The second time, the angle menu will be displayed.)

2. Pick the **90-0** option, and press ENTER .

3. Pick the sofa symbol.

4. Place it in the living room. Notice it's positioned at a 90-degree rotation angle, as in Figure 4.9.

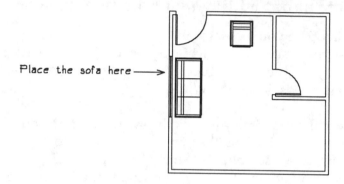

Place the sofa here ⟶

Figure 4.9: The symbol is rotated.

Getting a new template

Now you're done with the Furn template. You'll want to get the template called Tables.

1. Pick the **New File** option, found in the Template menu.

2. Pick the **TABLES** template.

3. The Tables template is displayed, as in Figure 4.10.

The Tables template ⟶

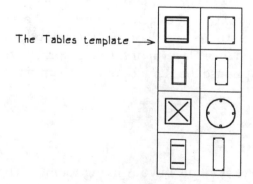

Figure 4.10: The Table template.

4.	Place the coffee table symbol in your drawing, shown in Figure 4.11. Notice that it's rotated too!

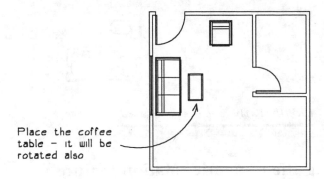

Place the coffee
table — it will be
rotated also

Figure 4.11: The coffee table will come in rotated.

Retrieving the plumbing templates

1.	Pick **New File**.

2.	Pick **New Path**.

3.	Pick the **..** option.

4.	Pick **PLUMB**. Notice the text line now says:
	\dcad6\tpl\plumb.

5.	Press ENTER .

6.	Once the plumbing templates are displayed, pick the **RESIDENC** template.

7.	The Residenc template should be displayed, as in Figure 4.12.

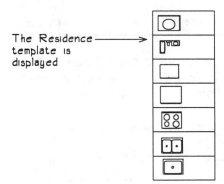

The Residence
template is
displayed

Figure 4.12: The Residenc template.

8.	Pick the **BathGrup** symbol. Notice that it comes in at the same 90-degree angle you set for the previous symbols. (You might try placing it on the drawing to see it better, as in Figure 4.13, then erase it by pressing the undo ◁ key.)

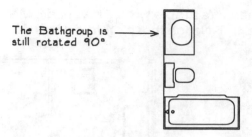

The Bathgroup is
still rotated 90° →

Figure 4.13: The bathgroup is still rotated.

Using the dynamic rotation feature

The dynamic rotation option allows you to place the symbol,
then rotate it by dragging the cursor on the screen.

1.   Pick the **DymnRot** option until it's active.

2.   Pick the **BathGrup** symbol again.

3.   Object snap to the corner of the bathroom shown in
     Figure 4.14.

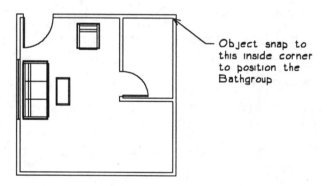

Object snap to
this inside corner
to position the
Bathgroup

Figure 4.14: Object snap to this corner for the bath group.

4.   Move the cursor out to the right until you see a line
     appear as in Figure 4.15. This is your "handle" for rotat-
     ing the symbol.

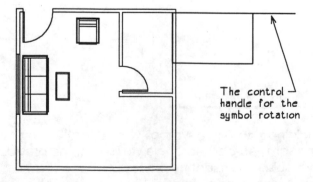

The control
handle for the
symbol rotation

Figure 4.15: The symbol rotation control handle.

5. Move the cursor down until the handle extends down in a vertical position, matching step 1 in Figure 4.16. Make sure you have orthomode ON! (Press Ⓞ for orthomode.)

6. Once the symbol box has the correct rotation, as shown as step 2 in Figure 4.16, pick to place it.

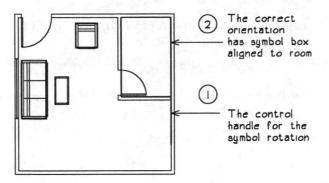

Figure 4.16: Rotating the symbol.

7. You might want to try this again. If so, press the undo Ⓒ key and repeat the procedure. You can try it with other symbols. Your drawing should look like Figure 4.17, but you might have added more symbols to it.

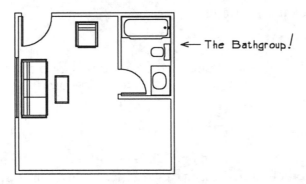

Figure 4.17: The bath group has been added.

8. Continue placing the symbols for your drawing that are found in this template, rotating as necessary. Use the second Wardrobe symbol as the double door refrigerator.

Renaming a symbol

Sometimes you might want to rename a symbol. As an example, for some reason the symbol you're using as a refrigerator is called a Wardrobe. Because this template is in the plumbing directory, it's probably better to rename this symbol. (If someone has renamed it already, try another new name!)

1. In the Template menu, pick **EditFlds** (Edit Fields). This option allows you to edit the template report fields that are connected with the symbols.

2. Pick the first **Wardrobe** symbol in the template window (it looks like a double door refrigerator).

3. Pick the **Item Nam** option.

4. Type in the new name for this symbol: **Small Refrigerator** and press ENTER .

5. Press mouse button 3 to quit.

6. Pick the second **Wardrobe** symbol in the template window (yes, there are two of them).

7. Pick the **Item Nam** option.

8. Type in the new name for this symbol: **Large Refrigerator** and press ENTER .

9. Press mouse button 3 to quit.

10. If you place your cursor over to the template window, you'll notice that the names for these symbols are *still* Wardrobe. You must reload the template (or individual symbol if you have used it in your drawing already). This is easy to do!

11. Pick the **Re-Load** option.

12. Pick **All**.

13. Pick **Yes**. The symbols will be reloaded, and the new names will be displayed for the refrigerators.

Identifying a symbol

You can inquire about an object or symbol to find out certain information about it. This is called "Identifying," and the option you'll use is called Identify. When you identify a symbol, you can find out the layer it's on, the color of the layer when the symbol was added (as specified by the handle point), and the lowest and highest points of the symbol (Z-base and height). This is useful for a number of reasons, one being that knowing the height of the table symbol will allow you to add a lamp on it, as you'll do in the following steps.

1. Pick the **[I]** button in the control panel to enter the Identify option, also found in the Edit menu.

2. Pick the table symbol. It will become gray and dashed.

3. Notice the information displayed in the message area of your screen. It will tell you the **Z-Min** (bottom) and **Z-Max** (top) of your symbol. The minimum should be

zero (unless someone has changed the table symbol), and the maximum could be about 1'-5" or 1'-6", depending on the actual symbol you used.

4. Write down the maximum height. You'll use this later, when you add the lamp on top of the table.

Identifying other items

As mentioned, identify is useful for many things. One practical purpose is to quickly tell you a wall length.

1. Pick one of your walls while you're in the Identify menu. It will become gray and dashed also. Notice the type of information that is displayed.

The following is a brief explanation of the Identify menu:

[F1] Item type (Line, arc, symbol, etc.)
[F2] Layer the item resides on.
[F3] Color of the item. If the item is a symbol, then color of the "handle point," which was the current color when the symbol was added.
[F4] Linetype (Solid, Dashed, etc.) If the item is a symbol, then linetype of the "handle point," as above.
[F5] Spacing for linetype, which is displayed in the message area at the bottom of the screen.
[F6] Line Weight, which is displayed in the message area.
[F7] Over Shoot factor, which is displayed in the message area.
[F8] and [F9] Z-base & height, which is displayed in the message area.

Another use for the Identify menu

While you're in identify, it's helpful to know that picking one of the menu options [F2-F9] will change the *current setting* to match the *selected item*.

As an example, if [F2] is showing that the layer for the selected item is *Walls*, picking [F2] will change the current active layer to Walls without having to [Tab] to it! To get back to *Furn*, you could pick the sofa symbol, which should be on Furn, and pick or press [F2] again.

The *Set All* option is frequently used. Picking Set All quickly changes *all* of the current settings to match the selected item.

1. Press mouse button 3 to quit.

Adding the lamp at table height

Later, you'll create a three-dimensional model from this floor plan. You'll want your lamp to set on top of the coffee table. To do this, you must adjust the Z-height of the symbol. The option to do this is called *Z Offset*. (The Z Offset remains set, like DymnRot. You'll want to change it it back to 0 after placing the lamp.)

1. Pick **New File**, in the Template menu.

2. Pick **New Path**.

3. Pick the **..** option.

4. Pick **FURN**. Press ENTER .

5. Now pick the **LAMPS** template choice.

6. The Lamps template will be displayed, as in Figure 4.18.

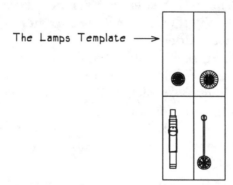

The Lamps Template ⟶

Figure 4.18: The Lamps template.

7. Pick the **Z Offset** option.

8. Type in the height of the table you identified earlier. This height will be around **1.5** or **1.6** (1'-5" or 1'-6"), depending on the table you used. Press ENTER .

9. Pick the lamp called **Ceramic**, and place it on your table, as shown in Figure 4.19.

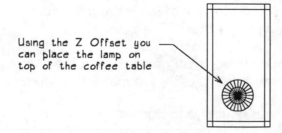

Using the Z Offset you can place the lamp on top of the coffee table

Figure 4.19: The lamp has been added.

10. Pick the **Z Offset** option again.

11. Change the offset value back to **0** and press ENTER .

12. File your drawing, pressing SHIFT F .

Turning off a template

1. To turn off the template when you're through working with it, pick the **TemplOff** option, in the Template menu.

Checking the size and accountability of your drawing

To check the size of your drawing, follow these steps.

1. Press ALT Y to go to the Directory menu, found in Utility.

2. The information of the current drawing will be displayed.

3. Look for the *"Current drawing size."* The drawing at this point will probably be around 40K if you have followed the steps in this book. The maximum for DataCAD is 6000K.

4. Also, the name of your file appears with the current directory path, under *"Drawing name"*.

5. You can check the amount of time you've spent on this drawing, under *"Total"* (total accumulated time), and *"This session"* (time spent during this drawing session since you pulled up the drawing file).

6. The *"Since last posting"* line is time spent during this drawing session since you last posted the information to a text file, which you haven't done, so it will be the same as *Total*.

7. The names of all your layers, along with their current active color and whether they are turned on or not, is also displayed.

8. The symbols you have used in your drawing can be listed by picking the **SymFiles** option.

Pausing the accounting time

Using the *Pause* feature, you can turn off the timing temporarily while you take a break. That way, if you're monitoring the actual time you've spent working on a project, it will be more accurate. Also, when you've walked away from your computer, people will be less tempted to play with your drawing. The pause feature turns off the mouse and keyboard, leaving only the [END] key functional.

1. Always file your drawing first by pressing [SHIFT] [F].

2. Pick the **Pause** option from the Directory menu.

3. The pause will be in effect until you press the [END] key.

4. Once you're out of pause, press mouse button 3 to exit this menu.

Exploding symbols

If you'll be using symbols that you know you'll want to change (for example, the color or erase some lines, etc.), then you'll have to explode the symbols. There are two ways to do this. First, you can add the symbols exploded, and there is an option in the Template menu to do just that. Secondly, you can explode symbols after they've been added.

Note: *Exploding symbols mean that they are no longer databased (connected with a report) or treated like a symbol. This also means they cannot be replaced or redefined in your drawing.*

To add symbols exploded

1. Press [T] to go to Template.

2. Pick the **SOFAS** template.

3. Pick **Explode** until it's active. Now symbols you add to your drawing will be exploded, and can be manipulated.

4. Pick the **SofaBed** and place it in your drawing.

5. Press [E] to go to the Erase menu.

6. Pick **Entity** to make it active.

7. Pick a piece of your sofabed. Notice that small chunks of it disappear at a time (it's made with 3D slabs). If it were still a symbol, all of it would erase at once.

8. Pick **Group** to make it active.

9. Pick a piece of your sofabed again. All of it will erase. Even though the symbol was exploded, it was still a *group.*

10. Press [T] to return to the Template menu.

11. Pick **Explode** to turn it OFF.

Exploding a symbol after it's placed in your drawing

1. Add another sofabed. You'll explode this one after you placed it.

2. Press SHIFT M to go to the Macros menu, found in Edit.

3. Pick the **SymExp** option (Symbol Explode).

4. Pick **Entity** or **Group**.

5. Pick the sofabed symbol you placed in step one. It will blink, indicating it was exploded. Let's try something new to do to your sofabed.

Changing items

Sometimes you've created items in the wrong color or linetype. You'll want to know how to change them.

1. Pick the **Change** tool from the tool bar, as shown in Figure 4.20. Or, you can press ALT C to go to the Change menu in Edit.

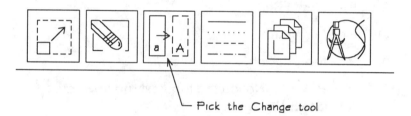

Pick the Change tool

Figure 4.20: The Change tool.

2. Pick the **Color** option.

3. Pick a new color for your sofabed. Don't worry too much, you'll be erasing it soon! Try picking **Yellow**.

4. Pick **Entity**.

5. Pick a piece of your sofabed. A section will change to yellow. Remember, the sofabed is made of 3D slabs (which are similar to boxes), so entire sections change together.

6. Try picking a symbol that hasn't been exploded. It won't change because it's protected!

7. Press E to go to Erase again, or pick the **Erase** tool, shown in Figure 4.21.

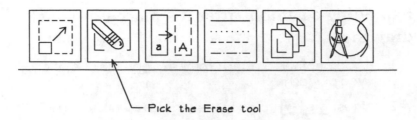

Pick the Erase tool

Figure 4.21: The Erase tool.

8. Pick **Group**.

9. Pick the sofabed in your drawing.

10. File your drawing, pressing SHIFT F .

Add the rest of the symbols

Use the Residence template to add a stove and sink to your drawing. Remember, the Residence template is in the tpl\plumb directory.

1. Press T .

2. Pick **New File**.

3. Pick **New Path**.

4. Pick the .. option.

5. Pick **PLUMB**. Notice the that text line now says: **\dcad6\tpl\plumb**.

6. Press ENTER .

7. Once the plumbing templates are displayed, pick the **RESIDENC** template.

8. Add the kitchen symbols, as shown in Figure 4.22.

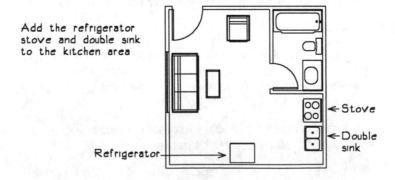

Add the refrigerator stove and double sink to the kitchen area

←Stove

←Double sink

Refrigerator

Figure 4.22: The completed space layout.

Quitting DataCAD

1. Press `ALT` `Q` , or pick **Quit** from the Edit menu.

2. Pick **Yes**, or press the `Y` key (for **Yes**), to save your drawing.

DataCAD Exercise 3

Please complete the following exercise by reading each question carefully, then circling the letter that corresponds to the correct answer.

1. To quickly change layers, you press the:
   a. ⌨Tab key.
   b. ⌨ALT ⌨L keys.
   c. ⌨L key.

2. DataCAD symbols are attached to:
   a. Other symbols.
   b. Symbol libraries.
   c. Templates.

3. To change a template directory, you use the:
   a. **New Dir** option.
   b. **New Path** option.
   c. **Tem Dir** option.

4. To use a symbol, you first have to:
   a. Pick a library.
   b. Pick a template.
   c. Call up a symbol file.

5. The quick way to enter the Template menu is to press the:
   a. ⌨ALT ⌨T key.
   b. ⌨T key.
   c. ⌨ALT ⌨S keys.

6. To pick a symbol off the template, you use mouse button:
   a. 1.
   b. 2.
   c. 3.

7. To quit placing the symbol, you use mouse button:
   a. 1.
   b. 2.
   c. 3.

8. To place a symbol at another angle, you use the:
   a. **Angle** option.
   b. **DymnRot** option.
   c. **NewAngl** option.

9. When you have set a rotation angle while placing a symbol, it:
    a. Automatically resets to 0 for the next symbol.
    b. Changes all of the rotation angles for the other symbols already placed in your drawing.
    c. Remains set for all new symbols you're adding, until you change it.

10. To open a new template, when you already have a template displayed, in the Template menu you pick:
    a. **New File**.
    b. **StrtFile**.
    c. **NewTempl**.

11. When you're working on the second floor of a 3D modeled building, before you place a symbol you would want to set the:
    a. **Z Base** option in the Template menu.
    b. **X Offset** option in the Template menu.
    c. **Z Offset** option in the Template menu.

12. To use coordinate input, you press the:
    a. `SPACE` .
    b. `ALT` `C` keys.
    c. `Tab` .

13. Exploding a symbol means:
    a. It's connected to a report and it's a single entity.
    b. It's no longer a single entity and you can change it.
    c. It's a single entity. You can't change a portion of it.

14. After renaming a symbol:
    a. The new name appears immediately when you move the cursor to the template window.
    b. You can only see the new name in another drawing that doesn't contain the symbol with the old name.
    c. Pick **Re-Load** to load the name in the drawing database.

15. Checking the size of your drawing is accomplished by using the:
    a. File I/O menu, **File size** option.
    b. Directory menu.
    c. Display menu, **File size** option.

16. Identifying a symbol is helpful to:
    a. Find out what layer it's on and what the Z-maximum and Z-minimum heights are.
    b. Identify what layer it should go on.
    c. Find out what items, such as lines and arcs, are in the symbol, along with the individual item colors.

17. The **Set All** option in the Identify menu allows you to:
    a. Change all of the current settings to match the identified item, such as layer, color, and Z-base and height.
    b. Set all of the selected items back onto their correct layer.
    c. Set all of the settings (layer, color, etc.) of the selected items to whatever you want with one pick.

18. Before changing the color of a symbol, you must:
    a. File your drawing.
    b. Explode it.
    c. Use the Change menu and pick a new color.

19. The Change menu is helpful if:
    a. You need the color or linetype of entities you already added to your drawing changed.
    b. You want to change the Z-height of your symbol.
    c. You need the current color or linetype settings changed for all new items you're about to create.

20. The **Replace** option in the Template menu is to:
    a. Change the symbol in the template box.
    b. Replace one template on your computer with another template quickly and easily.
    c. Replace a symbol in your drawing with another symbol quickly and easily.

CHAPTER 5

Viewing your drawing in 3D

The 3D drawing

Now that you have added walls, doors, windows, and symbols to your house floor plan, it will be interesting to view it in three dimensions. As mentioned previously, certain three-dimensional features were automatic as you drew your house.

Here are some of the things you'll learn in this chapter:

- Defining an isometric view.
- Adding a 3D view to your drawing.
- Creating a perspective view.
- Scaling the 3D view to fit in your border.
- Moving items by dragging and placing.
- Moving items by defining a point-to-point distance.
- Hidden line removal.
- Quick shading your 3D view.

3D views

You can create 3D views directly from your plan view drawings for presentations, spatial studies and illustration purposes. You can create three types of 3D views.

1. *Parallel* - which includes isometric, elevations and sections.

2. *Perspective* - including interiors and bird's eye.

3. *Oblique* - helpful for cabinetry specs and other details, and can be dimensioned.

During this chapter, you'll create *perspective views* as shown in Figure 5.1.

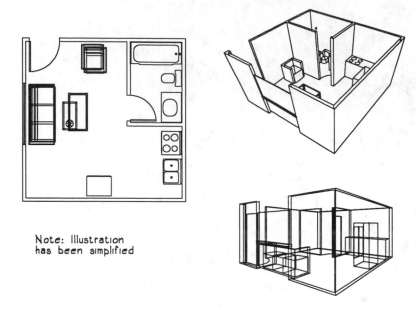

Note: Illustration has been simplified

Figure 5.1: The 3D views added to your drawing.

Turning off unnecessary layers

Before you create a 3D image, you'll want to turn off the layers that hold graphics you don't want to see in 3D, such as your border.

1. Press ⬚L to enter the Layers menu.

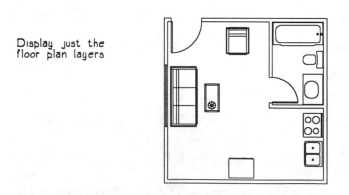

Display just the floor plan layers

Figure 5.2: Just the floor plan is displayed.

2. Pick the **On/Off** option.

3. Pick the layer called **Border** to turn it off.

4. Exit by pressing mouse button 3.

5. Now, only the plan view is displayed, as illustrated in Figure 5.2.

Creating the perspective view

1. Pick the **[V]** button in the control panel to quickly go to the 3D Views menu.

2. Pick the **SetPersp** option (Set Perspective View).

3. At this point there might be a triangular set of lines displayed on your drawing, as in Figure 5.3. This is a *cone of vision* default for your drawing. Don't worry if you don't see it, as it might be off your viewing window. You'll be defining a new one, regardless of how the cone is placed now.

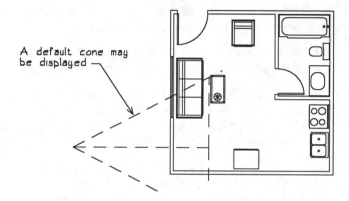

Figure 5.3: A default cone of vision might be displayed.

What is the cone of vision?

The cone shows where you have picked on the screen for the following definitions, as shown in Figure 5.4:

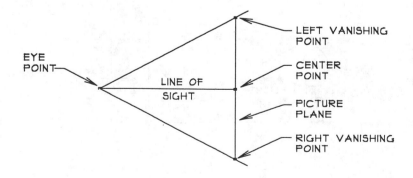

Figure 5.4: The definitions for the cone of vision.

1. *Eye point* (this will be pick 1).

2. *Picture plane*, with vanishing points, line of sight, and centerpoint (pick number 2).

Explanations of each perspective definition

The perspective control definitions are explained below, and pictured in Figure 5.5.

Eye point - Your point of vision, also called a station point. The eye point height (horizon line), in normal perspectives (those viewed from a standing position), is located 5'-0" above the ground line. The height of the eye point is adjustable using the *EyePnt Z* (eye point Z-height) option. The angle of the eye point (for three-point perspectives) is determined by also adjusting the *CentPnt Z* (Center point Z-height) option.

Picture plane - Items appearing in front of the plane look larger, items in back of the plane appear smaller. Items intersecting the plane retain true size.

Vanishing points - These are the vanishing points for your perspective, which are projected to the horizon line.

Line of sight - This is the line drawn from the eye point to the picture plane. Where it intersects the plane is the centerpoint. The angle of the line of sight is adjustable by using the *EyePnt Z* and *CentPntZ* options.

Centerpoint - This is the point where the line of sight meets the picture plane. The result is the horizon line. The height of the centerpoint is adjustable using the *CentPntZ* option. For a normal two-point perspective (horizon line height is the same as eye level) the centerpoint height is the same as the eye point setting. This provides you a level line of sight. For a three-point perspective (horizon line is at a different level than the eye level), adjust the centerpoint and the eye point heights to provide you with an angled line of sight.

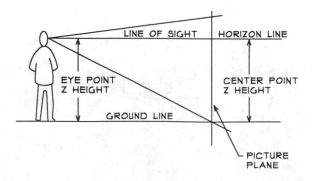

Figure 5.5: Illustrated perspective controls.

Setting the cone of vision

Sounds difficult, but it's really easy.

1. Press the ⬅ (move view left) key on your keyboard, until your plan view is moved over to the right-hand side (you could also pick the ⬅ button in your control panel). This will give you a better area to work with for positioning your cone of vision.

2. Press the ⬇ "move view down" key, (or pick the ⬇ button on the control panel), until the view is moved into the upper right-hand corner. Now you have a clear area to define a cone of vision.

3. Pick a point in the lower left of your drawing, as indicated in Figure 5.6. This will be your new eye point. (The height for your eye point is currently set to the default of 5'-0".)

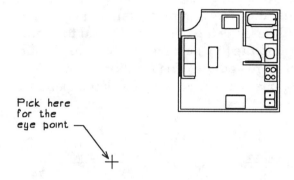

Pick here
for the
eye point

Figure 5.6: The first pick is the eyepoint.

4. Move your cursor around. You'll see the cone of vision attached to your cursor.

5. Now move your cursor all the way over to your house. Pick or object snap to the lower-left corner of your house, as indicated in Figure 5.7.

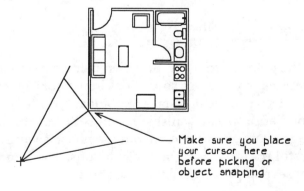

Make sure you place
your cursor here
before picking or
object snapping

Figure 5.7: Pick here for your centerpoint.

6. A textbook perspective will be displayed, and it should look similar to Figure 5.8.

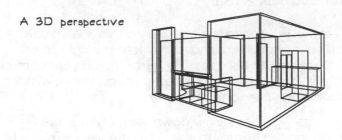

A 3D perspective

Figure 5.8: Your first 3D perspective view.

The globe

When you use any of the view options (perspective, parallel, oblique) except for orthographic, the "globe" will appear on the screen. What the globe is representing is a flattened-out world. The middle is the top of the world, and the bottom is spread out around the top, making a flat world. The idea is that you can change your viewing position by picking somewhere on the globe. The specific regions of the globe are explained in Figure 5.9, which shows the globe and its relationship to a round world.

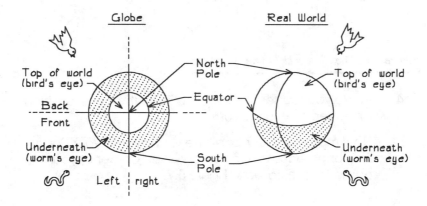

Figure 5.9: The globe illustrated.

Although the globe is very helpful when using a parallel view definition (as you'll see soon), it's clumsy for perspectives. This is because the original eye point and center point picks defined appropriate vanishing points. Picking on the globe changes your view position, but the house's vanishing points are still true to the original calculations. You might want to try several picking points to see how this looks.

1. Move your cursor up to the inside of the globe.

2.   Press mouse button 1 to pick a globe position. You must pick inside the globe, and you cannot use object snap.

After trying globe pick points, you can get close to your original view by picking in the bottom of the inside circle. The reason is, when you first defined your perspective, this is where your building was, as indicated in Figure 5.10.

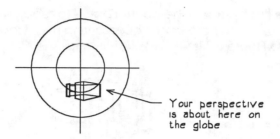

Your perspective
is about here on
the globe

Figure 5.10: The perspective view on the globe.

Although you didn't see your house dangling on the globe, it was there theoretically. Picking on the globe will get you close to the original perspective, but to get back to the true original perspective, you'll want to "Reset" it.

Resetting the perspective

1.   Pick **SetPersp**.

2.   Pick **Reset**.

Saving the 3D view

Once you're satisfied with your view, you can save in onto a layer, and add it to your plan view.

1.   Pick the **SaveImag** option (Save Image).

2.   Pick the **NewLayer** option. This will allow you to name a special layer for your 3D view.

3.   Type in the name for your new layer: **Persp1** and press `ENTER` .

4.   Pick **On** to keep this new layer displayed.

5.   Press mouse button 3 to exit.

Returning to the plan view (Orthographic)

The plan view is referred to as an *orthographic* in DataCAD.

1.   Pick the **[Ortho]** button in the control panel.

Displaying all layers

There is a layer option to display all layers.

1. Press [L] to go to the Layers menu.

2. Pick the **AllOn** option.

3. Pick **Yes**.

4. Pick the **[R]** button in the control panel to recalculate a full view of your drawing. Your drawing might look similar to Figure 5.11.

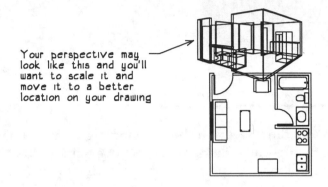

Your perspective may look like this and you'll want to scale it and move it to a better location on your drawing

Figure 5.11: The perspective appears in your drawing.

Reviewing the use of the tool bar

You'll use the tool bar for the next steps. As a review, you know the tool bar appears at the top of the drawing area. If you move your cursor over the icons, a description of the tool will be displayed in the the message area.

If you haven't used the tool bar yet, it might be because you feel comfortable using quick keys. (For example, pressing E to go to Erase might be much faster than finding the Erase tool to pick.)

Sometimes, scrolling the tool bar forward to find the tool would take more time than pressing a quick key (and, you'd have to scroll back!) The steps in this book concentrate on using a combination of quick keys and the main tools, and only scrolling through the tools when it saves steps in the long run.

Next, you'll scale your perspective, using the Enlarge tool that appears on your tool bar.

1. Move your cursor to the **Enlarge** tool, as shown in Figure 5.12.

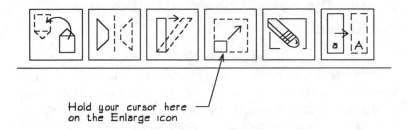

Hold your cursor here
on the Enlarge icon

Figure 5.12: The Enlarge tool.

2. Look at the message area, illustrated in Figure 5.13. It will display the name of the tool and a description.

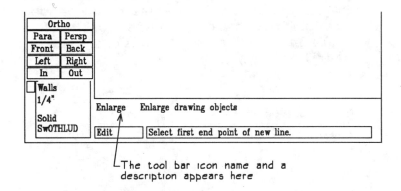

The tool bar icon name and a
description appears here

Figure 5.13: The description appears in the message area.

3. As a review, move your cursor over to the other icons and note what they are used for.

4. There are 25 tool icons in this tool bar. To see the other tools available, pick the **Scroll Forward** tool (arrow points right), as indicated in Figure 5.14. You'll have to pick it twice to see all of the tools, since only 11 are shown at a time.

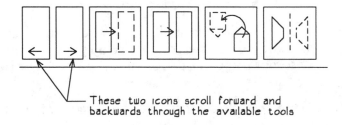

These two icons scroll forward and
backwards through the available tools

Figure 5.14: These icons control the tool list.

5. To go back to the main tools (first group of 11 icons shown), pick the **Scroll Back** tool (arrow points left), twice, until the tool bar doesn't scroll anymore.

6. You'll use the **Enlarge** tool for these next steps.

Scaling the perspective (enlarging and shrinking)

Because of the way the perspective is created, it rarely comes in at the desired size. You might want to enlarge it or scale it down, depending on what your 3D image looks like. (You use the same function to enlarge items in your drawing as you do to shrink them.)

1. Pick the **Enlarge** icon (shown in the previous Figure 5.12) to go to the Enlarge menu, found in Edit.

2. The message asks you to enter a centerpoint. This is the point that will stay stationary as the group is enlarged or shrunk. Pick in the center of your perspective to establish a center of enlargement, as indicated in Figure 5.15. (You'll move the image after it's been scaled, anyway.)

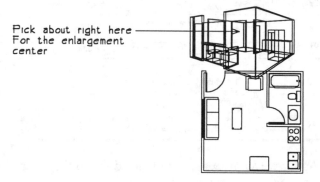

Pick about right here
For the enlargement
center

Figure 5.15: Pick in the center of the perspective.

3. Now the Enlarge menu is displayed. To set a scale, pick the **Enlrgmnt** option.

4. Make sure the layer that holds your perspective view: **Persp1**, is active, by using the [Tab] key.

5. Pick **Lyrsrch** to turn it off. This way, only the active layer can be edited, and you won't change the size of something else besides the perspective image by mistake.

6. Pick **Set All** to set the X, Y, and Z values at once.

7. Pick a scale factor that you want to change the size of the perspective by. For example, **.5** will shrink your items to half the present size. An enlargement factor of **2** will make items twice the present size. A **1.25** will make items larger a small bit at a time, while **.8** will shrink them a little.

8. Once you've decided on a scale, pick it or type it in and press [ENTER] .

9. Press mouse button 3 to return to the Enlarge menu.

10. Pick **Group** to make it active.

12. Pick a corner of your perspective, and it will change size. As shown in Figure 5.16, the image was reduced when a **.75** scale was used.

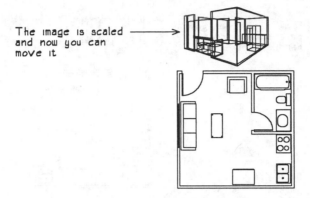

The image is scaled and now you can move it

Figure 5.16: The perspective image is reduced.

Note: *As you make your perspectives, you'll notice that they're created at all different sizes, some very large and some closer to correct size. This size is relative to the original viewing size of the building BEFORE you defined your perspective. Parallel views (such as elevations) come in at true size.*

Moving

Once the size of the perspective image is reduced, you'll want to "Move" it to fit better in your border with your house. Moving items in your drawing is an easy task.

1. Pick the **Move** tool icon, as shown in Figure 5.17. Or, you could press [M] , the Move quick key.

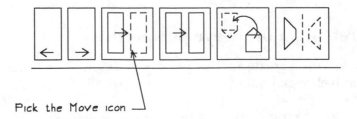

Pick the Move icon

Figure 5.17: Pick the Move tool.

2. Pick the **Drag** option.

3. Notice that **Group** is still active and **Lyrsrch** is still off.

5. Pick a corner of your perspective. It will become gray and dashed.

6. Now you'll be prompted to pick a point to move the perspective by. Pick a point on the perspective, as indicated in Figure 5.18.

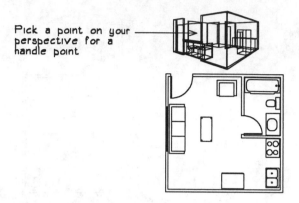

Figure 5.18: Pick to the left of the perspective.

7. A box outline showing the maximum size of your image will appear on your cursor (similar to a symbol as your placing it), and you'll be able to drag it to a new location.

8. Pick a spot over to the lower right of the original floor plan, as indicated in Figure 5.19. (You might want to turn OFF orthomode by pressing [O] .)

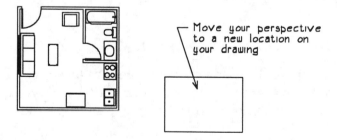

Figure 5.19: Pick for the new location.

Creating a birds-eye perspective

Now you'll create another perspective view. This time, you'll change your eye level and remove the hidden lines.

1. Pick the **Layer** tool, as indicated in Figure 5.20. Or, you could press [L] to go to the Layers menu.

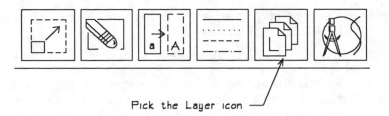

Pick the Layer icon ⎯

Figure 5.20: The Layer tool is handy to use.

2. Pick **On/Off**.

3. Turn off **Border** and **Persp1**. Press mouse button 3 to exit.

4. Pick the **[V]** button in the control panel.

5. Pick **SetPersp** to redefine your viewing orientation.

6. Pick **EyePnt** to change your eye point height.

7. Type in **30** and press ENTER . This will change your eye point height to 30 feet. Now you'll be able to look over the walls and into the room when you create your perspective.

8. Pick the points for your cone again, experimenting with the position. Just remember that the second pick will now define a viewing angle because the centerpoint is still set to 5'. In other words, move the cursor into the house before picking the second point.

9. Your new perspective will be displayed, and you'll have a bird's-eye view of the building, as shown in Figure 5.21.

Your bird's eye view

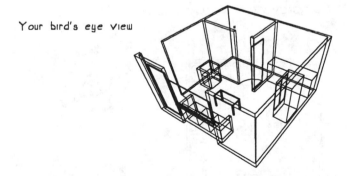

Figure 5.21: Your bird's eye perspective might look like this.

Hidden line removal

Once you have achieved the desired view, you'll want to remove the hidden lines from your view.

1. Press ⌈SHIFT⌉ ⌈Y⌉ to enter the Hide menu, found in the DCAD 3D, 3D Edit menus.

2. The Hide menu is displayed.

3. Pick **SavImag** until it's active, to save the image you'll be creating. You have to do this *before* creating the hidden line image in order to save it.

4. Another option you might want to set is **CropImag**. This way, if anything appears out of the 3D view, it will be cropped out of the picture like a photograph. (This is especially important for inside images.)

5. Pick the **Begin** option.

6. After the hidden line removal process is complete, pick the **NewLayer** option.

7. Type in the name this layer: **Persp2** and press ⌈ENTER⌉ .

8. Pick **On** to keep this layer displayed.

9. Press the ⌈:⌉ key to return to 2D DataCAD.

10. Follow the same steps as before to turn on the **Layers**, change the **Enlargement** scale of the image, and **Move** it to another location in your border.

Important Note: *If you decide you want to move your floor plan, turn on LyrSrch in the Move menu first! Otherwise, if you're on one of the Persp layers, nothing will move. If you ⌈Tab⌉ to another layer, like Walls, only the walls would move. Then, you would have a mess.*

---

11. Your drawing should now look like Figure 5.22.

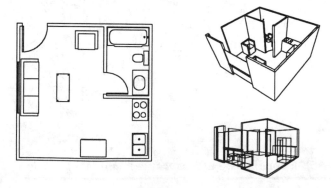

Figure 5.22: Two perspectives have been added.

12. Remember to press ⌈SHIFT⌉ ⌈F⌉ to quickly file your drawing.

Defining an isometric view

An isometric view is easy to define using these few steps.

1. Pick the Layer icon or press ⬜L to go to the Layers menu.

2. Pick **On/Off**.

3. Turn off **Border**, **Persp1**, and **Persp2**. Press mouse button 3 to exit.

4. Pick the **[V]** button in the control panel.

5. Pick **Isometrc**.

6. Pick the **[R]** button in the control panel to recalculate your viewing window.

7. Your isometric should look like Figure 5.23.

An isometric

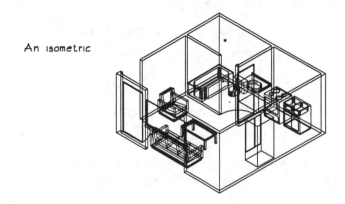

Figure 5.23: An isometric view.

Creating a shaded view

You can follow these steps if you configured the Quick Shader when you installed DataCAD. The Quick Shader is a quick way to see a surface-shaded image of your drawing. The colors of the shading depend on the colors of each item in your drawing.

1. Either the *isometric* or *perspective* view of your drawing works well for this.

2. Press ⬜J to go to the 3D Edit menu.

3. Pick **QShader**. If you don't see this option, check that you're in the 3D Edit menu. If you still don't see it, Quick Shader has not been loaded or is turned off. See Chapter 1, *Installing and Configuring DataCAD*.

4. Pick **LightL** to make it active (light from left side).

5. Pick **No Edge** to make it active, eliminating an edge line so that faceted edges blend together better.

6. Pick **Begin**. The house will be shaded.

7. Press 🔡 to quickly go to the 2D Edit menu.

Note: This image is a pixel shaded image. If you change your view or press ⟦ESC⟧ *, the shading will disappear.*

Printing the shaded image

If you have a printer that will print pixel format, you can print out the shaded image in color or black and white.

1. Once you have the shaded image, don't change your view, or the shading will disappear.

2. Press mouse button 3 to go to the Utility menu.

3. Pick the **File I/O** option.

4. Pick the **PixelOut** option.

5. Pick **AllDwg** to make it active.

6. Make sure **Inverse** is NOT active.

7. Pick **Lndscape** to make it active. This will turn the drawing 90 degrees to fit better on the paper.

8. Pick the **EnlrgFac** option. Try a 3 as a beginning value. (A factor of 1 makes a very small picture.)

9. If your printer is connected and turned on, pick the **ToPaper** option.

10. Press mouse button 3 to exit once the picture is generated.

Creating a pictogram of the shaded image

Since the image will not retain its shading when the viewing window size is changed, you must adjust the size you need first, then shade it.

1. In the **File I/O** menu, pick **PixelOut**.

2. Pick **Pictogram**.

3. Press ⟦ENTER⟧ to accept the name of the pictogram file.

4. Move the cursor into the drawing area.

5. Press the ⟦PG UP⟧ key on your keyboard until the 3D view of your house fits neatly into the small box.

6. Press [J] to go to the 3D Edit menu.

7. Pick **QShader**.

8. Pick **Begin**. The house will be shaded.

9. Press [:] to quickly go to 2D Edit menu.

10. Press mouse button 3 to go to Utility.

11. Pick **File I/O**.

12. Pick **PixelOut**.

13. Pick **Pictogram**.

14. Press [ENTER] to accept the name of the pictogram file.

15. Move the cursor into the drawing area. Now the shaded house should fit.

16. Pick to position the box over the image.

17. Press [SHIFT] [F] to file your drawing.

18. Press [ALT] [N] (new drawing) to leave this drawing and return to the drawing list.

19. Pick **Yes** to exit DataCAD.

20. Once the drawing list is displayed, hold your cursor over the drawing name for your house: **HOUSE1**. Is the shaded image showing up in the preview box?

DataCAD exercise 4

Please complete the following exercise by reading each question carefully, then circling the letter that corresponds to the correct answer.

1. Before creating a 3D view, you should:
   a. Make sure all of the layers are displayed.
   b. Turn off the layers that you don't want to view in 3D.
   c. Make sure the dimensions layer is displayed.

2. To help you create the perspective, DataCAD displays a:
   a. Cone of Vision.
   b. Option called Line of sight.
   c. View of Vision.

3. To create a new perspective, you use the:
   a. **MakePersp** option.
   b. **SetPersp** option.
   c. **Prspect** option.

4. To create a bird's-eye view, you need to adjust the.
   a. **CntrPntZ** option.
   b. **BirdsView** option.
   c. **EyePntZ** option.

5. The globe that's displayed when you're in perspective:
   a. Is really useful for redefining the perspective.
   b. Isn't correct for defining a perspective view. The vanishing points were calculated in Set Perspective.
   c. Shows you where your building is located.

6. The middle of the globe is really the:
   a. Top of the world.
   b. Bottom of the world.
   c. Worm's eye view.

7. Picking on the outer ring of the globe will display a view of your building from the:
   a. Top.
   b. Bottom.
   c. Side.

8. The 3D image is saved as:
   a. One group.
   b. Several different groups, depending on how many layers the items were on.
   c. The same amount of groups that were in the original building.

9. To "Move" objects by pulling them with your cursor
    dynamically, pick the:
    a. **Pull** option.
    b. **Drag** option.
    c. **Dynamic** option.

10. To save the 3D view, you use the:
    a. **SaveView** option.
    b. **NewView** option.
    c. **SaveImag** option.

11. When saving the 3D view, you:
    a. Must have a predefined layer to hold your views on.
    b. Are given the option to create a new layer for it.
    c. Cannot save in on any layer but the active one.

12. The saved perspective image:
    a. Usually will have to be moved to a better location.
    b. Pops into your drawing in the right spot.
    c. Automatically moves to an upper righthand corner.

13. The Enlarge option:
    a. Enlarges items only.
    b. Allows you to enter a new scale for plotting.
    c. Lets you enlarge or shrink items.

14. To increase the eye level height for viewing the perspec-
    tive, you use the:
    a. **BirdsEye** option.
    b. **EyePntZ** option.
    c. **EyeLevel** option.

15. If you want to save the view with hidden lines removed,
    you must:
    a. First set the **SavImag** option.
    b. Remove the lines, then pick the **SavImag** option.
    c. Remove the lines, then pick the **SaveView** option.

16. To display the plan view of your drawing after creating a
    perspective, you use the:
    a. **[Ortho]** button.
    b. **[PlanView]** button.
    c. Mouse button 3. The plan view is automatically
        displayed.

17. To permanently save a drawing, you must:
    a. Press ⌨SHIFT ⌨F ,or pick **Yes** when quitting DataCAD.
    b. Not do anything. The file is automatically saved.
    c. Quit DataCAD, and pick **Abort**.

Viewing your drawing in 3D

Adding dimensions and notes

Notating your drawing

Working drawings must have dimensions and notes to communicate. DataCAD makes dimensioning almost automatic, and typing in notes is very easy.

Here are some of the things you'll learn in this chapter:

- Creating horizontal and vertical dimensions.
- How to stringline dimensions.
- Adding notes to your drawing.
- Drawing arrows.
- Changing existing text.
- Modifying associated dimensions.

Dimensions

Dimensioning your drawing is fast in DataCAD. The text in a dimension is generated automatically. This is because the software calculates the lengths of your walls or other items. All you do is tell the system what you want dimensioned and where you want the dimension to appear. Figure 6.1 shows your house project with the dimensions you'll add during this chapter.

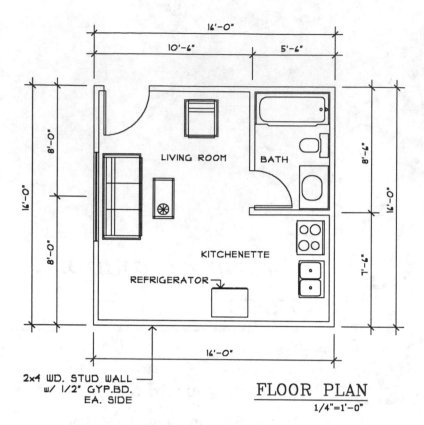

Figure 6.1: *Your house dimensioned.*

When you tell the system what corners you want dimensioned, remember to use object snap! This is to make certain you're "grabbing" the object you're dimensioning.

Four types of dimensions

There are four types of dimensioning available, and they are shown in Figure 6.2.

1. Linear   2. Angular   3. Diameter   4. Radius

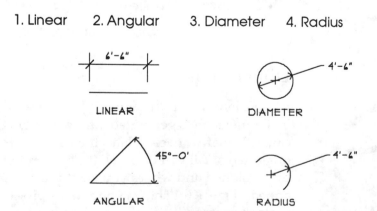

Figure 6.2: *Four dimensioning types.*

Snap increments

As you already know, when you move your cursor, it jumps to certain increments. This function is called *grid snap*. You can turn grid snap on and off, and the status is displayed as the S in SWOTHLUD, which appears in the status area of the screen.

1. To turn snap off, press ⌧ until the message reads: *Snap is OFF.*

2. To turn it on, press ⌧ again. The message reads: *Snap is ON.*

With snap ON, you'll be able to check the current cursor snap increments. Simply move your cursor on the screen and watch the coordinate readout, and you see what the measurements jump by. Is it 4" or 6"? Or maybe something else.

Snap is defined for *each layer*. In other words, you can have a 6" snap set on the Walls layer, and a 4" snap set for plumbing. Maybe you would have a 1" snap set for the electrical layer to make it easier to draw the electrical wiring line connecting the lighting and switches. For now, setting the snap to 2" for dimensions will make object snapping to corners and centers of walls easier.

Follow these simple steps to set your snap.

1. Press ⌨Tab to go to the layer you wish to set the snap on. In this case, tab to the **Dims** layer.

2. Press the ⌊S⌋ key. This is the quick way to enter the Grids, Gridsize, Set Snap menus.

3. The prompt will ask you to type in the X and Y increment values.

4. Type in **.2** (2") for the *X increment*. Press ⌊ENTER⌋ .

5. Notice that the *Y increment* automatically sets the same value, **0.2**. Press ⌊ENTER⌋ to accept it.

Creating linear dimensions to corners of walls

These steps will guide you through the creation of dimensions to the sides of wall versus the center. For dimensioning to centers, such as needed for steel studs, see that section. You'll notice that when using DataCAD, you start with the dimensions closest to the wall and work outwards. This is in contrast to manual drafting, where you start with the overall dimensions and work inward towards smaller dimensions.

1. Make sure the **Dims** layer is active.

2. Press ALT D . This is the quick way to enter the Dimension menu, Linear option, found in the Utility menu.

4. Pick the **Horiznt** option until it's active.

5. Make sure the **Assoc** option is also active. Associated dimensions change automatically when you stretch them. You'll see later how this works when you edit walls in your drawing.

6. Object snap to the first corner point of the wall to dimension, as illustrated in Figure 6.3. Remember to object snap with mouse button 2.

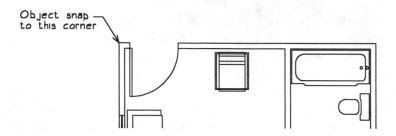

Figure 6.3: Object snap to the first corner.

7. Move the cursor over to the next corner of the wall, as shown in Figure 6.4. Object snap to it.

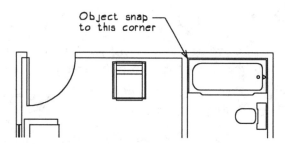

Figure 6.4: Object snap to the next point to dimension.

8. Move the cursor to place the height of the dimension, as shown in Figure 6.5, and pick with mouse button 1. Make it about 4' from the wall. Note that a distance of 4'-0" from the wall will be plotted as 1" in a 1/4" scale drawing. You might want another distance.

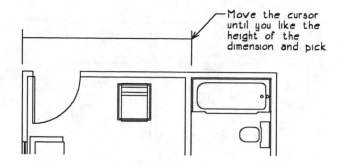

Figure 6.5: Pick for the dimension line placement.

9. The dimension and text will appear, as in Figure 6.6.

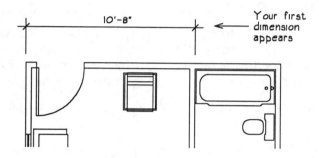

Figure 6.6: Your first dimension.

10. Pick the **StrngLin** option (String Line).

11. Now object snap to the *next* corner, as indicated in Figure 6.7. *(Don't object snap to the first corner again!)*

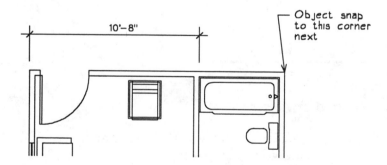

Figure 6.7: Grab the next corner.

12. The second dimension will pop up, as illustrated in Figure 6.8.

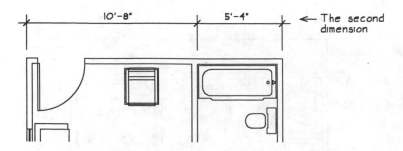

Figure 6.8: Your second dimension.

13. Now press mouse button 3 to exit StrngLin. You'll be returned to the Linear Dimensions menu.

14. Pick the **OverAll** option.

15. Pick to place the overall dimension, about 1'-6" away from the first stack of dimensions. This will leave a space of 3/8" when plotted. (You don't have to be this exact. Most people just pick a distance by eye.)

16. The overall dimension will appear, as in Figure 6.9.

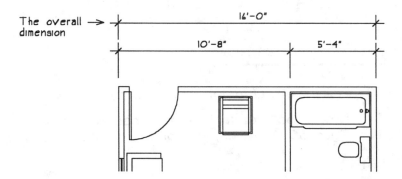

Figure 6.9: The "overall" dimension.

Stacking dimensions

Following a simple technique, you can create many levels of dimensions, as shown in Figure 6.10.

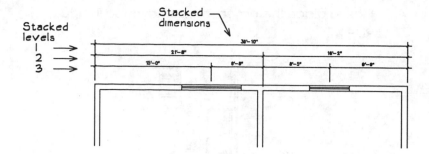

Figure 6.10: Stacking dimensions is easy.

To stack dimensions, all you have to do is "object snap" to the tic marks of the existing dimensions, as in Figure 6.11 This technique also avoids the little gap that occurs when using overall.

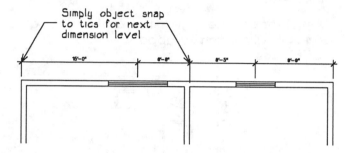

Figure 6.11: Stack dimensions by object snapping to tic marks.

1. Pick the **Verticl** option until it's active. This option allows you to create the vertical dimensions in your drawing

2. Object snap to the first corner of your vertical dimension, shown as step 1 in Figure 6.12.

3. Object snap to the center of the window, shown as step 2 in Figure 6.12.

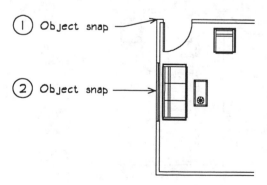

Figure 6.12: Creating your vertical dimensions.

4. Pick to place the dimension, as indicated in Figure 6.13.

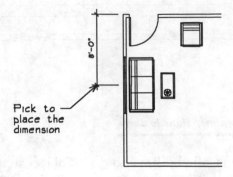

Figure 6.13: Placing the vertical dimension.

5. Pick **StrngLin**.

6. Object snap to the next corner, as shown in Figure 6.14. That dimension will appear.

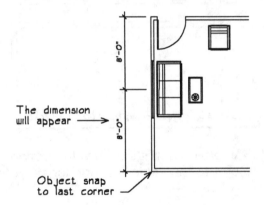

Figure 6.14: The stringline dimension appears.

7. Press mouse button 3 to exit the StrngLin menu.

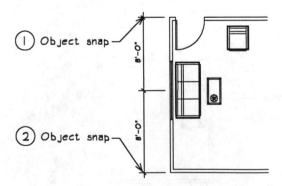

Figure 6.15: Object snap to these two tic marks.

8. Object snap to the tic mark of the first vertical dimension, as shown as step 1 in Figure 6.15.

9. Object snap to the second tic mark, as shown as step 2 in Figure 6.15.

10. Pick to place the dimension, as in Figure 6.16.

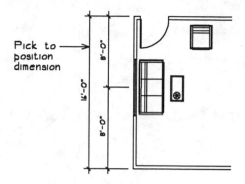

Figure 6.16: Pick to place the dimension.

Dimensioning to the centers of the walls

There are a few extra steps for this one using the Divide option, but it's worth it. Figure 6.17 illustrates how divide works.

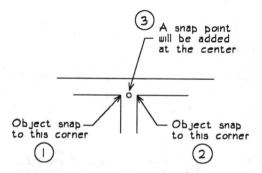

Figure 6.17: Divide locates the centerpoint.

1. Press ⌐ALT⌐ ⌐G⌐ to quickly go to the Geometry menu, found in Utility.

2. Pick the **Divide** option. Divide allows you to add a number of snap points between two points or on an entity (arc, circle, or line).

3. The message at the bottom should read: **Number of divisions = 2**. This means the points that you indicate will be divided to two pieces, putting a snap point in the middle.

4. If the number of divisions is *not* already set to 2, pick the **Dvisions** option, type in **2** and press ⌐ENTER⌐ .

5. Object snap to the two inside corners of the wall you wish to dimension to the center. This is illustrated in Figure 6.18.

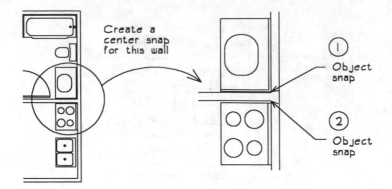

Figure 6.18: Creating the centerpoint in the wall.

6. A snap point will be added. (You might want to *zoom into* this area to see better.)

7. It would be a good idea to add all of the snap points you needed while you're in this option, instead of going back and forth. An example of this is found in Figure 6.19.

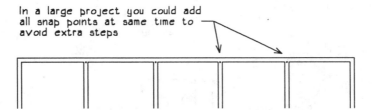

Figure 6.19: Many center points can be added at one time.

8. Press [ALT] [D] to return to Dimensions, Linear.

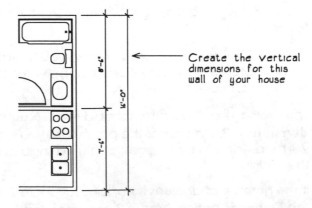

Figure 6.20: Object snap to your centerpoints.

9. Now continue dimensioning as required, making sure you object snap to the new snap points you've added. See Figure 6.20.

10. If you need a small centerline in your dimension, you can use the snap point as the beginning point for your centerlines. Then you can simply object snap directly to the end of the centerlines.

Inside dimensioning

When you're adding dimensions to the inside of a wall, against an outside wall, or against another item, you might want to turn off one or both extension lines. The reason is so that the extra line doesn't appear in the final plot if you're using a pen plotter. (You won't see this line if you use a laser plotter.) The effect of having an extension line drawn in a wall and plotted in wet ink is illustrated in Figure 6.21.

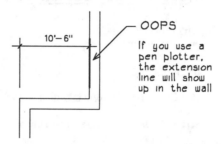

Figure 6.21: Oops, someone drew an extension line in the wall.

The dimension's extension lines are called line 1 and line 2. Which extension line is 1 or 2 depends on the order in which you pick the points you want to dimension. In other words, the first pick becomes line 1 and the second pick becomes line 2. Although the project that you're dimensioning during this exercise doesn't require inside dimensioning, some of your own projects will, so you can practice now.

1. From the Linear menu, pick the **Dim Style** option.

2. The Dimension Style menu will be displayed.

3. Now pick **Line1** until it's turned off (red). (If you want no extension lines drawn at all, you would turn off both lines.)

4. Press mouse button 3 to exit the Dimension Style menu.

5. Make sure **Horiznt** is active.

6. Object snap to the first inside wall, shown as step 1 in Figure 6.22. This will be the extension line that doesn't draw.

7. Object snap to the corner of the small room, shown as step 2 in Figure 6.22. This side will have an extension line.

8. Pick to place the dimension text line, as in step 3, Figure 6.22.

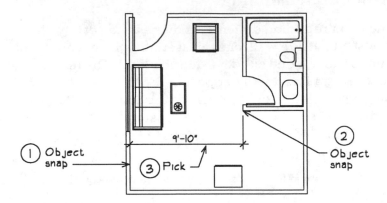

Figure 6.22: Creating an inside dimension.

9. Pick the **Dim Style** option.

10. The Dimension Style menu will be displayed.

11. Now pick **Line1** until it's active. *Remember to always turn it back on!*

12. Press mouse button 3 to exit the Dimension Style menu.

Adding notes to your drawing

Notes are referred to as *text* and are very easy to create. You just pick a spot to place the text, then type it in! There are two ways to add text. The first is *dynamically*. This means the text will show on your drawing as you type it in. The second way is to turn off Dynamic. With Dynamic OFF, the text shows up at the message area of your screen. This is extremely helpful in certain circumstances. However, you'll probably want to use Dynamic most of the time.

1. Press the ⟦Tab⟧ key to change the active layer to: **Notes**. (Reminder: If you use ⟦SHIFT⟧ and ⟦Tab⟧ together, you can scroll backwards through the layer list.)

2. Press ⟦ALT⟧ ⟦T⟧ to quickly enter the Text menu, found in Edit.

3. The Text menu will be displayed, as explained in Figure 6.23.

F1 Size	Size of Text
F2 Angle	The Angle of the text line
F3 Weight	Increases thickness of text
F4 Slant	Italics or Back-slant
F5 Aspect	Makes letters wide or skinny
F6 Factor	Adjusts the space between lines
F7 FontName	Different TYPE FACES
F8 TxtStyle	Saves text settings
F9 Dynamic	Type on drawing or in message area
F0 TxtScale	Scales size per plotter setting
S1 File I/O	Save to or load from a TXT file
S2 Arrows	Draws leader line with arrow

S4 Justify	Aligns text line
S5 Left	Aligns text to left of pick
S6 Center	Centers text around pick
S7 Right	Aligns text to right of pick
S8 Fit Text	Fits text size and aspect to fit in box

| S0 Exit |

Figure 6.23: The text menu.

4. Notice that the shape of your cursor has changed. The new shape and size of the cursor now represents the size that your text is currently set to.

5. Check to see if **Dynamic** is active. If it isn't, pick it to turn it on.

6. To set the correct font (typeface) that you want to use, pick the **FontName** option.

7. Notice that as you slide the cursor over the available fonts, pictures of what the typefaces look like appear in a little window, similar to the pictogram window!

8. Pick the style of type you wish to use. For example, **ARCWYDLC** was used for the figures in this book.

9. Pick the **Size** option.

10. Check that the size is set to **0.6** (which will be plotted as 1/8" at 1/4" scale). If not, type in **.6** to set this size. Press ENTER .

11. Pick the starting point of your **LIVING ROOM** note, as indicated in Figure 6.24.

    Important: Always make sure you pick the position for your text before you start typing.

12. Press the CAPS LOCK key in order to easily type in capitalized letters.

13. Type in **LIVING ROOM** and press ENTER .

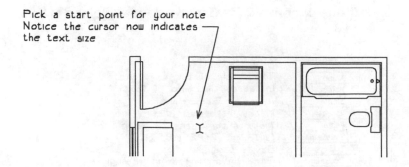

Pick a start point for your note
Notice the cursor now indicates
the text size

Figure 6.24: Pick the start point of your note.

14. If you desired a second line of text, you could type it in now. For example, **Area 10x9**.

15. When you're done typing in your note, press mouse button 3 to quit. The note appears in your drawing, as in Figure 6.25.

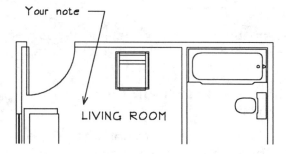

Your note

LIVING ROOM

Figure 6.25: The living room note.

16. Notice that the text for your refrigerator also has an arrow. This is easy to do. First, you add the text, then you add an arrow line.

17. Pick the starting position for the REFRIGERATOR note.

18. Type in **REFRIGERATOR** and press ENTER , as shown in Figure 6.26.

19. Press mouse button 3 once, to stop typing text.

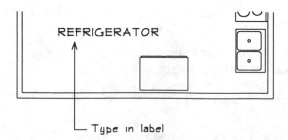

REFRIGERATOR

Type in label

Figure 6.26: Type in text.

Drawing arrows

1. From the Text menu, pick the Arrows option. This option allows you to draw a line that *ends* with an arrow. The last point of the line picked will be where the arrow appears.

2. Pick the start point of the leader line, indicated as step 1 in Figure 6.27.

3. Make sure **Orthomode** is ON, by pressing **O** until the message says "Orthomode is on" and the O is capital in SWOTHLUD. This way, the leader will be perfectly straight.

4. Pick the point for the elbow of the line, indicated as step 2 in Figure 6.27.

5. Now pick the last point of the line, in the position you wish the arrow to appear, indicated as step 3 in Figure 6.27. You can leave **Orthomode** on if you want a straight line, or turn it OFF if you want a line at a slight angle.

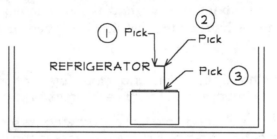

Figure 6.27: Steps for creating an arrow.

5. Press mouse button 3 to quit. The arrow will be drawn on the end of your line! See Figure 6.28.

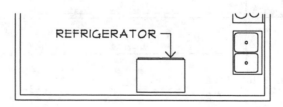

Figure 6.28: The arrow is drawn.

Right, Center and Left Justifying

All text at this point has been justified left, as shown in Figure 6.29. This option is used most of the time as you're annotating drawings and details.

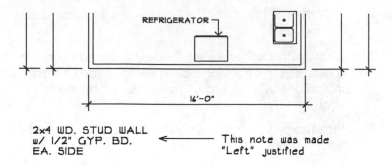

2x4 WD. STUD WALL
w/ 1/2" GYP. BD.   ←——————   This note was made
EA. SIDE   "Left" justified

Figure 6.29: Left justified notes.

There will be times when you want the text justified by center (maybe in a group of room notes) or right, such as in the note you're about to create, and as shown in Figure 6.30. This is done easily using the Justification options in the Text menu.

1. Pick the **Right** option, under the Justify option. (Justify is another option to realign existing text.)

2. Add the second note for your drawing, as shown in Figure 6.30. Your pick point will become the right side of your note. You might want to try this a couple times to get the hang of it.

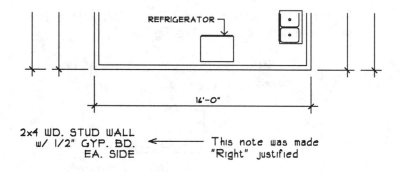

2x4 WD. STUD WALL
w/ 1/2" GYP. BD.   ←——————   This note was made
EA. SIDE   "Right" justified

Figure 6.30: Right justified notes.

3. When you're done using Right, pick **Left** to reset it. Don't forget to do this or it will really surprise you when your text jumps over later!

4. Add the arrow for this note.

Making the title

The drawing title, FLOOR PLAN, is larger than the rest of the notes. You'll change the text size and use another font.

1. Pick the **Size** option from the Text menu.

2. Pick the **1'-0"** option. This setting will make your text appear at 1/4" high on a final 1/4" scale plot.

3. Pick **FontNam**.

4. Look at the different fonts. You'll probably want a bolder typeface. For example, the title in the illustrations was made with **COMPLEX**, which is similar to Roman. Or you could use **HLV_BP** (Helvetica, bold, proportional).

5. When you find the font you wish to use, pick it.

6. You might also want to heavy up the stroke for your text. Pick the **Weight** option.

7. Type in **3** and press ENTER.

8. Pick to position the start point of your text.

9. Type in **FLOOR PLAN** and press **[Enter]**. Your drawing should look like Figure 6.31.

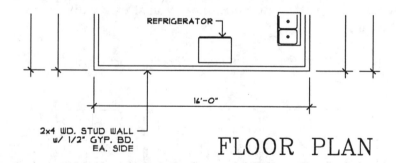

Figure 6.31: Add the Floor Plan note.

10. You might want to continue embellishing this title by adding an underline and a scale note, as in Figure 6.32. (Turn the text **Weight** back to **1** before adding the scale note!)

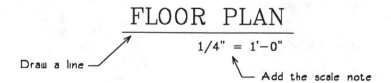

Figure 6.32: Add the underline and scale note.

11. When you're through adding text, press the CAPS LOCK key to turn it off.

Changing the text setting to match existing text

Once you have text in your drawing, you can change your current settings to match your existing text any time! This is very useful when going back and forth between fonts and sizes. You don't have to remember what the original settings were.

1. Pick the **[I]** button in the control panel.

2. Pick a small note to identify it.

3. Pick the **Update** option.

4. Press mouse button 3 to quit. Now try adding some more notes. That's all there is to it!

5. Remember to File your drawing by pressing SHIFT F .

Stretching the house walls

When you've added associated dimensions to your drawing (associated was active while you created them), the dimensions will update automatically as you stretch walls in your drawing.

1. Pick the **Stretch** tool from the icon bar, as in Figure 6.33.

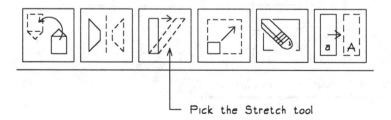

└─ Pick the Stretch tool

Figure 6.33: The Stretch tool.

2. Pick on the drawing a start point for your stretch, as shown in Figure 6.34.

3. Press the SPACE and type in a *negative* distance in the X direction:

   x = **-1.6** ENTER

   y = **0** ENTER

4. Make sure **Area** and **LyrSrch** are active.

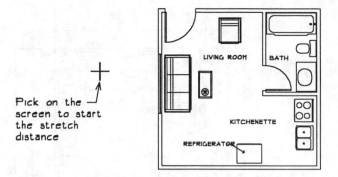

Pick on the
screen to start
the stretch
distance

Figure 6.34: Pick a start point.

5. Draw a box around the left side of your house by
    picking two points, as indicated in steps 1 and 2 in
    Figure 6.35. *Make sure you capture the dimensions in
    the stretch box!*

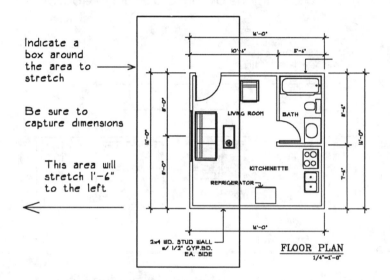

Indicate a
box around
the area to
stretch

Be sure to
capture dimensions

This area will
stretch 1'-6"
to the left

Figure 6.35: The stretch box.

6. Your house should stretch successfully, as shown in
    Figure 6.36.

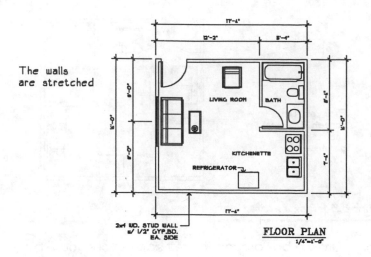

Figure 6.36: The living room got bigger.

7.   You'll notice that the dimensions changed too, as in Figure 6.37.

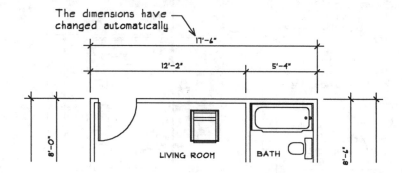

Figure 6.37: The dimensions change automatically.

8.   If you're unhappy with the results, pick the **Undo** option and try again.

9.   You might want to try using the **Fence** selection mode.

10.   There is also a **Point** selection mode, meant to be used with *object snap*. This mode stretches one corner at a time.

11.   Press mouse button 3 to exit the menu.

12.   As a reminder, you'll want to turn the [CAPS LOCK] key off when you're through using making text. If you leave it on, several quick keys work differently (such as [M] and [A]), and it would be hard to follow steps in this book. Later, you may want to leave it on and get used to the differences.

13.   Press [SHIFT] [F] to file your drawing.

DataCAD exercise 5

Please complete the following exercise by reading each question carefully, then circling the letter that corresponds to the correct answer.

1. To quickly change layers, you press the:
   a. `Tab` key.
   b. `ALT` `L` keys.
   c. `L` key.

2. To put the items (walls, dimensions, text, etc.) you're creating onto the right layer, you should:
   a. Change to the layer BEFORE you create the item.
   b. Change to the layer AFTER you create the item.
   c. Just create the item. It automatically goes to the correct layer.

3. To make a horizontal or vertical straight dimension, you would use the:
   a. **Angular** option.
   b. **Radius** option.
   c. **Linear** option.

4. If you're dimensioning a line that is the Y axis, you would pick the:
   a. **Horizontal** option.
   b. **Vertical** option.
   c. **Baseline** option.

5. To string a series of chained dimensions, you pick the:
   a. **Chain** option.
   b. **Strnglin** option.
   c. **Series** option.

6. To get the total length of the wall dimensioned after you have defined string line dimensions, you can use the:
   a. **Total** option.
   b. **Length** option.
   c. **OverAll** option.

7. To create text, you:
   a. Type in the text, then position it on your drawing.
   b. Pick a start point, then type in your text.

8. To create 1/8" text for a 1/4" scale drawing, text size should be:
   a. 1/8".
   b. 1'.
   c. 6".

9. To permanently save a drawing to your hard disk, you must:
   a. Press [SHIFT] [F] to periodically save your drawing.
   b. Not do anything. The file is automatically saved.
   c. Exit the system, and pick **Abort**.

10. When "stacking" dimensions or to avoid a gap from using "Overall," you can object snap to the:
    a. Wall corners again, because you cannot stack dimensions.
    b. Tic Marks of the first dimension.
    c. Text in the first dimension.

11. To make your text skinnier, you can adjust the:
    a. **Factor** option.
    b. **Justify** option.
    c. **Aspect** option.

12. To give your text a slight italicized look, you can use the:
    a. **Angle** option.
    b. **Slant** option.
    c. **Factor** option.

13. In order to add more space between text lines, you can use the:
    a. **Aspect** option.
    b. **Factor** option.
    c. **NextLine** option.

14. If you need to dimension to the center of your walls, it's a good idea to first create the center snap points, using:
    a. **Divide**, found in the GEOMETRY menu.
    b. **CntrSnap**, found in the ARCHITECT menu.
    c. **CntrPnt**, found in the ARCHITECT menu.

15. When you're adding text, in order for the text to appear at the MESSAGE area of your screen (in contrast to appearing on the drawing), you:
    a. Turn OFF the **Dynamic** option.
    b. Turn ON the **Dynamic** option.
    c. Turn OFF the **On Dwg** option.

16. To define another type face for your text, you use the:
    a. **FontName** option.
    b. **TypeFace** option.
    c. **Charctr** option.

CHAPTER 7

Plotting and printing your drawing

The final output

Your final plot or print of your drawing is very important. This chapter provides you with the necessary information you need to *plot* (with a pen plotter, electrostatic plotter, laser plotter, etc., or with a PostScript and HPGL printer), or to *print* (with any standard printer), and to send your *plot file* to a service bureau.

Here are some of the things you'll learn in this chapter:

- Moving the drawing in the border.
- Editing existing text.
- Defining pens.
- Setting up scale and layout.
- Changing the layout screen size.
- Choosing available plotters.
- Sending the plot to a plot file.
- Using different paper sizes.
- Loading in another tool bar.
- Printing to a printer.
- Using the DCPRINT software.
- Shelling out to DOS.

Settings

Certain plot settings were defined for you when you used the standard drawing sheet in chapter 2. This sheet, or "border" is called a *default drawing* in DataCAD. The idea behind using a default drawing is to eliminate repeated steps that you would have to do for drawing. Many of these steps are involved in the plotting setup.

Getting your drawing ready to plot

Before going to the plotter menu, you'll want your drawing ready to plot. One of these steps is to center everything within the drawing border.

1.   Pick the **Layer** tool from the tool bar, shown in Figure 7.1, or press the quick key ☐.

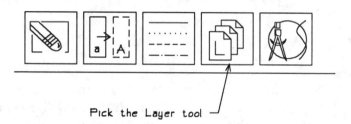

Pick the Layer tool

Figure 7.1: The Layer tool.

2.   Pick **All On**, **Yes**, to make sure all of your layers are displayed.

3.   Pick the **Move** tool, shown in Figure 7.2, or press Ⓜ.

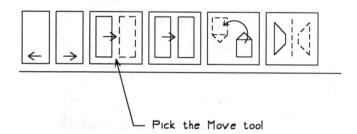

Pick the Move tool

Figure 7.2: The Move tool.

4.   Pick the **Drag** option.

5.   Pick **Group** to make it active.

6.   Make sure **LyrSrch** is active also.

7.   Pick on a line of your first perspective, as shown in Figure 7.3. The group will become gray and dashed.

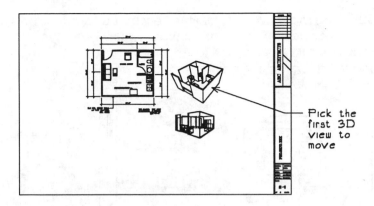

Figure 7.3: Pick a line of the first perspective.

8.   Pick in the center of the same perspective to define a move handle point.

9.   Drag it to a better location, as in Figure 7.4

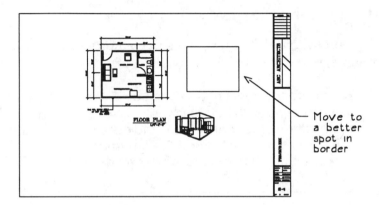

Figure 7.4: Move the perspective.

10.   Repeat the same procedure for the second perspective. Your drawing might look similar to Figure 7.5

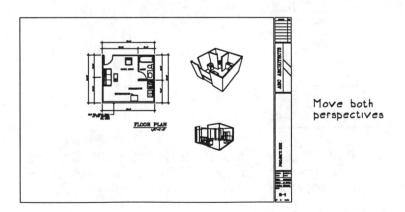

Figure 7.5: Both perspectives have been moved.

11.   Finally, move the house layout so that all of your drawing looks nicely centered in the drawing border.

12. You might want to use the Text menu to add labels for your perspectives, as shown in Figure 7.6.

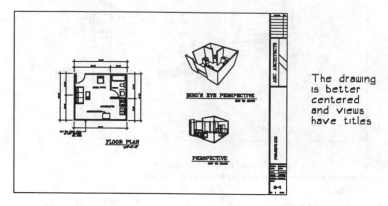

Figure 7.6: Add titles to the perspective views.

Editing the border text

You'll want to update the text that's in the border to include your name, name of your company, date, etc.

1. Zoom into the lower right portion of your border, using the **[W]** WindowIn button in the control panel and picking two diagonal points to indicate a box around the title block, as in Figure 7.7. Remember to press mouse button 3 to exit the WindowIn menu.

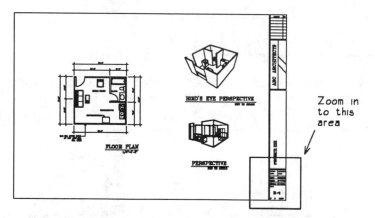

Figure 7.7: Zoom into this area.

2. Pick the **Change** tool, shown in Figure 7.8, to go to the Change menu (or press ALT C). You've used this menu before to change the color of items.

3. Pick the **Text** option.

4. Pick **Contents**, to change the content of your text line.

5. Pick **Area** until it's active.

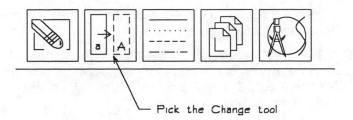

Pick the Change tool

Figure 7.8: The Change tool.

6. Indicate a box around the text to edit in the title
    block, as shown in Figure 7.9. All of the text in this area
    will come up into the message area of your screen,
    one line at a time, to be edited.

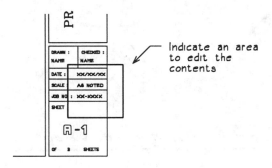

Figure 7.9: Indicate a box around the text.

7. As each section comes up, it disappears off your
    screen. This way, you can tell exactly where each
    piece of text goes.

8. When the text appears in the message area, you can
    type over the text.

9. If you want to change only a part of the text, you can
    press the ⇥ on the keyboard to move the text cursor
    to the spot in the line you wish to type over.

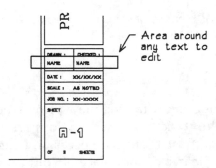

Figure 7.10: Draw a box around the next text.

10. Press ENTER when you're through editing each line.

11. When this section is edited, box around the next text to change, as in Figure 7.10.

12. When all of the title block is edited, you might want to edit the name of the company logo, which now says ABC ARCHITECTS, to the name of your company. Follow the same procedure.

13. If you use the **Entity** mode to select the text, you need to pick the text in a "sensitive spot" so that it's recognized by the cursor. The six spots are illustrated in Figure 7.11.

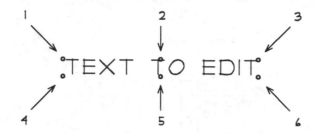

Figure 7.11: To pick text you must pick one of these points.

14. Once all of the text is edited, press SHIFT F to file your drawing.

Setting up the plot

Setting your drawing up for plotting consists of four main steps:

- Identify the *paper size* (the actual plotting area).

- Define the *layout,* or the plotting area of your drawing.

- Decide on the *scale* of the plot.

- Set the different *pens* (can also be used for line thicknesses in laser prints).

Going to the Plotter menu

You'll want to center your drawing view prior to entering the plot menu. The layout view is based on your *present drawing center.* This is because there is an occasion when you'll want this center to be in a certain place of your drawing, maybe because you're only plotting a small section of it. At that time, you center around that section.

1. Pick the **[R]** in the control panel to recalculate the view extents and center.

2. Press ALT P to go to the Plotter menu, found in Utility.

3. Pick **Select**.

4. Check the message area for the current plotter selected. Is it the plotter you wish to use?

5. Move the cursor over to the **Plotter1** option.

6. Look at the message area. The top line will display the type of plotter set for the Plotter1 option.

7. Move your cursor to the other options, **Plotter2** and **Plotter3**. The types of plotters set for those options will appear in the message area also.

8. Pick the type of plotter you'll be using.

9. When the correct plotter is specified, press mouse button 3 once to exit from the Select menu and return to the Plotter menu.

10. Pick **PaperSize**.

11. Notice that the paper size is set to Custom 23" x 34", shown in the message area. This is the maximum plot area for a D size sheet. (Some older plotters won't allow this enhanced size. If that is your case, and you'll want a D size sheet, you'll need to pick the **24x36 D** option, which sets the maximum plotting area to 21"x33".)

12. Pick the appropriate paper size you'll be using. For example, if you were plotting to a large D-size plotter, you could leave the setting as is, or select the **24x36 D** size paper. (You would probably plot at 1/4" scale.)

13. If you're going to use a laser jet plotter, you might want to pick the **8.5 x 11A** paper choice, in order to print on office paper.

14. Once you have picked the correct size, press mouse button 3 to exit the PaperSize menu and return to the Plotter menu.

15. Pick the **Layout** option.

16. Move your cursor out into the drawing area. You'll notice that you're dragging a box with your cursor, as in Figure 7.12. This *layout box* represents the plotting size of the paper you selected. If your drawing doesn't fit correctly, or is too small in the paper, you'll want to adjust the scale.

17. Pick to position the paper (don't worry, if you have to change the scale, you'll get another chance!)

18. If you need to change the scale, pick the **Scale** option.

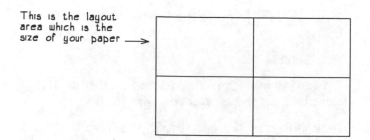

This is the layout area which is the size of your paper →

Figure 7.12: The layout box.

19. If you're trying to print on a 8.5" x 11" piece of paper, you might want to try the **1/16"** option. Try other scales until you find the best for your size drawing.

20. After you pick the scale you want to use, you'll be returned to the **Layout** mode. Position the paper with your cursor and pick.

Setting the pens

1. Make sure **ClrPlot** is active. (Otherwise, the SetPens option isn't displayed).

1. Pick the **SetPens** option.

2. Notice that the names of colors are displayed in the menu area. The colors listed represent the colors that can be displayed on your screen. You can connect a certain pen number to each color.

This pen number is used by your plotter in order to pick up a certain pen to draw with. Most pen plotters allow you to use eight different pens at one time. Pencil/pen plotters use the same pen numbers.

Laser plotters can also use these pens numbers. A small laser plotter can use pen number to plot thicker lines. For example, 1 will be skinny, and 7 would be thick. A large format laser can even have line textures connected with pen numbers. So, not only can the lines be thick or thin, but they can also appear screened.

In any case, it's essential that you standardize how colors, and subsequent pen numbers, will be used in your office. This is done by defining *Pen tables*. Pen tables are used to graphically connect colors and pen numbers to pen widths. This way, you can be confident that a certain color will be plotted with the correct pen. The following pen table, shown in Figure 7.13 is currently set for your drawings. (It was set in the default drawing.)

DEFAULT 1-4_PLAN PEN TABLE			
LINE	PEN SIZE	NUMBER	COLOR
——————	.10	4	WHITE YELLOW
——————	.50	3	LT MGTA
——————	.35	2	GREEN CYAN LT GRN
——————	.25	1	BLUE MAGENTA LT GRAY DK GRAY LT RED LT BLUE LT CYAN BROWN

Figure 7.13: The pen table for your default drawing.

3.   If you wish to check that these settings are correct in your SetPens menu, pick the **White** option.

4.   White should be set to pen number **4**. White items, then, will be drawn with pen number 4. Since this includes your walls, you would want a thicker pen then, say, the pen used for the dimension lines. In a pen plotter, you might put a *.70 pen* in slot number 4.

5.   Press ENTER .

6.   You can check the rest of the colors if you wish. They should all be set to **1**, except: *Green, Cyan*, and *Lt Grn*, which are set to **2**; *Lt Mgta*, which is set to **3**; and *White* and *Yellow*, which are set to **4**.

Note: *DON'T use 0 (zero) as a pen number. Most pen plotters can handle this (pen 0 just wouldn't be drawn). But on many raster-type plotters (including lasers) this could cause the plotter to halt, and your drawing wouldn't finish plotting.*

---

7.   When you're through with the SetPens menu, press mouse button 3 to exit and return to the Plotter menu.

8.   Press SHIFT F to file your drawing.

Changing the screen layout size

Sometimes you'll want the layout size of your paper and drawing to appear on the screen smaller. This would help you move the layout around easier. You can try this to see how you like it.

1.   Pick the **LyoutSet** option.

2.   Pick **Layout%**.

3. Type in a new size for your layout. For example, a size of 50% would show the layout at half the screen size. Type in **50** and press [ENTER] .

4. Press mouse button 3 to exit the LyoutSet menu.

5. Now your layout will be smaller.

Rotating your plot

It's easy to rotate the plot so it can fit on a paper differently.

1. Pick the **Rotate** option.

2. You'll be prompted to pick on the screen for the center of the rotation. Pick as close to the center of your drawing as you can.

3. Now you're asked for a rotation angle. Notice that **90** degrees is the default. Press [ENTER] to accept it.

4. Pick on your drawing to set the layout. Notice that your drawing is rotated, the layout isn't.

5. To return to the original rotation, pick the **Rotate** option until it's turned off.

Setting up a pen plotter

Before you send your drawing to the plotter, make sure that your plotter is ready to draw. This means that the paper is properly installed, the pens are wet and in the proper order, and the plotter is connected properly and online.

1. If you have a *multiple pen plotter* (has a pen carousel), check that your pens are set in the following order:

   1 = Smallest pen   Recommended = .25
   2 = Next size larger   Recommended = .35
   3 = Next size larger   Recommended = .50
   4 = Largest pen   Recommended = .70

2. If you have a *single pen plotter*, make sure the **Snglpen** option is active. Check that the smallest of your pen is inserted in the pen holder. The plotter will stop when it's time to insert the second pen.

3. Place the paper in your plotter. Make sure it's aligned properly and the paper holder (clamp) is firmly on the paper.

4. Turn the plotter on. It will probably view the paper and test the pens, depending on the type of plotter you have.

5. If you have made any changes to your drawing, *always* file it before plotting by pressing [SHIFT] [F] .

6. Make sure **ClrPlot** is active (Color plot). This option makes the plotter look at the colors for pen changes.

7. Pick the **Plot** option. Your plotter should start drawing!

Desktop Laser plotters

A printer is treated as a plotter if there is a plotter driver for it. There are drivers for HPGL and PostScript printers. If your printer is configured in DataCAD as a plotter, follow these steps.

Before you send your drawing to the printer, make sure your printer is ready. This means that the paper tray is filled, the printer is properly connected, the correct driver is installed for your printer (either HPGL or PostScript), and the printer is turned on and online.

1. If you're printing a large drawing at a small scale, you won't want to use pen thicknesses. If you do, most likely you'll be unable to read the results. Pick the **ClrPlot** option until it's off. (Now the printer won't look at the colors for pen changes, but instead it will plot everything in pen 1.)

2. If you're plotting a detail or other drawing where you can have a larger scale on a 8 1/2" x 11" paper (for example, 1" and 3" scales), you can use pen numbers. Make sure **ClrPlot** is active. You might want to adjust the pen numbers for more subtle changes (such as using 7 for White instead of 4), or edit the pen table in the printer for dot width.

3. Using the default settings for the Hewlett Packard LaserJet III, for example, you can set the following:

   Green, Cyan, Lt Grn = **3**
   Lt Mgta = **5**
   White, Yellow = **7**

3. If you've made any changes to your drawing, *always* file it before printing by pressing [SHIFT] [F] .

4. Pick the **Plot** option. Be patient. Unlike a pen plotter, the printer can't just start drawing a line at a time. First, the software will rasterize *all* of the lines for your plot. Then it will begin to send it to the your printer. Lights might start to blink, so you'll know it's working.

If your plotter or printer doesn't plot

This might be due to several problems:

- Your DataCAD is not configured to the correct plotter/printer.

- Your plotter/printer is plugged into the spot.

- You have not prepared your plotter/printer properly.

- The clamp isn't all the way down on your plotter.

- Reset all of your pens in the plotter.

- You have the wrong cable.

- You've moved your plotter/printer recently? Check that all cables are plugged in tight, including the power plug.

- The plotter/printer is offline, etc.

Check with the owner's manual, and the DataCAD *Up and Running* manual to assure that you have installed your plotter correctly and that you have followed the proper procedures. Also, see chapter 1, "Installing DataCAD" for further instructions.

Sending the plot to a file, for a plotting service or for printing with DC Print

You'll want to make a *plot file* if you're using a plotting service or if you're planning to use the DCPRINT program.

Sending a plot file to a plotter service is desirable because you'll have complete control over the actual layout and plot. They won't have a copy of your original drawing file, your settings can't be fooled with, and you won't have to worry about your typefaces.

Plot files end with the extension PLT (short for PLOT). Sometimes this is referred to as HPGL files (Hewlett Packard Graphics Language). Many desktop publishing programs can use PLT files, too.

1. Once all of your settings in the Plotter menu are correct, pick the **Config** option.

2. *If you're going to print using DC Print*, pick the plotter that you've configured for CADKEY Uniplot driver. Move the cursor over the **Plotter#1, Plotter#2,** and **Plotter#3** options to read what their setups are in the message area. Pick the option configured to *CADKEY Uniplot driver*.

3. *If you're going to send a file to a plotting service*, pick the plotter that you've configured for your service. This might be HPGL Large format, or other designated driver. driver. Move the cursor over the **Plotter#1, Plotter#2,** and **Plotter#3** options to read what their

setups are in the message area. Pick the option configured to the correct driver for your plotting service.

4   Once the correct plotter is set, pick the **ToFile** option.

5.   Pick **NewPath**.

6.   Type in: **plots** for the directory and press ENTER . The full path for your plot files will be: **\dcad6\plots**.

7.   If this is a new directory, pick **Yes**.

8.   The existing name of your drawing will appear as the name for your plot file. You can change it or use the same name. Then press ENTER .

9.   The file will be created in **DCAD6\PLOTS**, as mentioned earlier (if you have DataCAD 6), with a *.plt* extension.

Setting up a new tool bar

Ordinarily, you must exit to DataCAD and use DOS to start *DC Print*. DC Print is a software provided with DataCAD that allows you to print on an ordinary printer (one that doesn't have HPGL or PostScript format).

However, there is a tool for printing in the DCAD_2D tool bar.

1.   Press mouse button 3 until you're in the Utility menu.

2.   Pick the **Display** option.

3.   Pick **Menus**.

4.   Pick **IconFile**.

5.   Pick the **DCAD_2D** file. The new tool bar will be loaded.

6.   Press ⦂ to quickly go to the Edit menu.

7.   Pick the **Scroll Forward** tool until the **Utility** tools are displayed, as shown in Figure 7.14.

Pick Scroll Forward
until the Utility tools
are displayed

② Utility tools

Figure 7.14: Scroll to the Utility tools.

Using DC Print

Using the Printer Utility tool greatly speeds this process.

1. Press [SHIFT] [F] to file your drawing.

2. Pick the Printer Utility tool, shown in Figure 7.15. (Or, you could go to **File I/O**, **DOSShell**, and type in: **dcprint**.)

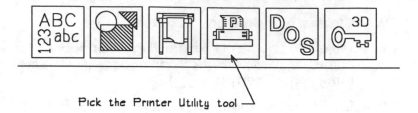

Pick the Printer Utility tool ⏤

Figure 7.15: Pick the DC Print "Printer Utility" tool.

3. To use DC Print:

    To move your cursor in this program, press the [↑] and [↓] arrow keys on your keyboard.

    Select an option by highlighting it with your cursor and pressing [ENTER].

4. Pick the **Setup** option from the main menu.

5. Pick **Set Paths**.

6. Pick **Get Plot File Path from DataCAD**. Check your path. It should be set to **PLOTS**.

7. If the path is not correct, pick **Plot Files**. Type in **plots** and press [ENTER]. Next time it should be set for you.

8. Press [ESC] to exit Setup.

9. Press [ENTER] to **Save Changes in Setup**.

10. Pick **Choose Plot File**.

11. Highlight all of the plot files you wish to print, by moving the cursor and pressing [ENTER].

12. When the plot files are selected, press [ESC] to return to the main menu.

13. Make sure your printer is ready to go.

14. Pick **Print (Go)**.

15. When the plots are completed, press [ESC] to leave the DC Print Utility program. You'll return to the Edit menu.

16. If you didn't use the Printer Utility tool, you'll be returned to the DOS prompt. Type in **exit** and press [ENTER] to exit the DOS shell and return to DataCAD.

To copy your file to diskette:

Service bureaus need to receive your *plot file*, either on a *diskette* or over the *modem*.

1. Press ⌈SHIFT⌉ ⌈F⌉ to file your drawing.

2. Pick the **DOS Prompt** tool, as shown in Figure 7.16. (Or, use **File I/O, DOSShell**.)

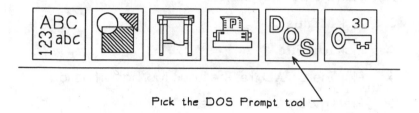

Pick the DOS Prompt tool

Figure 7.16: The DOS Prompt tools.

3. You'll exit DataCAD and a DOS prompt will be displayed.

4. If you have a menu shell that runs in DOS, and you want to use it to copy your file onto diskette, you can start it now. Just make sure you can exit the menu program and type: **exit** to reenter DataCAD. *Remember, you're in a DataCAD DOS shell!*

5. If you're using DOS, and own DataCAD version 6, simply type in: **cd \dcad6\plots** and press ⌈ENTER⌉ .

    If you have DataCAD 5, type in: **cd \dcad5\plots** and press ⌈ENTER⌉ .

6. Now type in: **dir/p** and press ⌈ENTER⌉ . The directory of PLOTS will be displayed.

7. Look for your file. If there is more than one screen page of files, you might have to press ⌈ENTER⌉ again to see your file. (Time for some house cleaning!)

8. Put a diskette into either drive A or B. If necessary, close the door handle.

9. If your diskette is in drive A, type in: **copy c:\dcad6\plots a:** and press ⌈ENTER⌉ .

    If your diskette is in drive B, type in: **copy c:\dcad6\plots b:** and press ⌈ENTER⌉

    You'll want to use the DCAD5 directory name for version 5, or even MTEC for earlier versions.

10. Once the copy is made, type in **exit** and press ⌈ENTER⌉ to exit the DOS shell and return to DataCAD.

Resetting the tool bar

You could keep the 2D_DCAD tool bar active, but several
steps in this book rely on the basic DCAD tool bar being
displayed. Later, you'll use the tool bar you like the most, or
make your own!

1. Press mouse button 3 until you're in the Utility menu.

2. Pick the **Display** option.

3. Pick **Menus**.

4. Pick **IconFile**.

5. Pick the **DCAD** file. The basic tool bar will be loaded.

6. Press mouse button 3 to exit.

Quitting DataCAD

1. Press `ALT` `Q` to Quit DataCAD.

2. Pick **Yes** or press `Y` to save your drawing.

DataCAD exercise 6

Please complete the following exercise by reading each
question carefully, then circling the letter that corresponds to
the correct answer.

1. To make plotting an easy, one-step process, you:
   a. Change the colors you use for different items, instead
      of standardizing the colors used for all of your draw-
      ings.
   b. Change the pen numbers every time you plot.
   c. Should have all of the information preset in your
      standard default drawing, and never vary your color
      standards.

2. To set the factor by which your drawing will be plotted,
   you pick:
   a. The **Factor** option.
   b. The **Scale** option.
   c. None of the options. You should always plot full size.

3. To pick the sheet size you'll plot your drawing on, you
   pick the:
   a. **Sheet** option.
   b. **Layout** option.
   c. **PaperSiz** option.

4. To adjust the position of the plotting area on the drawing,
   you pick the:
   a. **Layout** option.
   b. **Sheet** option.
   c. **Adjust** option.

5. If you wish to turn your plot 90 degrees counterclockwise, in the Plotter menu you use the:
   a. **Rotate** option.
   b. **LyoutSet** option.
   c. **Angle** option.

6. To change the size of the layout view, you use the:
   a. **LyoutSet, Size** options.
   b. **LyoutVu** option.
   c. **LyoutSet, Layout%** options.

7. If you want the plotter to make pen changes, you must
   have active:
   a. **ClrPlot**.
   b. **UsePens**.
   c. **MultiPen**.

Plotting and printing your drawing

8. When you're using multiple pens for your plots:
   a. Set your pen numbers for the colors you have used, and have a defined pen table for plotting purposes.
   b. Have all of your colors set to pen 1.
   c. Don't set pen numbers.

9. The final step in plotting your drawing, is:
   a. Setting the scale.
   b. Adjusting the layout.
   c. Picking the **Plot** option from the PLOTTER menu.

10. To use DCPrint:
    a. Make a plot file, then use the **DCPrint** option in the Plotter menu.
    b. Use **File I/O**, pick **DCPrint**, then pick **Go**.
    c. Make a plot file, pick the **Print Utility** tool, identify the plot file, then pick **Go**.

11. In order to use DOS commands while you're in a Data-CAD drawing, you would:
    a. Use the **File I/O, DOSShell** options.
    b. Use the **Window Out** option.
    c. Quit DataCAD. You can't use DOS while in a Data-CAD drawing.

12. The DCPrint program can be used:
    a. If your printer doesn't support HPGL or PostScript.
    b. Only if your printer supports HPGL or PostScript.
    c. By plotters only.

13. Before you enter the Plotter menu, it's a good idea to:
    a. Center your drawing using the **[R]** recalc button.
    b. Save your file using `SHIFT` `F` .
    c. Both a and b.

14. When you're in the DOS shell, to go back to DataCAD:
    a. Start DataCAD all over again.
    b. Type in: **quit** at the DOS prompt and press `ENTER` .
    c. Type in: **exit** at the DOS prompt and press `ENTER` .

15. To edit text that is on your drawing, use the:
    a. **Change, Text, Contents** options.
    b. **Change, Text, Edit** options.
    c. **Text, Edit** options.

16. In order to move your drawing details by dragging them to a new location, you use the:
    a. **Move, Slide** options.
    b. **Drag, Details** options.
    c. **Move, Drag** options.

CHAPTER 8

Setting up a site plan default drawing

Setting up default drawings

Default drawings are used as standard drawing formats that contain a border, defined layers, and other settings for your drawing sheet. In other words, the default drawing is a foundation for you to use over and over again. Creating a default drawing is easy in DataCAD.

Here are some of the things you'll learn in this chapter:

- Defining decimal scale input.
- Setting up polar bearings mode.
- Creating new layers.
- Naming layers.
- Changing the size of the border.
- Saving the default drawing.

Creating a 1:20 default drawing

In chapter 2, you used the default drawing called **PLAN_1-4**. The border in this "default sheet" was set up to equal a D-size sheet when plotted at 1/4" scale. Now you'll create a border for a 1:20 final plot scale. You'll learn the steps to change your dimensions, angles, and scales, and you'll find out how to save the drawing as a default drawing.

It's important to create a default drawing for every scale of drawing you'll use. This way, your text and dimensions and any other option will be set for that particular plot scale.

The different types of drawings you create will also influence how many default drawings you have. As an example, for the floor plan, an architectural (feet/inches/fractions) scale was set. For site drawings, you have all of the settings for decimal input and bearings mode. You'll accomplish this by changing your *scale settings*. And you'll need layers for your drawing that make sense for site work, such as property lines, easements, building, and more.

To make all of these steps easier, you'll use the PLAN_1-4 default drawing as a base for your new site default.

1. Start DataCAD. Or if you're already in a drawing, press ALT N to go to a new drawing, then pick **Yes**.

2. At the opening menu (drawing list), pick the **Default** option.

3. Pick the **PLAN_1-4** default drawing.

4. Now type in the new name for your drawing: **site1** and press ENTER .

5. The drawing border will be displayed, as in Figure 8.1

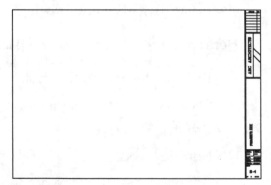

Figure 8.1: The 1/4" drawing border.

A visual check on border size

You'll need to change the size of the border so that it'll be a D-size sheet when plotted at 1:20 scale. Right now, this border would be extremely small at a 1:20 scale. You can get a visual check on how the border would look by changing the plot scale to 1:20 and viewing the layout.

1. Press ALT P to go to the Plotter menu.

2. Pick **Scale**.

3. Pick **1:20**.

4. Pick the **Layout** option.

5. Drag the cursor out into the drawing area, but *don't* pick to place the layout. Look at the size of your "paper" (the layout area) compared to the size of your border. It will look like Figure 8.2. It's obvious that you need to change the size of your border.

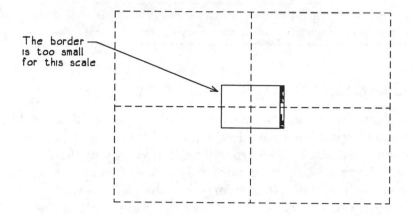

The border is too small for this scale

Figure 8.2: The border is too small for 1:20 plot scale.

6. *Don't* pick! You don't want to change the position of the layout. Press mouse button 3 to exit.

Finding the center point

Before you change the size of the border, you'll want to locate the center. That way, you can enlarge the border around this center point, and the layout will fit perfectly in the plot menu.

1. Press `ALT` `G` to go to the Geometry menu.

2. Pick the **Divide** option.

3. Object snap to the two corners of your borders, as shown as steps 1 and 2 in Figure 8.3.

4. The center snap point will appear, as step 3 in Figure 8.3.

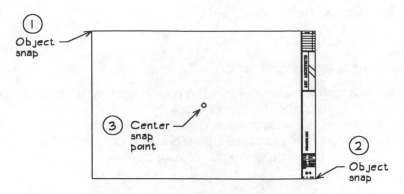

Figure 8.3: Steps to create a center snap point.

Changing the size of the border

It's easy to change the size of the border. You could calculate the difference between a 1/4" scale and 1:20 scale, and change the size of the border accordingly. Or you could shrink the existing border down 1/4" scale (which would make it "real size"), then enlarge it to the 1:20 scale factor. The latter is much easier, *and* it will work for any scale.

1. Pick the **Enlarge** tool, as in Figure 8.4.

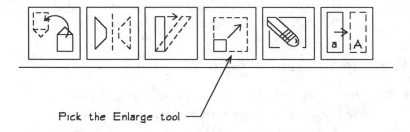

Pick the Enlarge tool

Figure 8.4: The Enlarge tool.

2. Object snap to the center snap point for the center of enlargement, as shown in Figure 8.5.

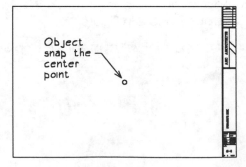

Figure 8.5: Object snap to the center.

3. When the Enlarge menu is displayed, pick the **Enlrgmnt** option.

4. Pick **Set All**.

5. Type in the scale factor for 1/4": **48** and press ENTER . 48 is how many times 1/4" goes into 12" (12x4).

6. Press mouse button 3 to quit back to the Enlarge menu.

7. Pick **Inverse**. This option will turn your factor (which was the enlargement scale), and reverse it to a reduction scale!

8. Your reduction scale is displayed in the message area of the screen: **.02083334**.

9. Pick **Area**.

10. Make sure **LyrSrch** is active.

11. Indicate an area around the entire border. It will shrink to a very small size. Now the border is *real size*. In other words, you could plot it at 12" scale (1:1) and it would be a D size sheet. At this point, you could enlarge the border to *any* scale.

    (Don't worry about zooming in; you'll enlarge it to the 1:20 size now.)

12. Pick the **Enlrgmnt** option again.

13. Pick **Set All**.

14. Type in the scale factor for 1"= 20': **240** and press ENTER . 240 is how many times 12" goes into 20 feet. (12x20).

15. Press mouse button 3 to quit back to the Enlarge menu.

16. You don't have to pick Inverse this time because you're enlarging the border, not making it smaller.

17. Indicate an area around the border. It will enlarge. (It might disappear from the present view window due to its size.)

18. Now pick the **[R]** in the control panel to recalculate your view window. The border will appear centered on your screen.

19. Press SHIFT F to file your drawing.

Checking the border size again

Check the plot size and layout again.

1. Press ALT P to go to the Plotter menu.

2.   Pick the **Layout** option.

3.   Does the layout look correct now? It should look like Figure 8.6. *Don't* pick to place the layout! Just press mouse button 3 to exit.

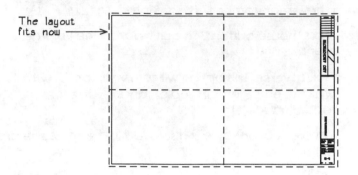

The layout fits now →

Figure 8.6: The border size is correct for 1:20 plot scale.

Changing the input types

Up to now you've been using an *architectural scale*. This means that you've typed your measurements in as Feet, Inches, and Fractions. You'll change this so that you can type in Feet in a *decimal scale*.

You'll also change your *angle type* so that you can type in North, East, South, and West directions. Currently, the angle type is set to *Normal* (normal "right" angle). The new setting will be *Bearings*.

1.   Press mouse button 3 until you're in the Utility menu.

2.   Pick the **Settings** option.

3.   Pick **ScaleTyp**.

4.   Pick **Decimal**.

5.   Move your cursor into the drawing area of your screen. Notice that the coordinate X and Y readout is now in *decimal feet*.

6.   You can try picking the other choices, each time moving your cursor out into the drawing area to see how the coordinates are displayed.

7.   Make sure the **Decimal** option is active again, then press mouse button 3 exit back to the Settings menu.

8.   Pick **AngleTyp**.

9.   Pick **Bearings** to make it active.

10. Move the cursor into the drawing area of your screen. Notice that the coordinate D and A readout (distance and angle) is now in *bearings*.

11. Pick **StrtAngl**. This option allows you to define the North direction of your drawing.

12. Pick a point in your drawing, as in step 1 of Figure 8.5.

13. Move your cursor. Notice that an arrow is attached to it. This is indicating the North arrow.

14. With Orthomode *ON* ([O] = orthomode), pick in an upward direction, as indicated as step 2 in Figure 8.7.

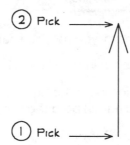

Figure 8.7: Two picks indicate the north direction.

15. Once the north direction is defined, press mouse button 3 to exit.

16. Press [SHIFT] [F] to file your drawing.

Setting the coordinate input mode

As before, in Chapter 2, you'll want to set the coordinate mode, this time in *Relative Polar*.

1. Press the [INS] key until *Relative polar* input is set.

Changing the layer names

Editing the layer names is easy.

1. Pick the **Layer** tool, as in Figure 8.8.

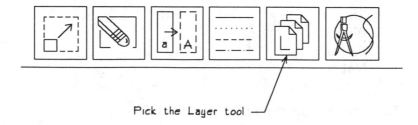

Pick the Layer tool ⸺

Figure 8.8: The Layer tool.

2. Pick **Name**.

3. The present layer list will be displayed, as in Figure 8.9.

The current
layer names ——→

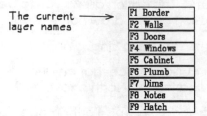

F1	Border
F2	Walls
F3	Doors
F4	Windows
F5	Cabinet
F6	Plumb
F7	Dims
F8	Notes
F9	Hatch

Figure 8.9: The current layer name list.

4. Pick the second name on the list: **Walls**.

5. The name will appear in the message area.

6. Type in the new name for this layer: **Property** and press [ENTER]. This layer will hold the property lines.

7. Pick the next layer: **Doors**.

8. Type in the new name for this layer: **EaseMnts** and press [ENTER]. This layer will hold the easement and setback lines.

9. Pick the next layer: **Windows**.

10. Type in the new name for this layer: **Street** and press [ENTER]. This layer will hold the Street lines.

11. Pick the next layer: **Cabinet**.

12. Type in the new name for this layer: **Bldg** and press [ENTER]. This layer will hold the building lines.

13. Pick the next layer: **Plumb**.

14. Type in the new name for this layer: **Parking** and press [ENTER]. This layer will hold the building lines.

15. Continue changing the names of the layers until you have layers named the following:

    Border
    Property
    EaseMnts
    Street
    Bldg
    Parking
    Notes
    Dimensions

16. Press mouse button 3 to exit the Name menu.

Deleting Layers

You'll have an extra layer left over from the floor plan layering scheme.

1. Pick the **DelLayer** option from the Layer menu.

2. Pick the last layer in your list: **Hatch**.

3. Pick **Yes** to delete it.

Adding Layers

1. If you needed to add more layers to your list, you would pick the **AddLayer** option.

2. Type in the number of layers you wish to add. Notice the default is set to **1**. Press [ENTER] .

3. Pick the **Name** option, to name your new layers.

4. Notice that the new layers are presently named with a number indicating their order in the layer list. For instance, if the new layer were the ninth layer created, it would be called *Layer9,* and it would appear at the end of the list. The tenth layer would be *Layer10,* and so on.

5. Pick the layer you just created and type in a new name for it, such as **Fencing**, pressing [ENTER] when you're through.

6. Press mouse button 3 to exit the Name menu.

Setting up the Dimensions

You need to change the text size and apply other minor adjustments to the dimension setup. Figure 8.10 illustrates the *style options* found in the dimension menu.

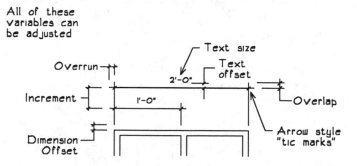

Figure 8.10: Styles that can be adjusted in dimensions.

1. Press [ALT] [D] to go to the Dimension Linear menu.

2. Pick the **TextStyl** option.

3. Pick **Size**. This option allows you to adjust the actual size of the dimension text, as shown in Figure 8.11.

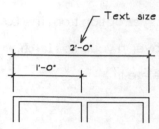

Figure 8.11: The dimension text size.

4. Type in: **2.5** and press ENTER .

   Why 2.5? First of all, now that you're using *decimal feet* as your scale, 2.5' = 2'-6". Since you're working in 1:20 scale (1" = 20') in order to get 1/8" text, you can divide 20 by 8, which is 2.5.

5. Pick the **Offset** option. This option allows you to adjust the text offset, shown in Figure 8.12.

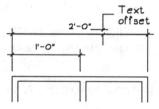

Figure 8.12: The dimension text offset gap size.

6. Type in **1.25** and press ENTER . This will make the offset gap 1/2 the size of text.

7. Press mouse button 3 to exit back to the Dimension Linear menu.

8. Pick **DimStyl**.

9. Pick **Offset**. This option adjusts the offset of the dimension extension line from the item, or wall, as shown in Figure 8.13.

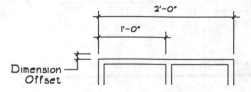

Figure 8.13: The dimension extension line offset gap.

10. Type in **2.5** and press ⎡ENTER⎤ to create a 1/8" offset gap.

11. Pick **Overlap**. This is the amount the extension line overlaps the dimension line, as shown in Figure 8.14.

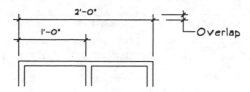

Figure 8.14: The dimension extension line overlap.

12. Type in **2.5** and press ⎡ENTER⎤ to create a 1/8" overlap.

13. Pick **Overrun**. This is the amount the dimension line overruns the extension line, as shown in Figure 8.15.

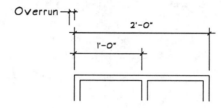

Figure 8.15: The dimension line overrun.

14. Type in **2.5** and press ⎡ENTER⎤ to create a 1/8" overrun.

15. Press ⎡SHIFT⎤ ⎡F⎤ to file your drawing.

Setting the linetype and spacing

1. Press ⎡ALT⎤ ⎡L⎤ to quickly go to the Linetype menu, found in Edit.

2. Move your cursor over to the available linetypes displayed. Notice that they're displayed in the preview window.

3. There are 24 linetypes. Pick the **ScrlFwrd** option. This option allows you to view the other linetypes.

4. Once the rest of the linetypes are displayed, you'll see a **ScrlBack** option. This option allows you to scroll back to the beginning of the list.

5. Find the **PropLine** option and pick it to set it as the current linetype.

6. The current linetype is displayed as PropLine in the status area, above SWOTHLUD, as in Figure 8.16.

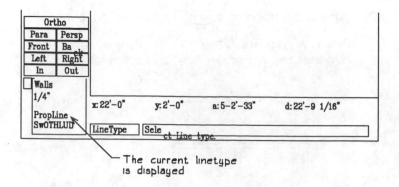

The current linetype
is displayed

Figure 8.16: The current linetype is displayed.

7.   Pick the **Spacing** option.

8.   Type in the spacing you refer and press [ENTER] . Every 20
     feet will plot as one inch in the final drawing. An
     illustration of this is shown in Figure 8.17.

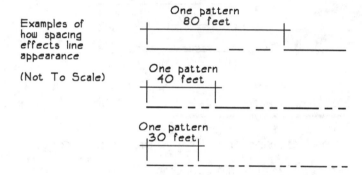

Figure 8.17: How spacing works with the line pattern.

Recommended spacings: (or you can chose your own)

   40 = 2" in final drawing
   50 = 2 1/2" in final drawing
   60 = 3" in final drawing.

4.   Once you've set your spacing, press mouse button 3
     to exit.

Saving the file for a default drawing

Now that you've taken the extra steps to set up your drawing
for a site plan, it would be nice if you didn't have to go
through the same steps again. That's what *default drawings*
are for! And, it's easy to save the current drawing to the
default directory. That way, you can use it over and over
again as a default drawing sheet.

1.   Press mouse button 3 until you're in the Utility menu.

2. Pick the **File I/O** option (Files In and Out).

3. Pick the **Save As** option. This allows you to save a copy of the current drawing under a new name. *It doesn't rename the current drawing file your in.*

4. Pick **New Path**. Using this option, you'll change the directory you want to copy the file to.

5. Type in: **default** and press [ENTER] . (*Or*, pick the **..** option, pick the **DEFAULT** directory, then press [ENTER] .)

6. Now type in the name for your new 1:20 drawing default: **site1-20** and press [ENTER] . Remember, you only have eight characters for a file name, and you can't use spaces.

Note: *Default drawings are regular drawings that have been put into a directory called "Default." To edit them, you can simply change to the default directory when you start DataCAD, using the NewPath option. But remember to return to your project directory before creating a new project drawing.*

Creating the pictogram for your default

You can even create a little preview pictogram for your default. Just remember to name it the same name and file it into the Default directory.

1. Pick the **PixelOut** option from the File I/O menu.

2. Pick the **Pictogram** option.

3. Pick **New Path**. You'll change the directory to Default again.

4. Type in **default** and press [ENTER] . (*Or*, pick the **..** option, pick the **DEFAULT** directory, then press [ENTER] .)

5. Type in the name of your default drawing: **site1-20** and press [ENTER] .

6. Press [PG UP] on the keyboard until the border fits into the little box on your cursor.

7. Pick to place the box over the border.

8. Press mouse button 3 to exit.

Checking your default drawings

Now you can go back to the drawing list and check for your default drawing you just made.

1. Press ALT N to go to a new drawing.

2. Pick **Yes** (or type in Y on your keyboard). Now the drawing list is displayed.

Note: *Anytime a Yes/No menu is displayed, you can type in a* Y *for Yes, or* N *for No as a keyboard shortcut.*

---

3. Pick the **Default** option.

4. The Default Drawing list will be displayed. Is your new *SITE1-20* default on the list?

5. Move your cursor to the drawing name. Is the pictogram displayed in the view window?

6. If you were going to use the Site1-20 default drawing sheet, you would pick it, then type in a new name for your drawing.

7. Pick **SITE1-20**, and you'll be returned to the main drawing list.

DataCAD exercise 7

Please complete the following exercise by reading each question carefully, then circling the letter that corresponds to the correct answer.

1. Default drawings allow you to:
   a. Change the type of drawing you're going to create, but not the scale or drawing borders.
   b. Preset several different "drawing formats" (blank drawing sheets) for the types and scales of drawings you'll be creating. This includes setting up special layers for your drawings also.
   c. Have the correct title block already set in your drawing only. The layers and scale cannot be preset in the default drawing.

2. To select your default drawing, when the original drawing list is displayed, you pick the:
   a. **New Path** option.
   b. **Default** option.
   c. **Set Deflt** option.

3. Your default drawings should all be stored in the (assuming you have version 6):
   a. **dcad6\dwg** directory.
   b. **dcad6\borders** directory.
   c. **dcad6\default** directory.

4. The different types of angle types are:
   a. Normal, Cartesian, Relative, Radians, and Gradians.
   b. Absolute and Relative.
   c. Normal, Compass, Bearings, Decimal Degrees, Radians, and Gradians.

5. Different lines (such as solid, dashed, dot-dash, etc.) are called:
   a. Line Weights.
   b. Linetypes.
   c. Line Scales.

6. When you create text or use different linetypes in your drawing, the spacing factor you define them in is dependent on the:
   a. Final plot scale.
   b. Color of the item.
   c. Size that looks good on the screen.

7. The option to adjust the line spacing is found in the:
   a. Measures menu.
   b. Plot menu.
   c. Linetype menu.

8. To set the angle mode to Bearings, you use the:
   a. [INS] key.
   b. [SPACE] .
   c. Settings menu, **AngleTyp** option.

9. To set the input mode to Relative Polar, you use the:
   a. [INS] key.
   b. [SPACE] .
   c. Settings menu, **AngleTyp** option.

10. To draw site plans using bearing angles, the Scale Type of your drawing should be set to:
    a. Engineering.
    b. Decimal.
    c. Civil.

CHAPTER 9

Site Plans

Site drawings

DataCAD provides many feature to help you plan the site of your building. You can develop the plot from the civil description, then work setbacks and easements to develop the limits of your design area.

Here are some of the things you'll learn in this chapter:

- Using decimal scale input.
- Typing angles in polar bearings mode.
- Creating site arcs using curve data.
- Measuring the site closing gap.
- Measuring lines and arcs.
- Aligning text to an angle.
- Setting the Z-base and height.
- Adding the measurements to the drawing.

Starting your drawing

1. Start DataCAD.

2. At the drawing list, pick the drawing name for your site drawing, **SITE1**. You created this drawing during the last chapter.

Or,

1. You can start a fresh drawing by picking the **Default** option.

2. Pick the **SITE1-20** default drawing.

3. Type in a new, unique name for this drawing, such as: **site-01** and press ENTER .

4. The site drawing border will be displayed, as in Figure 9.1.

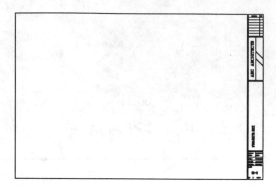

Figure 9.1: The site drawing border.

Your site project

You'll draw the site property lines from the project shown in Figure 9.2.

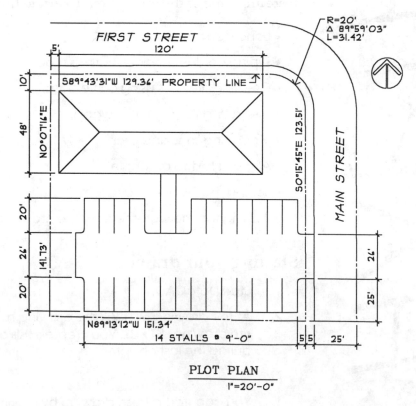

Figure 9.2: The site project.

Review of site plans and survey drawing information

Site plans are developed from information supplied by the civil engineer, in the form of a survey drawing. DataCAD has developed special options to allow the correct input of this information to your drawing. Correctly drawing the site is especially important when using a computer, because all subsequent plans will be developed from this information, in true scale and accuracy.

Using the exact information supplied by the survey drawing also helps you to screen problems during the initial site development. In manual drafting, when site information is traced, errors are often transferred to all of the proceeding drawings without being caught. The correction of these errors causes major impact to the original investment. Using DataCAD properly helps to eliminate many of these problems.

Survey drawings are supplied with *bearings information* calling out the length and direction of lines, in a North/East/South/West type of format. Radii in the drawings are notated with *curve data information* (length, bearings in, bearings out, radius, delta, etc.), as illustrated in Figure 9.3. As you refer to the survey drawing that will be used for the site layout project during this lesson, you'll notice the bearings and radius notations are similar to the survey information you usually find in your civil drawings. You'll use this data to create your site layout!

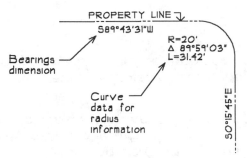

Figure 9.3: Sample of bearings and radii notation.

Bearing angle type

Bearings is a type of angle you can use for *polar input* (polar = distance + angle). This bearings information is also sometimes referred to as *metes and bounds*.

There are six types of polar angles you can choose from for site input. They are shown in Figure 9.4. Earlier, you set the *Bearing* option in the *Angle Type* menu (found in *Settings*), and that's what you'll use during this project.

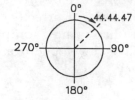

NORMAL

Based on a right
normal (90°) angle
Format:
Angle.minutes.seconds
Ex: 45.15.13

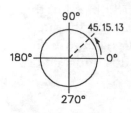

COMPASS

Clockwise 360°
Angle definition
Format:
Angle.minutes.seconds
Ex: 44.44.41

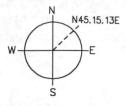

BEARINGS

North–east–
south–west–angle
Format:
Angle.minutes.seconds
Ex: N45.15.13E

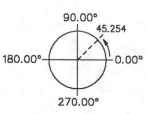

DECIMAL DEGREES

Based on a right
normal (90°) angle
Format:
Angle.decimal
Ex: 45.254

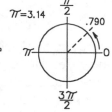

RADIANS

Counterclockwise
angle definition
Format:
radian.decimal
Ex: .790

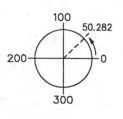

GRADIANS

Counterclockwise
400 Grad increments
Format:
Grad.decimal
Ex: 50.282

Figure 9.4: Angle input types.

An explanation of these types:

- *Normal* - used daily for typing in measurements of lines, walls, doors, windows, etc., when there are angles in the drawing.

- *Compass* - sometimes used in site plans, as seen in some overseas and European survey drawings. An example is Hawaiian and Japanese drawings.

- *Bearing* - used by architects in United States to transfer the plot information given by the civil engineer into DataCAD, if given in bearings.

- *Decimal Degrees* - helpful when using DataCAD for drawing mechanical details, because some are in decimal measurements. Also helpful if the main scale setting is a metric unit.

- *Radians* - used by civil engineers in developing site calculations using DataCAD.

- *Gradians* - another engineering angle. One grad is 1/100 of a right angle (90-degrees).

Setting the Z-base and height

You'll be viewing this drawing in 3D later, so it's a good idea to set the Z height of your property lines to 0 (zero).

1. Press [Z] .

2. Type in **0** and press [ENTER] for the Z-base.

3. Type in **0** and press [ENTER] for the Z-height.

Defining bearing angles

Every line is based on a major and minor axis. The major axis is either north or south. The minor will be east or west. Before you type in the bearing angle, you can figure which quadrant the line will fall in based on these axis. Is the line going northeast, southeast, northwest, or southwest?

The *quadrant* the line is angled into determines the actual direction. Why worry about direction? Because you're drawing on a CAD system, you must give the system a direction for the line, similar to how you typed in a X direction (to go right) or -X (negative to go left) before. The quadrants are illustrated in Figure 9.5.

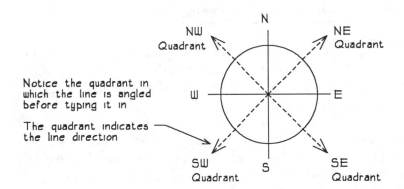

Figure 9.5: Bearing quadrants.

If the line is going northeast, the line will be drawn to the right, as shown in Figure 9.6. If the line is going southwest, it will be drawn to the left.

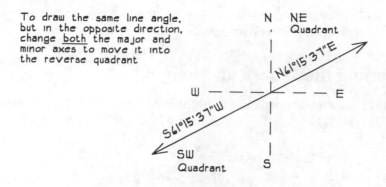

To draw the same line angle, but in the opposite direction, change <u>both</u> the major and minor axes to move it into the reverse quadrant

Figure 9.6: The quadrant shows the direction.

If you have a line that is angled to the *right*, but you wish it drawn to the *left*, you just change the major and minor axes, as in Figure 9.7. This way, you have drawn the same line, but in the direction you desire. (Another technique is to type in a negative distance, *not* direction.)

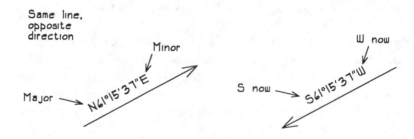

Same line, opposite direction

Figure 9.7: Changing both axes to change direction.

The technique of reversing a line angle is necessary when inputting site plans because you have to start in one place and work around the site in a single direction (clockwise or counterclockwise).

The lines in a plot are seldom angled all in one clockwise or counterclockwise direction. This is because plots are usually derived from subdivisions. The legal description of the line bearing must remain the same as the large unit being subdivided. You'll get the opportunity to reverse the direction of a line in your first project!

When you type in a bearing angle, you'll follow the format described in Figure 9.8. For example, an angle given as North 47 (degrees) 15′ (minutes) 35″ (seconds) West will be typed in as **n47.15.35w**. The N, E, S, or W can be typed in lower or uppercase letters. The angles, minutes, and seconds are separated by periods. *Don't* include spaces. Bearings are very easy to use, as you'll see.

Type in bearing angle by separating the angle, minutes and seconds with a period

Angle   Minutes   Seconds

N47.15.35W   *No spaces!*

Major Axis

Minor Axis

Figure 9.8: The format for typing in bearings.

The four site-plan checkpoint reminders:

1. In the setting menu, Angle Type = *Bearing*. Scale type = *Decimal*.

2. Input mode = *Relative polar*.

3. Angles typed in as: *n45.15.13e format*.

4. To change direction of the line, change both the *major and minor axes*.

Creating the property line

Figure 9.9 shows the property lines you'll draw. Use this figure as a reference while you follow the next steps.

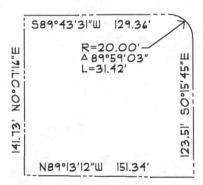

S89°43′31″W   129.36′

R=20.00′
Δ 89°59′03″
L=31.42′

N0°07′12″E   141.73′

S0°15′45″E   123.51′

N89°13′12″W   151.34′

Figure 9.9: The property lines of your project.

1. Pick a start point in your drawing to start your property line, as shown in Figure 9.10. (Always pick a start point before you use relative input.)

2. Press the SPACE .

3. Type in the relative distance of the first line: **123.51** and press ENTER .

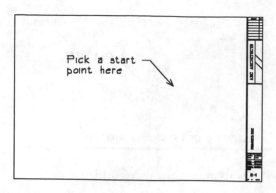

Figure 9.10: Pick a start point.

4. Now you'll be prompted to: Enter relative angle: A default of North might appear at the cursor area. Type in the bearing angle: **s0.15.45e** and press ENTER .

5. The line will be drawn.

6. Press the SPACE .

7. Type in the relative distance of the second line: **151.34** and press ENTER .

8. Type in the bearing angle: **n89.13.12w** and press ENTER . Your drawing should now look like Figure 9.11.

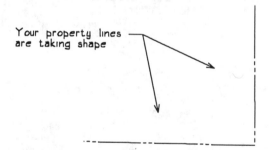

Figure 9.11: Your drawing should look like this.

9. Press the SPACE .

10. Type in the relative distance of the next line: **141.73** and press ENTER .

11. Type in the bearing angle: **n0.7.16e** and press ENTER .

12. Notice that the direction of the last line is *southwest* (S89.43.31W). This means it will be drawn to the left, when the desired direction is to the right. To change the direction of the line, simply change both the major and minor axes. This will result in a northeast line, drawn to the right.

13. Press the SPACE .

14. Type in the relative distance of the next line: **129.36** and press [ENTER].

15. Type in the bearing angle: **n89.43.31e** and press [ENTER].

16. Your drawing should look like Figure 9.12. You're ready to create the curve in your drawing.

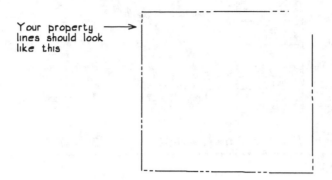

Figure 9.12: The lines are drawn.

Creating a curve using curve data

When you're given a drawing from the surveyor, the curves are described with data that can be used to recreate the curve using the DataCAD option called Curve Data. This information includes:

- Radius
- Cord length
- Arc length
- Delta angle (included angle)
- Bearings in
- Bearings out, etc.

1. Pick the **Curve** tool in the tool bar, as shown in Figure 9.13. (The quick key is [ALT] [A] for Arcs.)

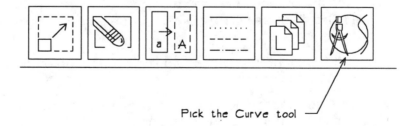

Pick the Curve tool

Figure 9.13: The Curve tool.

2. Pick the **CurvData** option.

3. The Curve Data menu is displayed, as shown in Figure 9.14. This illustration shows the menu divided into three parts: *Point placement*, *Arc definition*, and *Bearing angle*. You'll only need to use four options in this menu to create your arc - one from the point section, two

from the arc section, and one from the bearing section.

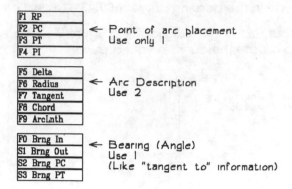

Figure 9.14: The Curve Data menu is divided into 3 parts.

Definitions of point and arc options

RP (Radius Point) The center of the radius, or "arc" to be defined.

PC (Point of Curve) The starting point of the arc. Remember curve is created in a clockwise direction!

PT (Point of Tangency) The ending point of the arc.

PI (Point of Intersection) The point where the tangent lines through PC and PT intersect. (Lines are tangent to the resulting arc.) See Figure 9.15.

Delta Once you have defined the point for your curve, it's like nailing it into place by that point. Now the arc has to be defined.

Radius The radius of the arc.

Tangent The distance from the *start point* of the arc to the *PI*. This distance will be identical to the distance from the *endpoint* to the *PI*.

Chord The straight line from the starting point to the ending point of the arc.

ArcLnth (Arc Length) The distance along the arc from the starting point to the ending point.

The following illustration, Figure 9.15, shows how all of the choices in the Curve Data menu are related to your curve.

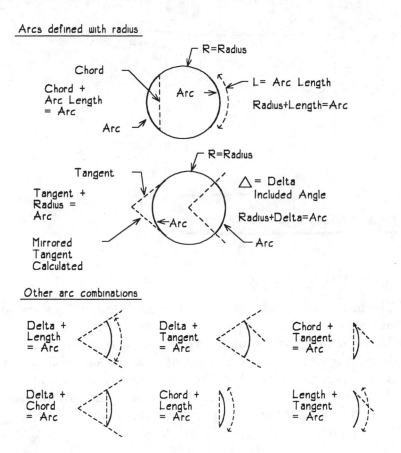

Figure 9.15: Curve data described graphically.

Placing the arc

The first part of the menu is to help you place a point of the arc on your drawing. You'll use the beginning point, PC. The PC and PT are the most commonly used point definitions. (See Figure 9.16.)

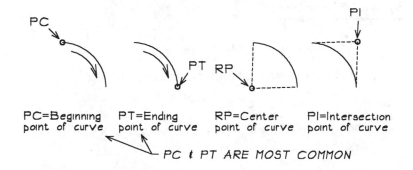

Figure 9.16: Point definitions.

1. Pick the **PC** option.

2. Object snap to the start point position, indicated in Figure 9.17.

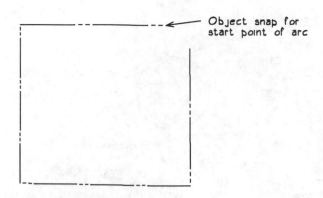

Figure 9.17: Object snap to start the arc.

Describing the arc

The most common arc annotations you'll find in the site plan are: *arc radius* (R=), *length* (L=), and *delta* (included angle, shown with a small triangle). You need two options to describe an arc. If possible, use Radius and Delta. The radius is usually a whole number, and the delta includes angle, minutes, and seconds. This calculation is equivalent to three decimal places, where all other dimensions have been rounded to two places. See Figure 9.18.

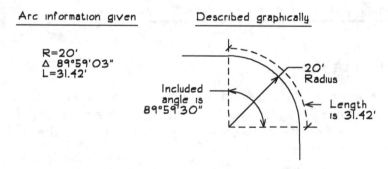

Figure 9.18: Describing the arc.

1. Pick the **Radius** option.

2. Type in the radius of your arc: **21** and press ENTER .

3. Pick the **Delta** option.

4. Type in the included angle of your arc: **89.59.03** and press ENTER .

Bearing definitions

Next, the *bearing information* (what you might think of as the tangency) must be supplied. Figure 9.19 illustrates how the arc is swiveling around the point. Once a tangent slope (bearing in or bearing out), or a slope defining the cross tangency (bearing PC or bearing PT) is defined, then the arc can be placed!

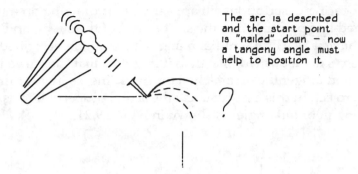

The arc is described
and the start point
is "nailed" down — now
a tangeny angle must
help to position it

Figure 9.19: Tying the arc into place with an angle.

Brng In (Bearing In) The tangent line going into the start of the arc.

Brng Out (Bearing Out) The tangent line coming out of the end of the arc.

Brng PC (Bearing Point of Curve) The line created from the center-point of the start point of the arc.

Brng PT (Bearing Point of Tangency) The line created from the center-point to the end-point of the arc.

4 Examples of Curve Bearings

Bearing In   PC

Bearing PC

Bearing PT   PT

Bearing Out

Bearing In

Bearing PC

Bearing PT   PC

Bearing Out   PT

Bearing PC

Bearing In   PC

Bearing PT

PT   Bearing Out

Bearing Out

Bearing PT   PT

Bearing In   PC

Bearing PC

Figure 9.20: Examples of arc bearing notations.

Figure 9.20 shows how to identify the correct bearing choice to describe your curve.

The bearing description will appear in your drawing on a dashed line pointing into the start or end of the curve, and will have a "RAD" identifier along with an angle described. If there's not a dashed line, then it might be that the curve is assumed tangent to an attached property line, as in your first site project. In this case, you use the actual property line as a bearing in or out angle, as shown in Figure 9.21.

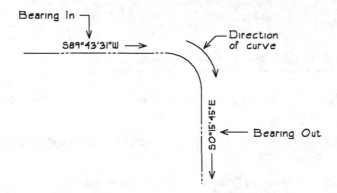

Figure 9.21: The property line supplies the bearing angles.

1. Pick the **BrngIn** option.

2. You'll use the same line that you object snapped to for the start of your arc. This line qualifies as the bearing-in.

3. Type in the angle for the bearing in of your arc: **n89.43.31e** and press ENTER .

4. Notice now the **Add** option appears. Pick it.

5. Your arc is added, as shown in Figure 9.22.

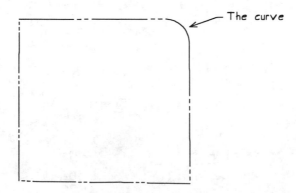

Figure 9.22: The arc is added.

6. Press SHIFT F to file your drawing.

Validating the closing point of your site

The point where you started drawing the property line and where you ended is called the *closing point*. The end point of the first line and the end point of the last line, or arc, will never actually be 100% closed. They'll be slightly off, due to the decimal round off (to two decimal places) in the dimensions of the site plan.

In other words, one inch is .0833333..., but it would be rounded off to .08 in your drawing dimensions, so it's easy to see how the site plan's final closing point would have a gap. It's important how large this gap is (it should be very small). The civil engineer is limited to a *.01* tolerance on calculations. This is around 1/8", which of course wouldn't show up in any drawing after being plotted, and it wouldn't show up on the screen unless you zoomed in.

Sometimes, through mistakes in calculations, the closing point might have a large discrepancy that's easily seen. One site I drew was 27 feet off once it was checked with Data-CAD! (Two numbers were transposed in the legal description and the site was resurveyed.) To check the closing point of your site, you can use the *Measures* option.

1. Press ALT X to go to the Measures menu, found in Utility.

2. Pick the **PntToPnt** option.

3. If grid snap is on, you'll want to turn it off by pressing the X key until the message reads "*Snap is off.*"

4. If necessary, pick the **[I]** button on the control panel, then pick the arc to identify it, in order to see where it ends. Press mouse button 3 to return to Measures.

5. Object snap to the end point of the arc (right side), which was the final end point of your property line, as in step 1 in Figure 9.23. You might want to "zoom in" to make object snapping easier.

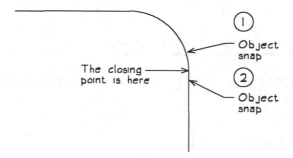

Figure 9.23: Object snap to find gap size.

4.   Now object snap to the end point of the line, which was the starting point of the property line, as in step 2 in Figure 9.23.

5.   The distance between the two points will be displayed in the message area of the screen.

The measured distance

If you've done everything correctly, the distance between the start point and the end point of this site will be around .008. When you perform this check on your own drawings, you might find that a .01 or .009 is common for a closing point distance. (If you got 0.0, try again, you must have gotten the same point twice.)

If you get a .08 or .1, remember that this is still a very close distance, and you could start your working drawings. If you get a distance reading any larger than this, you might want to make it a rule to check back with your civil engineer with your findings.

You can add this measurement to your drawing, if you wish.

1.   Pick the **ToDrwing** option.

2.   Move the cursor out to the drawing area, and you'll notice it's a text cursor. A text menu is displayed.

3.   Pick to place the start point of the text, as shown in Figure 9.24. The measurement will be added to your drawing.

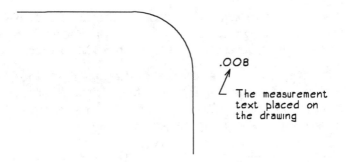

.008

The measurement text placed on the drawing

Figure 9.24: The measurement text is added.

4.   Press mouse button 3 to exit back to the Measures menu.

Measuring arcs and lines

You might want to use measure to quickly check on the angles of your lines, their length, or even the size of your arc.

1. Pick the **LineAngl** option.

2. Pick one of the property lines. The angle will be displayed in the message area of the screen. Continue picking the lines you want to check. When you're done, you can return to the Measures menu by pressing mouse button 3 once.

3. If you want to check the length of the line, you can use the **Line** option and pick the lines you want to check.

4. To check the arcs in your drawing, you can use the **Radius, Chord**, and **ArcLnth** options.

5. Another way to check the line lengths and angles is to use the Identify menu. Pick the **[I]** button in the control panel.

6. Pick the line you wish to check. The length and angle will appear in the message area of the screen. Identify will only display the radius for arcs.

7. Press mouse button 3 to exit the Identify menu and return to the Measures menu.

Dimensioning the property lines

To annotate your site, you could use the Text menu and simply type in the dimensions of your lines. But you can also use the Measures menu to add dimensions to your plot drawing.

1. Pick the **LineAngl** option in the Measures menu.

2. Pick one of your property lines that you wish to dimension. You'll notice the angle of the line will appear in the message area.

3. Picking the **ToDrwing** option.

4. A text menu will be displayed, and the cursor will now appear as a text cursor. Pick by the line to add the measurement. (This is shown in Figure 9.25.)

To align the text to the line

To align the text to the angle of the line you're dimensioning, you can use the *Angle* option.

1. Once you've selected the line to measure using **LineAngl**, pick the **ToDrwing** option.

2. Pick **Angle**. This option controls the angle of the text line. You could type in the angle, or use Match.

3. Pick **Match**.

4. Pick the line you're dimensioning. The angle of the line will appear in the message area of the screen.

5. Press mouse button 3 to exit back to the Angle menu. The angle of your line will appear in the message area of your screen.

6. Press ENTER to accept this angle. You'll return to the ToDrwing menu. Notice that the text cursor now appears aligned with the line you're dimensioning.

7. Pick near the line to place your text. The text will be aligned to the line's angle.

8. Once you have placed the text, continue by pressing mouse button 3 once, which returns you to the LineAngle menu. Pick the next line you want dimensioned.

9. Follow steps 1 through 7 again to add all the dimensions. *If your text comes in the opposite angle* that you want during the match, as in Figure 9.25, see the next section; "To reverse the match angle."

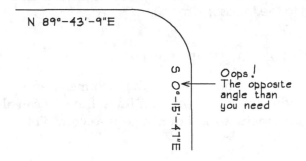

Figure 9.25: The text came in at the wrong angle.

To reverse the match angle

Sometimes the angle will be the opposite that you want the text to be. In other words, the angle goes down but you want your text pointed up to be read from the right. The text will come in upside down. (You could avoid this by typing in the angle instead of using Match, remembering to reverse the angle when necessary.) When using Match, you can quickly reverse the angle by following these steps:

1. Pick **Match**.

2. Pick the line you're dimensioning. The angle of the line will appear in the message area of the screen.

3. Pick **Inverse**.

4. Pick **Supplement**. The angle will be reversed.

5. Press mouse button 3 to exit back to the angle menu.

6. Press ⏎ENTER to enter the angle and return to the ToDrwing menu.

7. Pick near the line to place your text. It should appear correct now.

Note: *The angle set in this option remains as the set angle in the Text option also, so you can go back and forth between menus and your text will be aligned. The Angle option in Text works the same. To return the angle to a horizontal position while in the Bearings Angle mode, type in **E** as the angle (East). If you are in the Normal Angle mode, type in 0 (zero).*

Visually checking the lines

The final step in checking the property lines is to perform a visual check, which is double-checking them against the original lines of the civil engineering drawing. This is easy to do. Plot out your DataCAD drawing to the same scale as the engineering drawing you were working from. Then hold the DataCAD drawing over the original drawing so that the lines can be seen through the paper.

Of course, it's easier to see through the paper if you used vellum or have a light source to backlight the drawings, but you can also hold them against a window to let the sun-light shine through. Look closely at the lines. If there is a discrepancy, you might want to contact your civil engineer. The question becomes: which is correct, the calculations or the line?

DataCAD exercise 8

Please complete the following exercise by reading each question carefully, then circling the letter that corresponds to the correct answer.

1. Default drawings allow you to:
   a. Change the type of drawing you're going to create, but not the scale or drawing borders.
   b. Preset several different "drawing formats" (blank drawing sheets) for the types and scales of drawings you'll be creating. This includes setting up special layers for your drawings also.
   c. Have the correct title block already set in your drawing only. The layers and scale cannot be preset in the default drawing.

2. The different types of angle types are:
   a. Normal, Cartesian, Relative, Radians, and Gradians.
   b. Absolute and Relative.
   c. Normal, Compass, Bearings, Decimal Degrees, Radians, and Gradians.

3. Before you use a relative input mode, you should:
   a. ALWAYS pick a start point.
   b. NEVER pick a start point.
   c. Only pick a start point if the drawing tells you to.

4. When you use Bearings, the following angle would be correctly entered:
   a. **90-15-13**
   b. **n90.15.13w**
   c. **n 90.15.13 w**

5. The Bearings input mode in DataCAD is usually used:
   a. By civil engineers only, to create survey drawings. The architect will never use it.
   b. To quickly input survey information supplied by civil engineers, to correctly create the site plan.
   c. When first creating the survey drawing only. It's never used while drawing site plans, since you only have to trace the survey drawing on the computer.

6. To recreate Radii found in the survey drawing, you can use the:
   a. Survey menu, **Curve** option.
   b. Curves menu, **Radius** option.
   c. Curves menu, **CurvData** option.

7. If a line's bearing direction goes to the right, and you wish to draw the same line but to the left direction, you must:
   a. Change just the minor axis from east to west.
   b. Change both the major and minor axis in order to draw the same angle, or type in a negative distance.
   c. Draw the line going to the right, then move it later.

8. When using the Curve Data menu, you need to describe:
   a. One point, two arc definitions, and one bearing angle.
   b. Every option in the menu.
   c. Two points, two arc definitions, and two bearing angles.

9. To measure the line angle, you can use the:
   a. **Measures**, **LineAngl** options.
   b. **Dimension**, **Linear**, and **LineAngl** options.
   c. **Measures**, **PntToPnt** options.

10. To validate your site plan, you should:
    a. Run the **S** option, which will check the site for you. Then visually check it against the original drawing.
    b. Check the closing points for a large gap and the final plotted lines against the original drawing.
    c. Not worry about it, since civil drawings are always correct.

11. The site plan will:
    a. Never have a gap. If it does, just use CleanUp to correct it.
    b. Sometimes have a gap, but will usually close completely.
    c. Always have a gap at the closing point, due to the round off of the decimal places.

12. To align your text with a line angle, you can use the:
    a. **Angle**, **Align** options.
    b. **Align**, **ToLine** options.
    c. **Angle**, **Match** options.

Some review questions:
13. The quickest way to turn from lines to walls, or from walls to lines, is to use the:
    a. Menu option choices.
    b. ◁ key.
    c. ▤ key.

14. In order to define a reference point, you press the:
    a. SPACE .
    b. ~ key.
    c. X key.

15. To clean up wall intersections after you create them, you pick the:
    a. **Cleanup** option, then pick **T** or **L Intsect**.
    b. **Cleanup** option, then pick **Corner**.
    c. **Architect** option, then pick the **Clean** option.

16. To erase the last item you created, you use the:
    a. **Delete** option.
    b. < key.
    c. > key.

17. To turn on and off grid snap, press the:
    a. G key.
    b. X key.
    c. < key.

CHAPTER 10

Copying techniques

Copying

In this chapter, you'll add easements, streets, a building, and a parking lot to the site you created in chapter 9. Many of the lines and arcs you'll use to create these additions will be "copied" from other items in your drawing.

Here are some of the things you'll learn in this chapter:

- Offsetting copies of existing lines and arcs.
- Changing the attributes of items.
- Copying in a rectangular pattern.
- Moving items to different layers.
- Mirroring copies of items.
- Trimming lines.
- Erasing parts of lines.
- Extending lines.
- Adding fillets to round the corners of existing lines.

Why copy?

Whenever possible, you should always copy. Why? Because copying existing geometry saves time, eliminates steps, increases accuracy, and reduces error. As an example, note that the parking lot, which was shown in your earlier project and is illustrated in greater detail in

Figure 10.1, is made up of repeated lines (parking stripes). One line is drawn and copied many times.

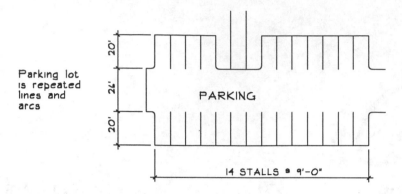

Parking lot
is repeated
lines and
arcs

Figure 10.1: The parking lot is repeated geometry.

Copying techniques include:

- Copying in patterns
- Offsetting copies
- Mirroring and copying
- Point to point copying

Or you might make symbols of items or a part of a building, and use the symbols in several drawings.

Preplanning your drawing

If you spend a few minutes organizing your steps prior to starting your drawings, you'll be able to scan for repeated patterns. Look for the "best" way to create the drawing. This is called *preplanning*. How long it takes depends on the experience of the user and the complexity of the project.

Some beginning users have found it very effective to rough out a "quick-and-dirty" sketch, only penciling the major steps, as in Figure 10.2. Later, when you're more experienced, you'll find that you preplan mentally.

Sometimes a
quick sketch
helps you to
preplan your
drawing

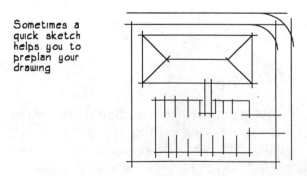

Figure 10.2: Sometimes, quick sketches help you preplan.

1. Examine your project for repeated geometry. In this case, the street lines are lines and an arc moved a certain constant distance from the property lines. This can be achieved by "copying" the property lines or "offsetting" them at an equal distance.

2. Although the linetypes are not the same, as shown in Figure 10.3, it becomes an easy task to simply change the linetype of the copied lines.

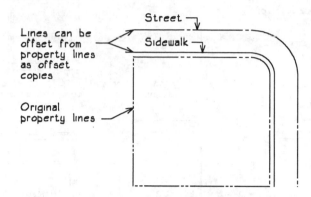

Figure 10.3: Look for duplicate lines in your drawing.

3. Look for repeated patterns in your drawings. As mentioned, the parking lot is a very good example of a repeated pattern.

4. Look for ways to eliminate steps, using your natural thinking process. For instance, although the entire parking lot could be made by a complex repeat pattern, it's more of a "no-brainer" to just mirror the first pattern over to the other side, as shown in Figure 10.4.

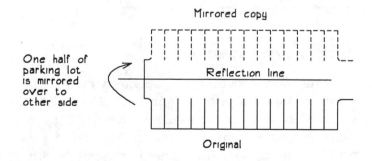

Figure 10.4: Mirroring is easy and saves time.

5. Plan how you'll start and what the progression will be in creating the geometry. What is your first step? What will you do next? Can you lump together some related steps to perform at one time, without having to change back and forth through menus?

    It would be faster, for example, to offset all the street lines in one step. Then the second step would be to change the offset copies to the correct linetype all at one time. This avoids needless changes of menus and unnecessary steps.

Examine Figure 10.5, which graphically illustrates the creation steps you'll use for your next project. These steps appear in a storyboard to help you understand the preplanning process.

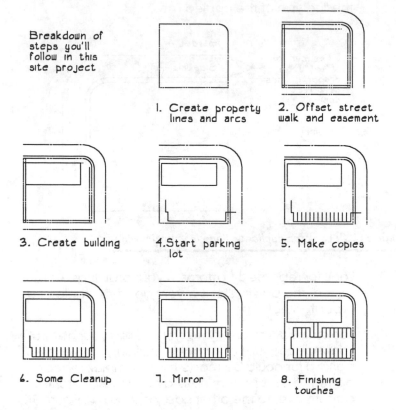

Breakdown of steps you'll follow in this site project

1. Create property lines and arcs

2. Offset street walk and easement

3. Create building

4. Start parking lot

5. Make copies

6. Some Cleanup

7. Mirror

8. Finishing touches

Figure 10.5: The step-by-step pictorial breakdown.

Creating the easements

The Offset function is found in the Geometry menu. Offset allows you to make a copy of an item at a defined distance. You'll use Offset to create copies of the property lines to draw lines for your easements, sidewalk, and street. This way, you'll avoid drawing these lines from scratch with input coordinates or figuring out the correct radius for the arc. Let DataCAD do it for you!

Figure 10.6 shows the easements, sidewalk/curbs and street lines for your reference.

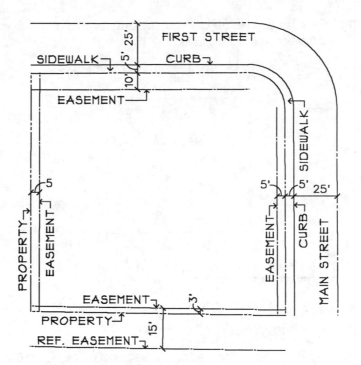

Figure 10.6: Project dimensions.

1. Pull up your **SITE1** drawing.

2. Press ⌊ALT⌋ ⌊G⌋ to go to the Geometry option found in the Utility menu.

3. Pick the **Offset** option.

4. Make sure the **LyrSrch** option is active.

5. Pick **Dynamic** to turn It OFF (red). Otherwise, the PerpDist option won't be displayed.

7. Pick the **PerpDist** (perpendicular distance) option.

8. Type in the distance for the first property easement: **10** and press ⌊ENTER⌋ .

9. Pick the first line to offset, shown as step 1, Figure 10.7.

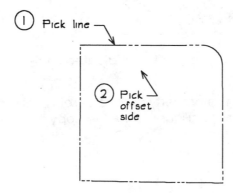

Figure 10.7: Pick this line, then pick side to offset.

10. Pick on the inside of the property for the offset copy to appear, as in step 2, Figure 10.7.

11. The copy will be created, as in Figure 10.8.

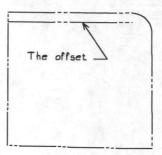

The offset

Figure 10.8: The offset is drawn.

12. Pick the **New Dist** option.

13. Pick **PerpDist** again.

14. Type in the distance for the second easement: **5** and press ENTER .

15. Pick the line to define the second easement, as shown as step 1 in Figure 10.9.

16. Pick inside the property to offset the copy, shown as step 2 in Figure 10.9.

17. The copy is created, as in step 3, Figure 10.9.

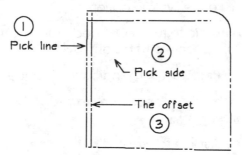

Pick line →
② Pick side
The offset
③

Figure 10.9: Steps for offsetting.

18. Pick the next line to offset, indicated as step 1 in Figure 10.10.

19. Pick inside the property area to offset a copy of this line, as in step 2, Figure 10.10. The copy is made, shown by step 3.

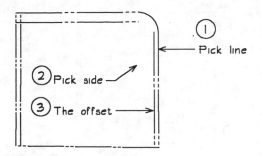

Figure 10.10: Offsetting the next easement.

20. Pick the **New Dist** option.

21. Pick **PerpDist** again.

22. Type in the distance for the final easement: **3** and press ENTER .

23. Pick the line to define the second easement, as shown as step 1 in Figure 10.11.

24. Pick inside the property to offset the copy, shown as step 2 in Figure 10.11.

25. The copy is created, as in step 3, Figure 10.11.

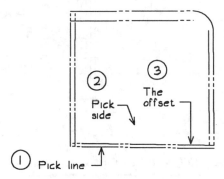

Figure 10.11: Offsetting the parking lot easement.

26. This easement must be shown with a 15' easement allowance. Pick the **New Dist** option, then pick **PerpDist** again.

27. Type in the distance for the easement allowance: **15** and press ENTER .

28. Pick the easement line you just created, as shown as step 1 in Figure 10.12.

24. Pick inside the property to offset the copy, shown as step 2 in Figure 10.12. The copy is created, as in step 3.

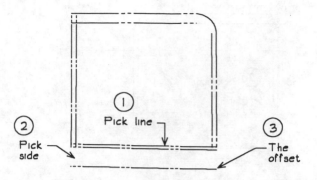

Figure 10.12: Offsetting the easement allowance.

25.   Press [SHIFT] [F] to file your drawing.

Creating the sidewalk

1.   Pick **New Dist**, then **PerpDist**.

2.   Type in **5** and press [ENTER].

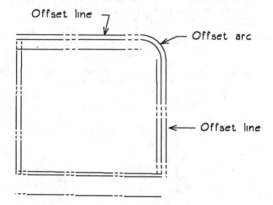

Figure 10.13: Offsetting curb lines for the sidewalk.

3.   Offset all of the property lines and arc indicated in Figure 10.13 for the sidewalk.

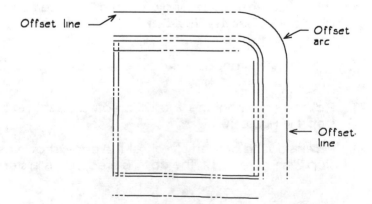

Figure 10.14: Offsetting for the street.

Drawing the Street

1. Pick **New Dist**, then **PerpDist**.

2. Type in **25** and press ENTER .

3. Offset all of the property lines and arc indicated in Figure 10.14 for the street.

Changing the color and linetype of existing items

1. Pick the **Change** tool from the icon bar, as shown in Figure 10.15. (Or press ALT C .)

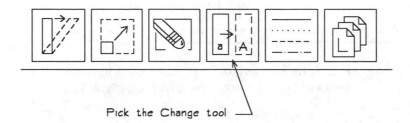

Pick the Change tool

Figure 10.15: The change tool.

2. Pick **LineTyp**.

3. Pick the **CentrLn** linetype.

4. Pick **Color**.

5. Set the color to **Green**.

6. Pick **Entity** to make it active.

7. Pick all of the easement lines you want changed to the new color and linetype, indicated in Figure 10.16.

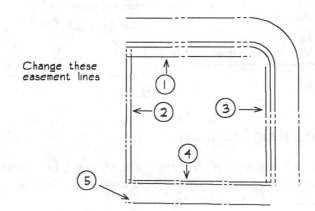

Change these easement lines

Figure 10.16: Change these easement lines.

8. Pick **Color** again, twice. The first time will turn it off; the second time the color list will be displayed.

9.   Set the color to **Cyan**.

10.   Pick the street lines, as shown in Figure 10.17.

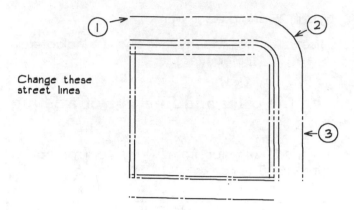

Figure 10.17: Change these street lines.

11.   Pick **LineTyp** twice. The first time will turn it off; the second time the linetype list will be displayed.

12.   Set the linetype to **Solid**.

13.   Pick all of the curb lines you want changed, indicated in Figure 10.18.

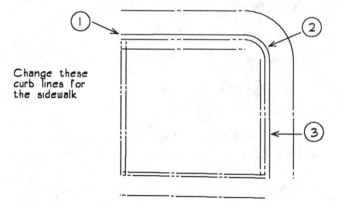

Figure 10.18: Change these curb lines.

14.   Press ⌨SHIFT ⌨F to file your drawing.

Moving items to a layer

Offset creates copies of the original line or arc, on the same layer the original item was on. You'll want to "Move" them to the easement and street layer.

1.   To confirm what layer the easement lines are on, you can use Identify. Pick the **[I]** button in the control panel.

2. Pick one of the easement lines until it becomes gray and dashed. Look at the (F2) option in the menu, which tells you what layer the item is on. If you have drawn your site correctly, it will still be on the Property layer.

3. Pick the **Move** tool, shown in Figure 10.19, or press ⌨M to quickly enter the Move option, found in the Edit menu.

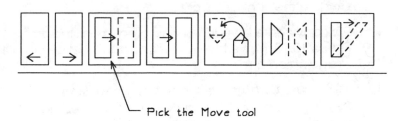

Pick the Move tool

Figure 10.19: The move tool.

4. Pick the **To Layer** option.

5. Now pick the layer name you want the easement lines *moved to.* In this case, pick the **Easement** layer.

6. Pick **Entity** to make it active.

7. Pick all of the lines that should go on the easement layer. Sometimes you can see them blink a little when you pick them, but the real indicator is in the message area of the screen. It should read "1 entity selected" as you pick the items.

8. When you have picked all of the easement lines, pick **New Layer**.

9. Pick the **Street** layer name.

10. Now, pick all of the lines and arc that should go on the Street layer.

11. When you're done moving the street items, press mouse button 3 to exit.

Changing the settings for architectural design

Now that you're ready to draw the architectural features of your site, you can change your scale settings.

1. Press mouse button 3 until you're in the Utility menu.

2. Pick the **Settings** option.

3. Pick **ScaleTyp**.

4. Pick **Architct**.

5.   Press mouse button 3 to exit this menu and return to Settings.

6.   Pick the **AngleTyp** option.

7.   Pick **Normal** to return the angle setting back to normal (360-degrees).

8.   Pick **StrtAngl**. Currently, your Start Angle (0 degrees) is set to the North position. You need to change this back to the right 3:00 position.

9.   Pick anywhere in your drawing area, as in step 1 of Figure 10.20. Move the cursor, and you'll notice you're dragging an arrow.

10. Make sure *Orthomode is active*, by checking the O in SwOTHLUD. If the O is small, turn it on by pressing [O] until the message reads Orthomode is ON.

11. Pick to the right, as shown by step 2 in Figure 10.20, to indicate that the starting of the normal angle is at the 3:00 position.

Figure 10.20: The steps to indicate a starting angle.

12. Press mouse button 3 to exit.

Drawing the building

Reference Figure 10.21 for the architectural plan of your site layout. You can use the rectangular feature to draw the building.

1.   Press [Tab] to go to the Bldg layer.

2.   Press the **Z** key to set your Z-base and height. (You'll give your building some 3D height.)

3.   Type in **0** and press [ENTER] for the base of your building.

4.   Type in **26** and press [ENTER] to make the height of your building 26 feet.

5.   To set the coordinate input mode to Relative Cartesian coordinates, press the [INS] key until the message reads *Relative Cartesian*.

6.   Press [ALT] [R] to go to the Polygon (Rectangle) menu.

7.   Make sure the **Rectangl** option is active.

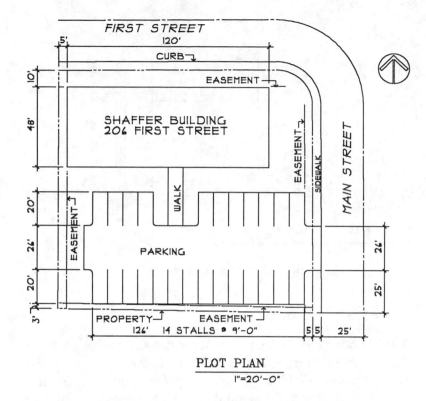

FIRST STREET

PLOT PLAN
1"=20'-0"

Figure 10.21: You'll add the building and the parking lot.

8. Object snap to the upper-left intersection of the easement lines, as shown in Figure 10.22.

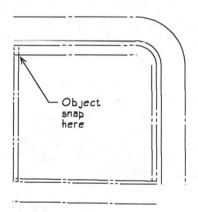

Object snap here

Figure 10.22: Object snap to this intersection.

9. Press the [SPACE] to invoke coordinate input.

10. For the X distance, type in **120** and press [ENTER] .

11. For the Y distance, type in **-48** (negative to go down) and press [ENTER] .

12. The building will be drawn, as in Figure 10.23.

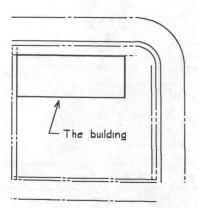

Figure 10.23: The building is drawn.

13.　Press `SHIFT` `F` to file your drawing.

Creating the parking lot

You'll notice the dimension that locates the parking lot is in the lower-left corner. You'll locate this spot on the easement line by using Offset to create a temporary construction line which intersects the easement. Since situations like this occur frequently in drawings, you'll find the following technique helpful for a variety of circumstances.

1.　Press `ALT` `G` to go to the Geometry menu, found in Utility.

2.　Pick the **Offset** option.

3.　Pick **PerpDist**.

4.　Type in **126** and press `ENTER` . This is the distance of the left corner of the parking lot to the right corner, as dimensioned on your drawing.

5.　Pick the line shown as step 1 in Figure 10.24. This is your dimensioned reference line. Pick the side shown in step 2 to offset.

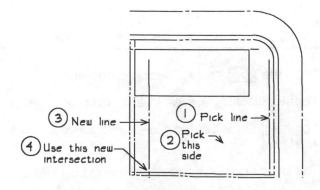

Figure 10.24: Steps to find an intersection point.

6. Your new line is shown as step 3 in Figure 10.24. Note that step 4 shows the new intersection point you'll use to create your parking lot. (You'll erase this line later.)

7. Press the [Tab] key to change the active layer to **Parking**.

8. Press the **Z** key to set your Z-base and height back to zero elevation.

9. Type in **0** and press [ENTER] for the base of your parking stripes.

10. Type in **0** and press [ENTER] for the height.

11. To start your parking lot, object snap to your new intersection point, as shown in Figure 10.25.

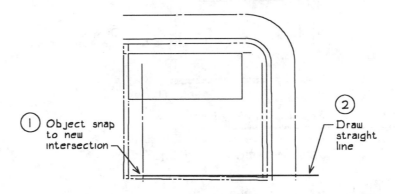

Figure 10.25: Object snap to the easement intersection.

12. With *orthomode still on*, draw a horizontal line that crosses over the right side easement line, as shown as step 1 in Figure 10.26. This creates another intersection point.

13. Press mouse button 3 to quit the line.

14. Object snap to the intersection of the easement and the parking lot line, shown as step 2 in Figure 10.26.

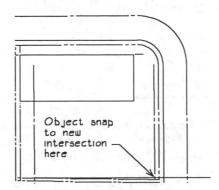

Figure 10.26: Object snap to this intersection now.

15. Press the [SPACE] .

16. Press [ENTER] to accept **0** for the X direction.

17. Type in **20** and press [ENTER] for the Y direction. The line will be drawn.

18. Now move your cursor to the right to draw the line for the driveway, allowing it to cross over the sidewalk curb line, as shown in Figure 10.27.

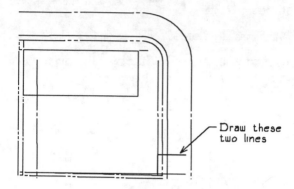

Figure 10.27: Draw the driveway lines.

19. Press mouse button 3 to quit this line.

Using a "two-pick" copy

You can use copy quickly by indicating "from" and "to" points.

1. Pick the **Copy** tool in the icon bar, as shown in Figure 10.28. (Or press [C] to go to the Copy menu.)

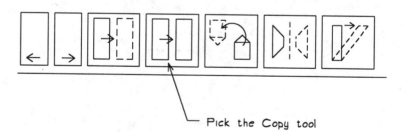

Figure 10.28: The Copy tool.

2. Object snap to the lower-right intersection of the easement and lot line, indicated as step 1 in Figure 10.29. This will be your "from" point.

3. When you move your cursor, you'll drag an arrow. Object snap to the lower-left intersection of the easement lines, as shown as step 2 in Figure 10.29.

4. Now, with **Entity** still active, pick the 20' line you created, indicated as step 3 in Figure 10.29.

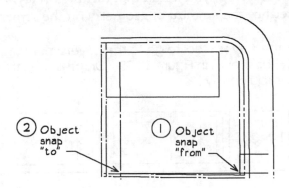

Figure 10.29: Step to copy "from" a point, "to" a point.

5. The line is copied, as shown in Figure 10.30.

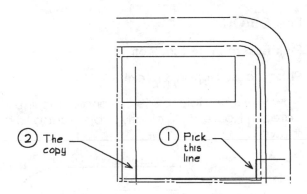

Figure 10.30: The new line.

6. Press mouse button 3 to exit the Copy menu. *Don't forget to exit the copy menu when you're done using it.*

7. Pick the **Erase** tool, or press Ⓔ , and erase the line shown in Figure 10.31.

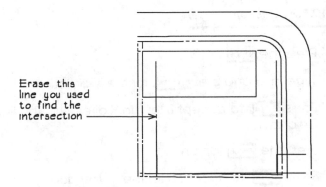

Figure 10.31: Erase this temporary line.

Turing off layers

Often, when drawing, you'll find that turning off layers is helpful to reduce the amount of geometry on the screen.

1. Pick the **Layers** tool to go to the Layers menu, found in Utility, as shown in Figure 10.32. (Or, press $\boxed{L}$, the Layers quick key.)

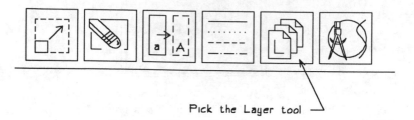

Pick the Layer tool ⎯

Figure 10.32: The Layers tool.

2. Pick **On/Off**.

3. Pick **Easement** to turn it off.

4. Press mouse button 3 to exit.

5. Now you'll be able to see the end of the line indicated in Figure 10.33 clearly. Object snap to it, as shown.

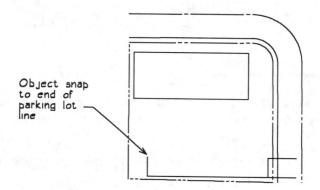

Object snap to end of parking lot line ⎯

Figure 10.33: Object snap here.

6. Press the $\boxed{\text{SPACE}}$.

7. Type in **-5** and press $\boxed{\text{ENTER}}$ for the X direction.

8. Press $\boxed{\text{ENTER}}$ to accept **0** for the Y direction. The line will be drawn.

9. Press the $\boxed{\text{SPACE}}$ again.

10. Press $\boxed{\text{ENTER}}$ to accept **0** for the X direction.

11. Type in **26** and press [ENTER] for the Y direction. The line will be drawn. Your drawing should now look like Figure 10.34.

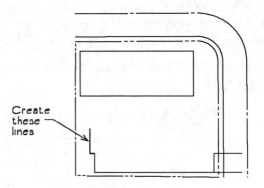

Figure 10.34: Your drawing should look like this.

14. Press mouse button 3 to quit.

15. Press [SHIFT] [F] to file your drawing.

Creating repeated copies

You can create a copy pattern using the Copy menu. This way, you can create all of the parking stripes using one of the existing lines.

1. Pick the **Copy** tool from the icon bar, as shown in Figure 10.35. (Or press [C] .)

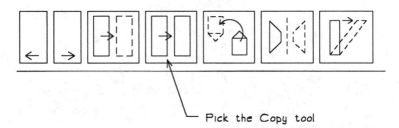

Pick the Copy tool

Figure 10.35: Pick the Copy tool.

2. Pick the **RectArry** option.

3. Pick a start point on your drawing. (It doesn't matter exactly where you pick because you'll type in a relative distance.)

4. Press the [SPACE] .

5. Type in **9** and press [ENTER] for the X distance.

6. Press [ENTER] to accept **0** in the Y distance.

7. Now the message is asking for the *total* number of items you want (including the original line), in the X direction. Type in **14** and press ENTER .

8. For the Y direction, you must have at least 1 to create copies at all, which is why 1 appears as the default (the original item counts as 1). Press ENTER to accept **1**.

9. Pick the line you'll use as the stripe original, as shown in Figure 10.36.

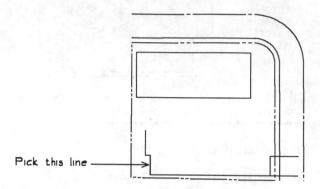

Pick this line ——

Figure 10.36: Pick this line to create your stripes.

10. The copies will appear, as shown in Figure 10.37.

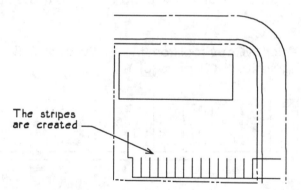

The stripes
are created ——

Figure 10.37: Your stripes.

11. *Remember* to press mouse button 3 to exit out of the Copy menu!

Note: *Many people forget to exit out of copy, and the next item they object snap to creates another set of copies.*

Trimming up your sketch lines

Before you mirror this side of the parking lot over for the other side, clean up the sketch lines and round the corners as necessary.

1. Press [ALT] [F] to go to Fillets, which is found in Cleanup, in the Edit menu.

2. Pick **Radius** to define the size of the round.

3. Type in **2** and press [ENTER].

4. Pick the first line to fillet, as shown as step 1 in Figure 10.38, where the arrow is pointing in the illustration. This is important because you have to pick the line on the part you wish to *keep*, versus the part that will be erased when the fillet is created. Also, *don't object snap!*

5. Pick the second line to fillet, as shown as step 2 in Figure 10.38. Again, be careful where you pick, or the fillet will come in with the wrong results. (You might want to draw some lines on the side of your drawing and practice what results you get with different picks.)

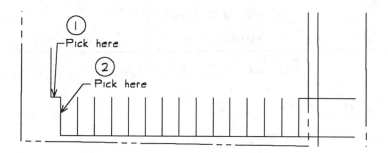

Figure 10.38: Take care when picking while creating a fillet.

6. Follow steps 1 and 2 in Figure 10.39 to create the next fillet.

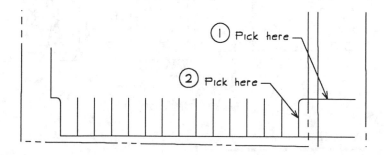

Figure 10.39: Create the second fillet.

7. Press [ALT] [J] to go to 2 Line Trim (Join 2 lines), found in Cleanup, in the Edit menu. This option works like fillet, only a radius isn't drawn when the corner is cleaned up.

8. Pick the first line to trim, as shown as step 1 in Figure 10.40. Make sure you pick the line where the arrow is pointing in the illustration.

9. Pick the second line, shown as step 2 in Figure 10.40.

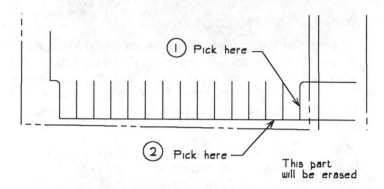

Figure 10.40: Two picks for 2 Line Trim.

10. The corner will be cleaned.

11. Press mouse button 3 to exit to the Cleanup menu.

12. Press [SHIFT] [F] to file your drawing.

Erasing part of a line

You can use the Erase, Partial options to clean up the end of the overlapping driveway line.

1. Pick the **Erase** tool in the icon bar, shown in Figure 10.41, to go to the Erase option found in the Edit menu. (Or, you could press [E] !)

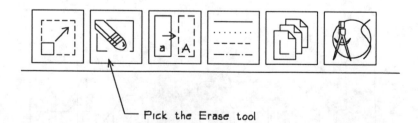

Figure 10.41: The Erase tool.

2. Pick **Partial**. This option allows you to pick select an item, then make two picks to erase a part of it. The erased area will be between the two picks. Examples of this are shown in Figure 10.42.

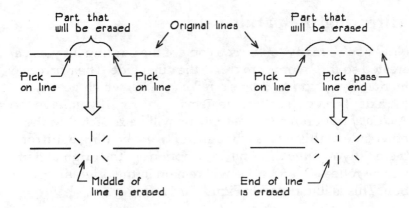

Figure 10.42: Examples of how a partial erase works.

3. Pick the driveway line, shown as step 1 in Figure 10.43. It will become gray and dashed.

4. Object snap to the intersection of the driveway line and the curb line, as shown as step 2 in Figure 10.43. This will be the first point on the line which defines the section to erase.

5. Pick out beyond the end of the line, as shown as step 3 in Figure 10.43. This pick will define the second point, and erase the entire end of the line.

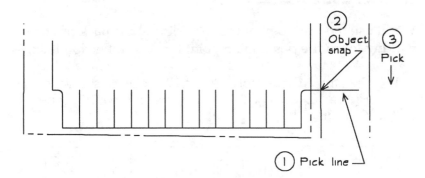

Figure 10.43: Steps to erase the end of the line.

6. Press mouse button 3 to exit, until you're back in the Edit menu.

Note: *Partial erase can also be used to "break" a line. Simply select the line to break, then object snap to the same point on the line twice. It will break at that point, leaving two lines. (This is useful if a part of a line must be in a Dashed linetype.)*

Mirroring the parking stripes

Now you're ready to *mirror* a copy of the parking lot you've created so far, in order to create the other side. The Mirror menu allows you to define a *reflection line*, which acts like the axis. Then you collect the items to mirror. If you have the *AndCopy* option active, these items will be reflected to the other side of this line, as though you were holding a mirror there. If you have the AndCopy option *off*, the original items will be reflected, and none will remain in the original location. This is illustrated in Figure 10.44.

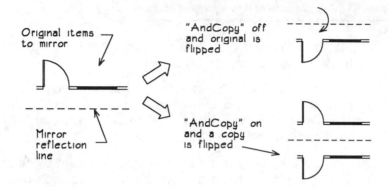

Figure 10.44: Mirroring items.

You'll use the midpoint of the 26'-0" line at the back of your parking lot as the positioning point for your reflection line..

1. Pick the **Mirror** tool from the icon bar, as shown in Figure 10.45, to go to Mirror option in the EDIT menu. (The quick key is [ALT] [M].)

Pick the Mirror tool

Figure 10.45: The Mirror tool.

2. Object snap to the midpoint of the 26' line, indicated as step 1 in Figure 10.46, to define the start point of your reflection line.

3. Drag your cursor out to the right, making sure *Orthomode is on* so that your line is straight. Pick the second point for your reflection line, as shown as step 2 in Figure 10.46.

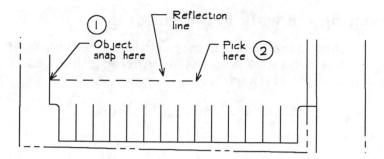

Figure 10.46: Creating the reflection line.

4. Pick **Area** to make it active.

5. Pick the **AndCopy** option until it's active.

6. Pick two points to indicate a rectangle around the area you wish to copy, as in Figure 10.47. Make sure you don't surround the entire 26' line because you don't need this line copied. Only the lines you completely surround will be mirrored.

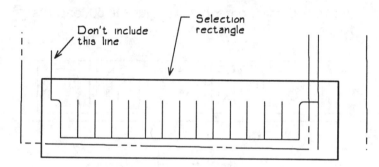

Figure 10.47: Pick to define an area to mirror.

7. The mirrored copy is created, as in Figure 10.48.

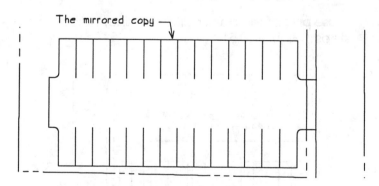

Figure 10.48: The mirrored copy.

8. Press mouse button 3 to exit.

9. Press SHIFT F to file your drawing.

Copying techniques

Creating the walk to the building

1. Draw a line by object snapping to connect the fourth line to the seventh line of the mirrored pattern, as indicated in Figure 10.49.

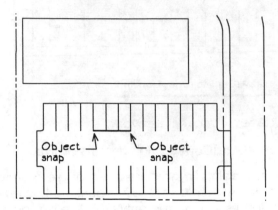

Figure 10.49: Object snap to draw a line.

2. Pick the **Erase** icon, shown in Figure 10.50, or press 🄴 to go to the Erase menu.

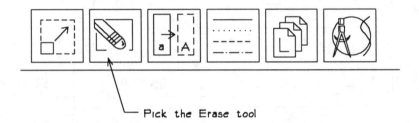

Pick the Erase tool

Figure 10.50: The Erase icon.

3. Pick the **Partial** option.

4. Erase part of the back parking lot line, indicated as steps in Figure 10.51.

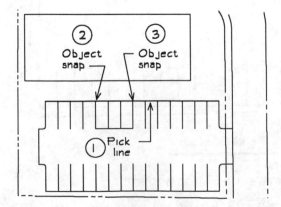

Figure 10.51: Erasing part of the parking lot line.

5.   Your drawing should look like Figure 10.52.

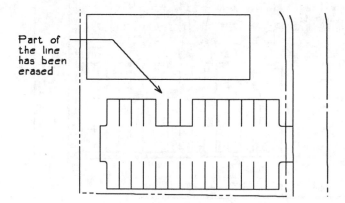

Figure 10.52: You drawing should now look like this.

Using 1 line trim

You can use the 1 line trim option to extend the walk lines to the building.

1.   Pick the **CleanUp** option, found in the Edit menu.

2.   Pick the **1LnTrim** option.

3   Pick the **Entity** option. This will allow you to pick an entity to trim to, in this case a line of your building.

4.   Make sure **LyrSrch** is active.

5.   Pick the bottom line of the building, as indicated as step 1 in Figure 10.53. This is the line you'll want to trim *to*.

6.   Pick anywhere on the other side of the line, as in step 2, Figure 10.53. This pick defines which side of the line should be erased. The necessity for this pick may seem confusing, since your lines don't actually cross the building line. However, this function is designed to allow you to trim several lines at once, many which might cross the trim line. Any that don't cross will be extended *to* the trim line! You'll see how this works.

7.   Pick **Entity** to make it active.

8.   Now pick the two lines to extend, shown as step 3 in Figure 10.53.

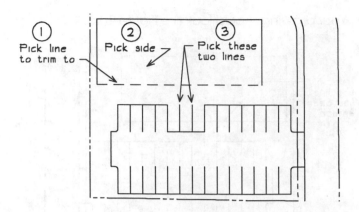

Figure 10.53: The steps to extend the lines.

9. Your walk lines are extended! (Notice there's an **Undo** option if you've made a mistake.)

10. Press ⌑ALT⌑ ⌑F⌑ to go to Fillet.

11. Pick lines for the two corners to round, as in Figure 10.54.

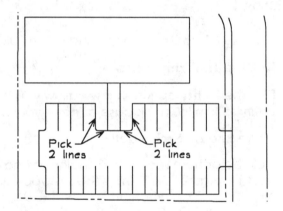

Figure 10.54: Round these corners.

12. Press ⌑SHIFT⌑ ⌑F⌑ to file your drawing.

Setting up a 3D view

Follow these hints to add a perspective view of your plot plan to your drawing. If you need additional help, review chapter 5, "Viewing Your Drawing in 3D."

1. Use the Layer tool to turn off your **Border** layer.

2. Using the **[V]** button in the control panel, pick the **SetPersp** option.

3. Create a bird's-eye view of your drawing, setting the **EyePnt Z** to **50** feet.

4. Create a hidden view of your drawing, using **Hide,** **SaveImag,** and **Crop.** Pick Begin, naming your **NewLayer**: **Hide1** and leaving it **On.**

5. Use the Layer tool to turn on all layers, and pick the **[Ortho]** button to return to the Plan view.

5. **Move, Drag** this 3D image by **Group** to a desirable location.

6. Use **Area** if you want to **Move** the plan view, if necessary, making sure your **Easement** layer is on and **LyrSrch** is active.

7. Use **Erase, Entity** to erase the extra lines that appear in your 3D-view building (the lines that make it look hollow.) Your drawing might look like Figure 10.55.

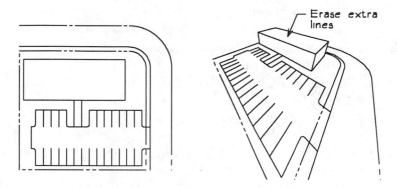

Figure 10.55: Your plot plan and 3D view.

8. Press ⌊SHIFT⌋ ⌊F⌋ to file your drawing.

DataCAD exercise 9

Please complete the following exercise by reading each question carefully, then circling the letter that corresponds to the correct answer.

1. Before starting to create your project, you should:
    a. Preplan the steps you'll use in drawing it.
    b. Not waste time preplanning the steps you'll take in drawing it.

2. Part of the preplanning stage consists of:
    a. Creating the walls in your drawing.
    b. Looking for repeated patterns and the "best" way to create your drawing.
    c. Looking for repeated patterns in your drawing. There is never a "best" way to create it.

3. To copy geometry in a repeated pattern, in the X and Y directions, you use the:
    a. **Move**, **AndCopy** options.
    b. **Copy**, **RectArry** options.
    c. **Copy**, **Repeat** options.

4. To reflect entities, or copies of entities, to another location, you use the:
    a. **Reflect** option.
    b. **Mid Pnt** option.
    c. **Mirror** option.

5. When defining an area to copy, items that are included only partially in the rectangle will:
    a. Not be copied.
    b. Will be copied.
    c. Will only be copied if the Include option is active.

6. To create a hole in a line, you use the:
    a. **CleanUp**, **Partial** options.
    b. **Erase**, **Partial** options.
    c. **CleanUp**, **1LnTrim** options.

7. To extend lines to a trim line, you use the:
    a. **Erase**, **Partial** options.
    b. **CleanUp**, **Stretch** options.
    c. **CleanUp**, **1LnTrim** options.

8. If you wish to place a copy of an entity by defining a distance by picking two points, you use the:
   a. **Copy** option, pick two points defining the move distance, then pick the item(s) to copy.
   b. **Copy**, **Drag** options, pick two points defining the move distance, then pick the item(s) to copy.
   c. **Stretch** option, pick two points defining the move distance, make sure **AndCopy** is active, then pick the item(s) to copy.

Some review questions

9. Default drawings allow you to:
   a. Change the type of drawing you're going to create, but not the scale or drawing borders.
   b. Preset several different "drawing formats" (blank drawing sheets) for the types and scales of drawings you'll be creating. This also includes setting up special layers for your drawings.
   c. Have the correct title block already set in your drawing only. The layers and scale cannot be preset in the default drawing.

10. To select your default drawing, when starting a new drawing, you must:
    a. Enter the name of your default drawing as your new drawing name.
    b. Change the current directory using the **New Path** option, setting it to **Default**.
    c. Pick the **Default** option and pick the name of your default drawing, then enter a new name for your drawing.

11. Three possible choices for angle types are:
    a. Normal, Cartesian, and Bearings.
    b. Relative, Cartesian, and Bearings.
    c. Normal, Compass, and Bearings.

12. Different lines (such as solid, dashed, dot-dash, etc.) are called:
    a. Line Weights.
    b. Linetypes.
    c. Line Scales.

13. To set the angle type to Bearings or Normal, you use the:
    a. **[Insert]** key.
    b. **[Space bar]**.
    c. Settings menu, **AngleTyp** option.

14. To set the input mode to Relative Polar or Relative Cartesian, you use the:
    a. **[Insert]** key.
    b. **[Space bar]**.
    c. Settings menu, **InputTyp** option.

15. Before you use a relative input mode, you should:
    a. ALWAYS pick a start point.
    b. NEVER pick a start point.
    c. Only pick a start point if the drawing tells you to.

16. The quickest way to turn from lines to walls, or from walls to lines, is to use the:
    a. Menu option choices.
    b. ◁ key.
    c. ▤ key.

17. In order to define a reference point, you press the:
    a. SPACE .
    b. ~ key.
    c. X key.

18. To clean up wall intersections after you create them, you:
    a. Pick the Change tool, then pick the **Cleanup** option.
    b. Press C , to enter the Cleanup menu.
    c. Pick the **Cleanup** option, and use **T** or **L intersection**.

19. To erase the last item you created, you use the:
    a. **Delete** option.
    b. ◁ key.
    c. ▷ key.

20. To erase an entire area at one time, you use the:
    a. Pick the Erase tool, then pick the **Area** option.
    b. Pick the Change tool, then pick **Erase**, **Area**.
    c. ◁ key.

CHAPTER 11

Setting up detail default drawings

Detail defaults

In chapter 8, you set up a default drawing for a 1:20 site plan. Now you'll set up two more defaults - one for 1" details and one for a full-sized detail sheet, on which you add many different scaled details.

Here are some of the things you'll learn in this chapter:

- Dividing lines into a number of even sections.
- Changing the setup for 12"-scale (full size) drawing.
- Changing the setup for 1"-scale drawing.
- Modifying your scales.
- Adding distances to your settings.
- Copying to a layer.
- Using the Clip It macro to create a clipped copy of an area.
- Saving and loading a layer file.

Detail drawings

Details are first created at full size, then scaled down to fit on a detail sheet. Many differently scaled details can be added to one sheet. The sheet itself is full size.

You'll want to create a detail default drawing for every scale of detail you work on. That way, the dimensions

and notes, along with other options, are preset to the proper size.

Changing the drawing directory

As you already know, having created a default drawing already, defaults are stored in the *\dcad6\default* directory. You'll change your present directory, which is *\dcad6\dwg*, to the default directory, in order to create your detail defaults.

1. Start DataCAD.

2. Pick **New Path** to change your directory.

3. Pick the ".." option to move up one directory.

4. Pick the **DEFAULT** directory name from the list.

5. Press ENTER .

6. Now your default drawing names are displayed in the drawing list, as in Figure 11.1. At this point, you can edit your defaults just as you would any drawing. For instance, you could pull up the PLAN_1-4 default and add your own title block.

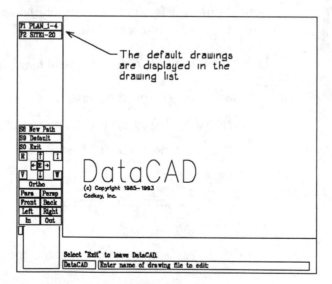

Figure 11.1: The default drawing list.

Creating the detail drawing sheet

To create this sheet, you'll use the PLAN_1-4 as a default.

1. Pick the **Default** option.

2. Pick **PLAN_1-4**.

3. Type in the new name for your detail sheet: **detsheet** and press ENTER .

4. The 1/4" plan border will be displayed, as shown in Figure 11.2.

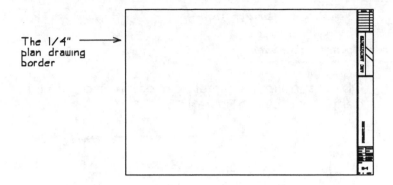

The 1/4" plan drawing border

Figure 11.2: The 1/4" drawing border.

Changing the size of your border

Just as before, you'll need to change the size of your border for this new detail sheet scale, which will be 12" or 1 to 1. First, divide the border so you can use the centerpoint as an enlargement center.

1. Press ALT G to go to the Geometry menu.

2. Pick **Divide**. Note that the default divide number is 2.

3. Object snap to the outer corners of the border, as shown as steps 1 and 2 in Figure 11.3. A snap point will appear in the center.

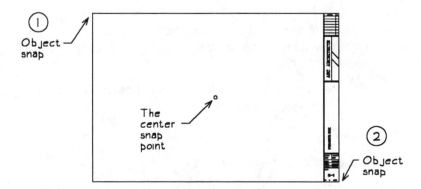

Object snap

The center snap point

Object snap

Figure 11.3: Object snap to the corners for a center point.

4. Pick the **Enlarge** tool, shown in Figure 11.4.

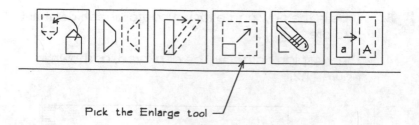

Pick the Enlarge tool

Figure 11.4: The Enlarge tool.

5. Object snap to the center point as the enlargement center, as shown in Figure 11.5.

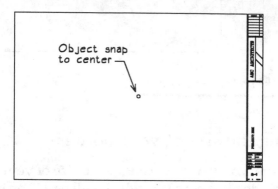

Object snap to center

Figure 11.5: Object snap to the center snap point.

6. Pick the **Enlrgmnt** option.

7. Pick **Set All**.

8. Type in the scale factor for 1/4": **48** and press ENTER . Forty-eight is how many times 1/4" goes into 12" (12x4).

9. Press mouse button 3 to quit back to the Enlarge menu.

10. Pick **Invert**. As before, this option will take your factor (which was the enlargement scale) and reverse it to a reduction scale.

11. Your reduction scale is displayed in the message area of the screen: **.02083334**.

12. Pick **Area**.

13. Make sure **LyrSrch** is active.

14. Indicate an area around the entire border. It will shrink to a very small size. It's now *real size*. In other words, you could plot it at 12" scale (1:1), and it would be a D-size sheet.

15. Pick the **[R]** button in the control panel to recalculate the view window. The border will appear centered on your screen.

16. Press [SHIFT] [F] to file your drawing.

Turning on and off grid snap

You'll want to turn of the grid snap as you work in this drawing.

1. Press [X] until the message says Grid snap is OFF and the S is small in swoTHLUD.

2. The grid snap is set on each layer, so you have to turn it off again as you move to different layers.

Naming layers for the detail box layout

You can create a few sheet layouts for different size details. The first you'll create is for a 3x4 layout of detail boxes. You'll put these boxes on a 3x4 division layer.

1. Pick the **Layer** tool, as in Figure 11.6, or press [L].

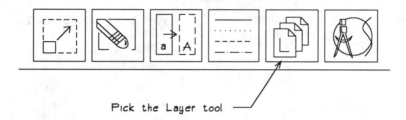

Pick the Layer tool

Figure 11.6: The Layer tool.

2. Pick **Name**.

3. The present layer list will be displayed. Pick the second name on the list: **Walls**.

4. The name will appear in the message area. Type in the new name for this layer: **3x4Boxes** and press [ENTER].

5. You might want to create a division layout for a 2x3 layout, also. Pick the next layer: **Doors**.

6. Type in the new name for this layer: **2x3Boxes** and press [ENTER].

7. Pick the next layer: **Windows**. You can name this layer for a 2x2 layout.

8. Type in the new name for this layer: **2x2Boxes** and press [ENTER].

9. While you're at it, you'll want to name a layer to hold the details. Pick the next layer: **Cabinet**.

10. Type in the new name for this layer: **Details** and press ENTER .

11. Press mouse button 3 to exit the Name menu.

12. Use the **DelLayer** option to delete extra layers from the list. You can always add some later, if you need them. Pick **Yes** when prompted.

Dividing the drawing for boxes

1. Press Tab to go to the **3x4Boxes** layer.

2. Press ALT G to go to Geometry, found in the Utility menu.

3. Pick **Divide**.

4. Pick **Entity**, an option that allows you to divide a line or circle into equal parts.

5. Pick **Divisons** to change the number of divisions.

6. Type in: **3** and press ENTER .

7. Pick the vertical line of the drawing area border, as indicated in Figure 11.7.

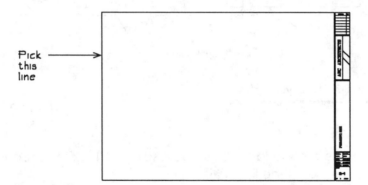

Pick this line

Figure 11.7: Pick this line to divide.

8. Two points will appear on the line. The line has been equally divided into three parts. This is illustrated in Figure 11.8.

9. Pick **Divisons** to change the number of divisions again.

10. Type in: **4** and press ENTER .

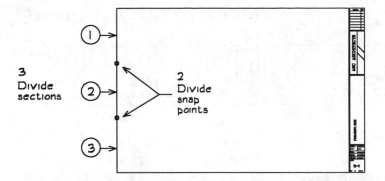

Figure 11.8: The line is divided into 3.

11. Now, pick the horizontal line of the drawing area border, as indicated in Figure 11.9.

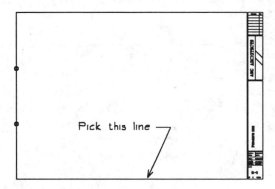

Figure 11.9: This time, pick this line to divide.

13. Three points will appear on the line. This line has been equally divided into four parts, as shown in Figure 11.10.

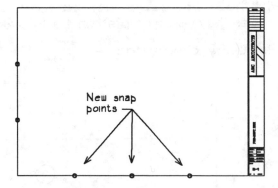

Figure 11.10: The line is divided into 4.

Copying lines

You can use these points as snap to copy new lines.

1.   Pick the **Copy** tool, shown in Figure 11.11, or press Ⓒ .

Figure 11.11: The copy tool.

2.   Object snap to the first point on the vertical line, shown as step 1 in figure 11.12.

3.   Object snap to the second point, shown as step 2 in Figure 11.12. These two points defined the distance of the copy.

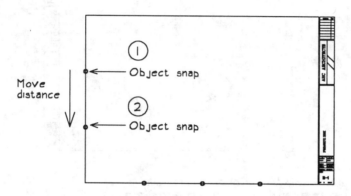

Figure 11.12: Defining the copy distance.

4.   Pick **ToLayer**.

5.   Pick the **3x4Boxes** layer name. Now, as you make your copies, they will be created on the 3x4Boxes layer.

6.   Pick **Entity** to make it active.

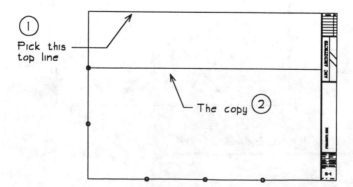

Figure 11.13: The line is copied.

7. Pick the horizontal line, shown as step 1 in Figure 11.13. It will copy to the new location on the snap point, as in step 2.

8. Pick the new line, shown as step 1 in Figure 11.14. It will copy, too, as shown in step 2.

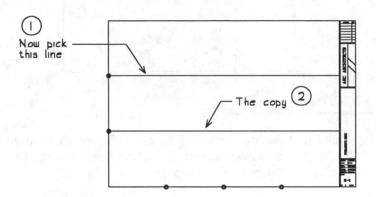

Figure 11.14: The line is copied again.

9. Pick the **NewDist** option to define a new distance and still copy to the defined layer.

10. Object snap to the first point on the horizontal line, shown as step 1 in figure 11.15.

11. Object snap to the second point, shown as step 2 in Figure 11.15. Now a new copy distance is defined.

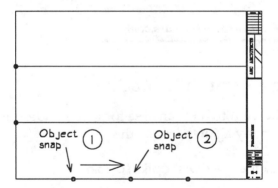

Figure 11.15: Defining the copy distance for the next line.

12. Pick the vertical line, shown as step 1 in Figure 11.16. It will copy to the new location on the snap point, as in step 2.

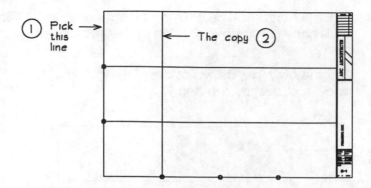

Figure 11.16: The line is copied.

13. Pick the new line, shown as step 1 in Figure 11.17. It will copy too, as shown in step 2. Pick that line to create the last copy, shown in step 3.

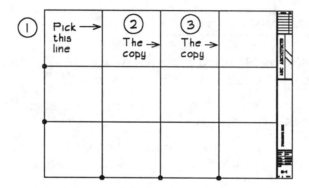

Figure 11.17: The division lines are complete.

Adding a detail title block

You might want to have an area for a title under each detail. You'll use copy again to create this.

1. Pick the **NewDist** option again.

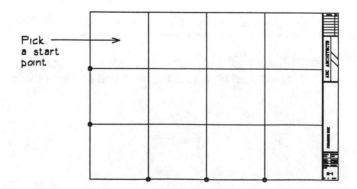

Figure 11.18: Pick for a start point.

2. You'll type in the distance for this copy, so pick on the drawing anywhere for a start point, as shown in Figure 11.18.

3. Press the [SPACE] to invoke the coordinate mode.

4. Press [ENTER] to accept **0** in the X distance.

5. Pick **0 1/2"** and press [ENTER] to define a Y distance of 1/2".

6. Pick the lines shown in Figure 11.19.

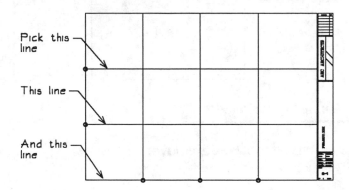

Figure 11.19: Pick these lines to copy.

7. The copies are created, as shown in Figure 11.20.

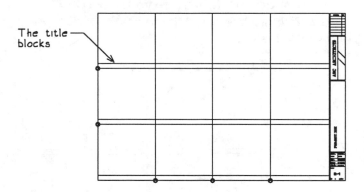

Figure 11.20: The detail boxes now have a title block area.

Creating the 2x3 and 2x2 divisions

Follow the same procedure, and these hints, to create the 2x3 and 2x2 layouts.

1. Turn off the **3x4Boxes** layer, and press [Tab] to make the **2x3Boxes** layer active.

2. Press [ALT] [G] and use **Divide**, **Entity**, setting the **Divisons** as needed, to create the snap points for the 2x3 detail grid layout shown in Figure 11.21.

3. Use the **Copy** tool, and define your distances by object snapping. Make sure you define the **ToLayer** as **2x3Boxes**. Use **NewDist** to create the detail title area, as before.

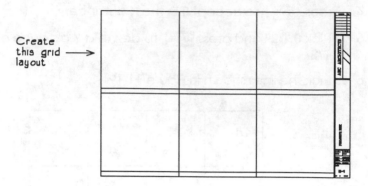

Create this grid layout →

Figure 11.21: The 2x3 detail layout.

4. Turn off the **2x3Boxes** layer, and press [Tab] to make the **2x2Boxes** layer active.

5. Press [ALT] [G] and use **Divide, Entity**, setting the **Divisons** as needed, to create the snap points for the 2x2 detail grid layout shown in Figure 11.22.

6. Use the **Copy** tool, and define your distances by object snapping. Make sure you define the **ToLayer** as **2x2Boxes**. Use **NewDist** to create the detail title area, as before.

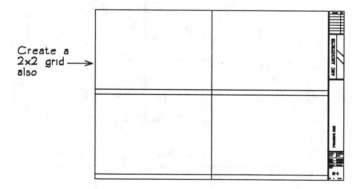

Create a 2x2 grid also →

Figure 11.22: The 2x2 detail layout.

7. Press [SHIFT] [F] to file your drawing.

Changing the drawing title block

1. You might want to take a few minutes to modify the drawing sheet title block to reflect your own company's name.

2.   You can use the **Change** tool, **Text**, **Contents** if you wish to edit the existing text in the title block.

3.   When you're done, press [SHIFT] [F] to file your drawing.

Setting up distances

When you setup your dimensions for this default, you'll use a 1/8" distance for many of the options. You can actually add this to the *distance list* that comes up whenever a measurement is needed. Then all you have to do is pick it off the list! (You'll recognize the distance list once you see it.)

1.   Press mouse button 3 until the Utility menu is displayed.

2.   Pick the **Settings** option.

3.   Pick **EditDefs** (Edit defaults).

4.   Pick **Distnces**.

5.   Pick **List**. The current distance list will be displayed, as in Figure 11.23. (Now does it look familiar?)

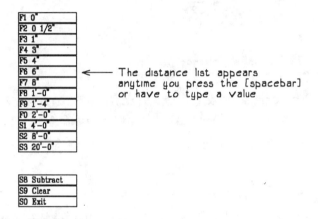

The distance list appears anytime you press the [spacebar] or have to type a value

Figure 11.23: The distance list.

6.   Press mouse button 3 to exit back to the Distnces menu.

7.   Pick **Add**.

8.   Type in: **..1/8** and press [ENTER].

9.   Pick Add again, to add 1/16" to the list also.

10.   Type in: **..1/16** and press [ENTER].

11.   Now pick Add to add 1/4" to the list also.

12.   Type in: **..1/4** and press [ENTER].

13.   Use the same procedure to add a **1 1/2"** distance.

14. When you try to add any more distances, you'll get a *"No room to add any more distances"* message. That's okay because you can use the Change option and change existing distances.

15. Pick **Change**.

16. Pick the **12'-0"** distance.

17. Type in: **.2** and press ⌷ENTER⌷ to set a 2" distance.

18. Pick **List**. Your new distance choices will appear, as in Figure 11.24.

Figure 11.24: *Your new distances are listed.*

19. You can save these distances to a file in order to share it with other drawings. Pick **SaveFile**.

20. Type in: **small** for the name, and press ⌷ENTER⌷ .

Setting up the dimensions

You might not have to dimension very often in this drawing, since your details will be completed with dimensions before you add them to this sheet. However, it would be helpful to have them set if you need to make last-minute edits. Figure 11.25 is included here for your reference, and shows the dimension options you'll set.

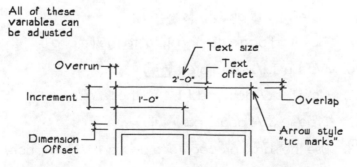

Figure 11.25: *The features that can be adjusted in dimensions.*

1. Press [ALT] [D] to go to the Dimension Linear menu.

2. Pick the **TextStyl** option.

3. Pick **Size**.

4. Pick **1/8"** and press [ENTER] .

5. Pick the **Offset** option.

6. Pick **1/16"** and press [ENTER] .

7. Press mouse button 3 to exit back to the Dimension Linear menu.

8. Pick **DimStyl**.

9. Pick **Offset**.

10. Pick **1/8"** and press [ENTER] .

11. Pick **Overlap**.

12. Pick **1/8"** and press [ENTER] .

13. Pick **Overrun**.

14. Pick **1/8"** and press [ENTER] .

15. Press [SHIFT] [F] to file your drawing.

Aren't you glad you added and changed those distances?

Setting up notes

You might want to set your text size and font also.

1. Press [ALT] [T] to go to the Text option, in the Edit menu.

2. Pick **Size**.

3. Pick **1/8"** and press [ENTER] .

4. Pick **FontName**.

5. Pick the font you'll use for details, such as **ARCWY2LC**.

6. Press [SHIFT] [F] to file your drawing.

Setting the plot scale

You'll want to adjust the plot scale and check the layout.

1. Press [ALT] [P] to go to the Plotter menu.

2. Pick the **Scale** option.

3. Pick **12"**.

4. Pick the **Layout** option.

5. Does the present layout look correct? It should look like Figure 11.26. *Don't* pick to place the layout! Just press mouse button 3 to exit.

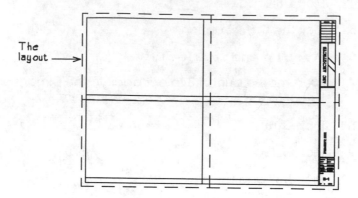

Figure 11.26: Checking the layout.

Extracting a detail box

You can extract a detail box from this sheet and save it off to a layer. Then, when you set up the detail default sheet, you can simply bring in the detail box and enlarge it to the necessary scale. And then the detail will fit into the detail sheet layout exactly!

First create a layer for your extracted box.

1. Pick the **Layer** tool, as in Figure 11.27.

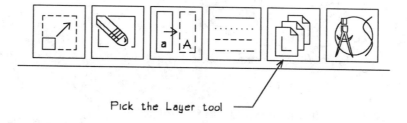

Figure 11.27: The Layer tool.

2. Pick **NewLayer**.

3. Press ENTER to accept **1**.

4. Pick **Name**.

5. Pick the last name on the layer list.

6. Type in the new name for this layer: **Box** and press ENTER .

7. Pick **On/Off**.

8. Turn on the **3x4Boxes** layer.

9. Make sure **2x3Boxes** and **2x2Boxes** layers are turned OFF.

10. Press mouse button 3 to exit.

Using the ClipIt macro

To extract the box, you'll use an option in your Macros menu, called ClipIt.

1. Press ⌨Tab to go to the **Box** layer. This way, the copy of the detail box will go on the Box layer.

2. Press ⌨SHIFT ⌨M to go to the Macros menu, found in Edit.

3. Pick the macro called **CLIPIT**. Now, you'll want to set some options in this macro.

4. Pick **Area** to make it active.

5. Pick **Boundary** to turn it OFF.

6. Pick **LyrSrch** to make it active.

7. Pick **Copy** to make it active.

8. Pick **Clip** to make it active.

9. Now indicate a rectangle area around one of the detail boxes, as shown in Figure 11.28.

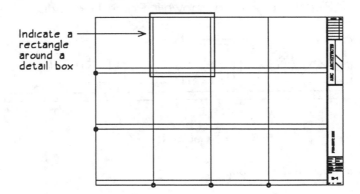

Indicate a rectangle around a detail box

Figure 11.28: Pick a rectangle as shown.

10. The system will take a few moments to process the lines, then you'll be asked to pick a handle point. Pick in the center of the box, then move your cursor over to the side of the detail sheet and pick to place your copy, as illustrated in Figure 11.29.

11. Press mouse button 3 a few times to completely exit the ClipIt macro.

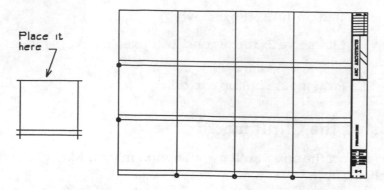

Place it
here

Figure 11.29: Place your copy to the side of the border.

Important Note: *Don't use a quick key or a tool to exit this macro, as the undo buffer will not clear properly, and this could cause a unrecoverable error later. Always exit ClipIt using mouse button 3 to exit. If you forget, simply go back to the ClipIt macro and exit again. The buffer will clear.*

Saving the layer for your detail default

You can save layers out of the drawing file to share with other drawings. When you save your layer, it becomes a .LYR file and is saved to the DCAD6\LYR directory.

1. Pick the **Layer** tool, shown in Figure 11.30, or press L .

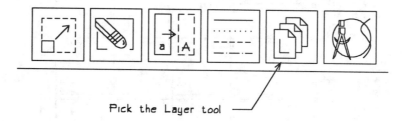

Pick the Layer tool

Figure 11.30: The Layer tool.

2. Pick the **[I]** button in the control panel, and pick the detail box you extracted to check that it's on the Box layer. Is it? (Look at F2; the layer should say *Box*.)

3. Press mouse button 3 to return to the Layers menu.

4. Pick **SaveLayer**.

5. Pick the **Box** layer name from the list.

6. A message asks you to name the layer file, and the current name will be defaulted to **Box**. Press ENTER to accept this name.

7. The layer file will be created.

8. Pick **DelLayer**.

9. Pick **Box** to delete the layer and its contents from your drawing. You don't need it anymore, since you saved it to a file. Pick **Yes**, or press Y.

10. Pick the **[R]** button in the control panel to recalculate the view window.

Creating the pictogram for your default

You might want to create a little preview pictogram for this default.

1. Pick the **PixelOut** option from the File I/O menu.

2. Pick the **Pictogram** option.

3. Press ENTER to accept the drawing name as the name for your pictogram.

4. Press PG UP on the keyboard until the border fits into the little box on your cursor.

5. Pick to place the box over the border.

6. Press mouse button 3 to exit.

Saving your default

You're done with this default and are ready to create the detail box default.

1. Press Tab until the **Details** layer is active.

2. Press ALT N to go to a new drawing. Pick **Yes** to save your default drawing.

3. The default drawing list will be displayed.

Creating the 1" detail default drawing

You can use the PLAN_1-4 default again. You'll erase the border, but the settings will save you a lot of setup time.

1. Pick the **Default** option.

2. Pick **PLAN_1-4**.

3. Type in the new name for your 1" detail default: **det_1** and press ENTER.

4. The border is displayed.

5. Pick the **Erase** tool, as shown in Figure 11.31.

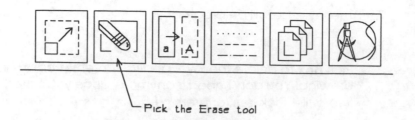

Pick the Erase tool

Figure 11.31: The Erase tool.

6. Pick **Area** to make it active.

7. Indicate a box around the entire border to erase it, as shown in Figure 11.32.

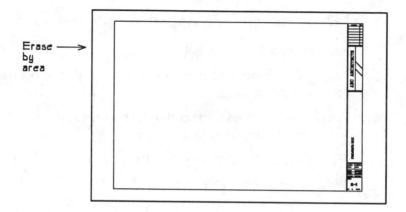

Erase by area

Figure 11.32: Erase the border by area.

Bringing in the detail box layer file

When you load the **Box** layer, it will rename the current layer to match.

1. Press ⌷Tab⌷ to go to the **Border** layer.

2. Pick the **Layer** tool, shown in Figure 11.33.

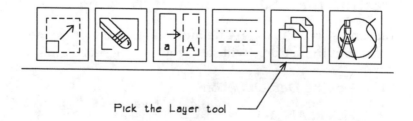

Pick the Layer tool

Figure 11.33: The Layer tool.

3. Pick **LoadLyr**.

4. Pick **Yes**.

5. Pick the **BOX** layer file. Notice that the layer name now says **Box**.

6. Pick the **[R]** button in the control panel. Your detail box will be displayed, as in Figure 11.34.

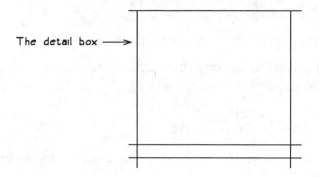

The detail box ⟶

Figure 11.34: Your detail box.

Scaling the box

Since this default will be a 1" = 1'-0" scale drawing, you need to enlarge it for scaling later.

1. Pick the **Enlarge** tool, shown in Figure 11.35.

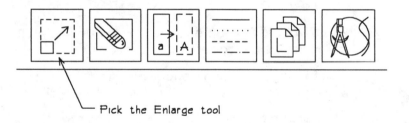

Pick the Enlarge tool

Figure 11.35: The Enlarge tool.

2. Pick near the center of the box, as in Figure 11.36.

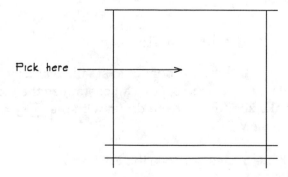

Pick here ⟶

Figure 11.36: Pick for the enlargement center.

3. Pick the **Enlrgmnt** option.

4. Pick **SetAll**.

5. Type in **12** and press `ENTER` . (1" into 1'-0" = 12 times.)

6. Press mouse button 3 to exit back to the Enlarge menu.

7. Pick **Group** to make it active.

8. Pick a line of the detail box. It will enlarge.

9. Pick the **[R]** button in the control panel to recalculate the view window.

Loading in your distances

You can bring in the distances you edited earlier to use in this default.

1. Press mouse button 3 until the Utility menu is displayed.

2. Pick **Settings**.

3. Pick **EditDefs**.

4. Pick **Distnces**.

5. Pick **List**. Notice that the present distances are the DataCAD default distances.

6. Pick **LoadFile**.

7. Pick **SMALL**, the name you gave your file earlier. The distances will be loaded.

8. Pick **List** again. Your distances are listed. You can load these distances into any of your drawings!

9. Press mouse button 3 to exit.

10. If you ever want the original distances back, you can pick the **DCAD** choice in **LoadFile**.

11. Press mouse button 3 to exit back to the EditDefs menu.

Changing the View Scales

Sometimes you'll want to zoom in to small areas as you draw details. Like distances, you can customize the view scales to make zooming up and down with the `PG UP` and `PG DN` keys easier.

1. Pick the **Scales** option in the EditDefs menu, found in Settings.

2. Pick **Change**. Since the scales are already full, you'll only be able to change an existing one.

3. Pick **1:1000**.

4. Type in the new scale name for your new scale: **1.5x** and press ENTER .

5. Type in the new scale: **1.5** and press ENTER . This scale will allow you to zoom in 1 1/2 times the real size.

6. Pick **Change** again.

7. Notice that your new scale appears as the first scale in your list. This time, pick **1:40**.

8. Type in the new scale name for your next scale: **2x** and press ENTER .

9. Type in the new scale: **2** and press ENTER . This scale will allow you to zoom in 2 times the real size.

10. If you need more, remember that you can change the scales, but don't use a scale you would need for plotting. *This is the same scale list that appears in the plotting menu!* You wouldn't, for example, want to change the 1" scale, because you'll need it for plotting.

11. To save these scales in order to use them in different drawing, pick the **SaveFile** option.

12. Type in the new name for your scale set: **small** and press ENTER .

13. If you ever want to return to the original scale, use **LoadFile** to return the **DCAD** scales.

Setting up the dimensions

You need to change the dimensions for 1" scale drawings.

1. Press ALT D to go to the Dimension Linear menu.

2. Pick the **TextStyl** option.

3. Pick **Size**.

4. Pick **1.1/2"** and press ENTER .

5. Pick the **Offset** option.

6. Type in: **..3/4** and press ENTER . (Or pick **0.1/2"** and **0.1/4"** and they'll add together.)

7. Press mouse button 3 to exit back to the Dimension Linear menu.

8. Pick **DimStyl**.

9. Pick **Offset**.

10. Pick **1.1/2"** and press ENTER .

11. Pick **Overlap**.

12. Pick **1.1/2"** and press `ENTER` .

13. Pick **Overrun**.

14. Pick **1.1/2"** and press `ENTER` .

15. Press mouse button 3 to exit back to the Dimension Linear menu.

16. Pick the **Assoc** option to turn it off. This way, you can scale your detail later, and the dimensions won't change. Also, you can add notes in place of dimensions, or have N.T.S. (not-to-scale) dimensions.

17. Press `SHIFT` `F` to file your drawing.

Setting up notes

You might want to set your text size and font also.

1. Press `ALT` `T` to go to the Text option in the Edit menu.

2. Pick **FontName**.

3. Pick the font you'll use for the detail title, such as **COMPLEX**.

4. Pick **Size**.

5. Type in: **.3** and press `ENTER` . This size will result in 1/4" text when you plot at 1", which is a good size for the title. After you add the title, you'll change the size to 1 1/2", for 1/8" text.

6. Pick in the title block area of your detail box to start your text string.

7. Type in: **TITLE** and press `ENTER` , as shown in Figure 11.37.

8. Press mouse button 3 to quit typing notes.

9. Pick **FontName** again.

10. Pick the font you'll use for detail notes, such as **ARCWY2LC**.

11. Pick **Size**.

12. Now pick **2"** and press `ENTER` . Add the scale note, also shown in Figure 11.37.

13. Pick **Size** again.

14. Now pick **1.1/2"** and press `ENTER` . This will be the size of your 1/8" notes.

15. Press `SHIFT` `F` to file your drawing.

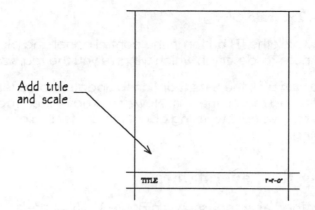

Add title
and scale

TITLE   1"-1'-0"

Figure 11.37: Add the title and scale note.

To find the correct size for your text - Text Scale

Some people have no problem with the scales involved with text, they just pull out an architectural scale and measure notes on existing drawings. Sometimes the size is easy to figure out. It's easy to understand, for instance, that in a 1/4"=1'-0" scale drawing, text created at 1'-0" high will plot at 1/4". Half of that is 6" text, resulting in 1/8".

But what about the size for odd detail scales? Once again, we can let the computer figure it out for us. There is an option called *TxtScale* in Text. "Text Scale" works with the current setting in the plot menu to calculate your scale. If you had 1" set in the *Plotter menu*, you could turn on TxtScale and set the size of your text to ..1/8. The size would automatically adjust to create 1/8" text when plotted at 1" scale. (Existing text is not effected.)

You must be aware that any time you change the plot scale, your text size (for new text) changes also. If the plot scale changes frequently during the development of your drawing, (for example, you might print sections to a 8.5x11 piece of paper for checking on your laser printer), TxtScale wouldn't be a desirable setting.

There is a way to use TxtScale temporarily in order to find the correct text size for a plot scale:

1. Set the **Plotter, Scale** you'll use for the final print of your drawing.

2. Turn **Text, TxtScale** *ON*.

3. Set the **Size** for your text to **1/8"** and create a note on your drawing.

Setting up detail default drawings

11

4. Turn **TxtScale** *OFF*.

5. Now pick the **[I]** button in the control panel and pick the note to identify it, which will give you the *real size*.

6. You can pick the **SetAll** option to update the current settings to match the text. Now, you'll have the proper size text, without worrying about the plotter scale setting.

Changing the Layer names

1. Pick the **Layer** tool, shown in Figure 11.38, or press **L**.

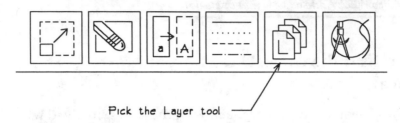

Pick the Layer tool —

Figure 11.38: The Layer tool.

2. Pick the **Name** option.

3. Pick **Walls**.

4. Type in: **Detail** and press **ENTER**.

5. Pick **Doors**.

6. Type in: **Hatch** and press **ENTER**.

7. Press mouse button 3 to return to the Layers menu.

8. Pick **DelLayer**.

9. Delete the extra layers, leaving just five layers: **Box**, **Detail**, **Hatch**, **Dims**, and **Notes**.

10. Press mouse button 3 to exit.

Setting the plot scale

You'll want to adjust the paper size and plot scale for creating prints of your details.

1. Press **ALT** **P** to go to the Plotter menu.

2. Pick **PaperSiz**.

3. Pick the size you want for your paper. For example, if you'll be making small prints of your details, either for checking or for stickyback, pick **8.5x11A**.

4. Press mouse button 3 to exit the paper size menu.

5. Pick the **Scale** option.

6. Pick **1"**.

7. Pick the **Layout** option.

8. Place the layout over the box and pick. It should look like Figure 11.39.

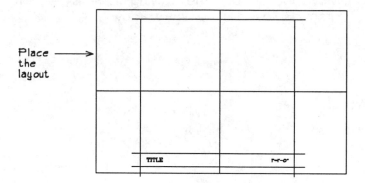

Place the layout →

Figure 11.39: Placing the layout.

Creating the pictogram for your default

You might want to create a little preview pictogram for this default also.

1. Pick the **PixelOut** option from the File I/O menu.

2. Pick the **Pictogram** option.

3. Press ENTER to accept the drawing name as the name for your pictogram.

4. Press PG UP on the keyboard until the border fits into the little box on your cursor.

5. Pick to place the box over the border.

6. Press mouse button 3 to exit.

Saving this default drawing

1. Press Tab to make the **Detail** layer active.

2. Press ALT N to go to a new drawing.

3. Pick **Yes** (or type in Y on your keyboard). Now the drawing list is displayed.

Going back to your project directory

1. Pick the **New Path** option.

2. Pick the ".." option.

3.   Pick the **DWG** directory name.

4.   Press ENTER . Your drawing list will be displayed.

5.   Pick the **Default** option.

6.   The *default drawing list* will be displayed. Are your new defaults on the list?

7.   Move your cursor to the drawing name. Is the pictogram displayed in the view window?

DataCAD exercise 10

Please complete the following exercise by reading each question carefully, then circling the letter that corresponds to the correct answer.

1. Default drawings allow you to:
   a. Change the type of drawing you're going to create, but not the scale or drawing borders.
   b. Preset several different "drawing formats" (blank drawing sheets) for the types and scales of drawings you'll be creating. This includes setting up special layers for your drawings also.
   c. Have the correct title block already set in your drawing only. The layers and scale cannot be preset in the default drawing.

2. To select your default drawing, when the original drawing list is displayed, you pick the:
   a. **New Path** option.
   b. **Default** option.
   c. **Set Deflt** option.

3. Your default drawings should all be stored in the (assuming you have version 6):
   a. **dcad6\dwg** directory.
   b. **dcad6\borders** directory.
   c. **dcad6\default** directory.

4. To change to the Default directory in order to edit the default drawings, you use the:
   a. **Default** option.
   b. **NewPath** option.
   c. **Directory** option.

5. To share graphics with another drawing, as you did with the detail box, you can use a:
   a. Layer file.
   b. Share file.
   c. Merge command.

6. The list that appears when you press the [SPACE] for coordinate input, is called:
   a. Coordinates.
   b. Scales.
   c. Distances.

7. The options to customize your scales are:
   a. **Custom, Scales.**
   b. **Settings, EditDefs, Scales.**
   c. **Change, EditDefs, Scales.**

8. The options to customize the distances are:
    a. **Custom, EditDefs, Distnces.**
    b. **Settings, EditDefs, Scales.**
    c. **Settings, EditDefs, Distnces.**

9. To copy items to a layer, you:
    a. Can pick the distance to copy, then pick the **ToLayer** option.
    b. Have to copy first, then move the items to the layer.
    c. [Tab] to the correct layer, then copy. Copies are always made to the active layer.

10. When adjusting the Dimension style settings, you:
    a. Can set the options to 1-1 real size measurement, such as the **Overlap** to 1/8". Then, when you turn on **PlotScale**, the settings are adjusted automatically to the scale set in the Plotter menu.
    b. Just change the **Scale** option in the Dimension, Linear menu.
    c. Must consider the final plot scale.

11. To use Clip It, you:
    a. Go to the Macros menu, then pick the **ClipIt** macro.
    b. Go to the Utility menu, and pick **ClipIt**.
    c. Press the [ALT] [C] key.

12. When exiting ClipIt:
    a. In order to properly clear the Undo buffer, press mouse button 3 until you're completely out of the macro.
    b. You can use a quick key or pick a tool.
    c. Don't pick the **Exit** option.

13. Once you have edited the distances, you can:
    a. Save the edited list to a file to use in that drawing only. Then you can go back and forth between distance lists as needed.
    b. Save the edited list to a file to use in any other drawing.
    c. Zoom into the new distance by pressing [PG DN] .

CHAPTER 12

Drawing Details

Details

In this chapter, you'll use your new detail default drawings to draw your detail. You'll make a symbol with this detail and add it to your detail sheet.

Here are some of the things you'll learn in this chapter:

- Using the wall function to draw double lines with caps.
- Drawing the insulation with a linetype.
- Creating earth, cement, and other textures using hatching.
- Using unassociated dimensions.
- Editing associated hatch.
- Drawing arcs and circles.

Detail drawings

Detail drawings are drawn full size, then scaled for your detail sheet. The detail you'll draw is shown in **Figure 12.1**.

1. Start DataCAD.

2. Pick the **Default** option.

3. Pick the new default you created: **DET_1**.

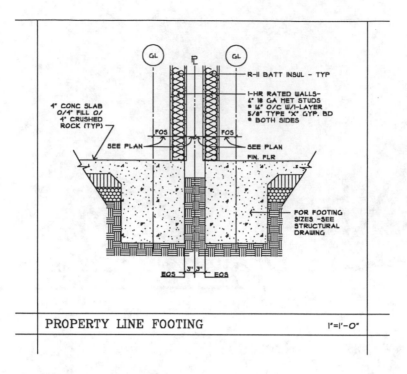

Figure 12.1: The detail project.

4. Type in the new name for your detail drawing: **ftgdet1** and press ENTER .

5. Your detail box is displayed, as in Figure 12.2.

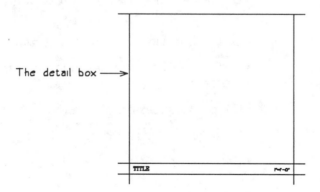

Figure 12.2: The detail box you created.

Drawing the concrete footing

To make the drawing of this footing easier, you can set your snap to 1" increments and use Orthomode.

1. Press ⑤ to set the snap.

2. Pick **1"** and press ENTER for the X direction.

3. Press ENTER again to accept **1"** in the Y direction.

4. Press ⎡K⎤ until the color is **Lt Gray**.

5. Press ⎡O⎤ until orthomode is ON.

6. Draw the outline for the concrete, as shown in Figure 12.3.

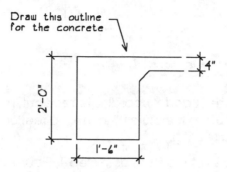

Figure 12.3: Draw the concrete outline.

Drawing the stud

You'll use the Walls feature to draw the metal stud. The dimensions for the stud are shown in Figure 12.4.

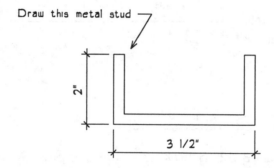

Figure 12.4: The stud dimensions.

1. Press the ⎡A⎤ key to go to the Architect menu.

2. Pick **Walls** to make it active.

3. Pick **Caps** and **Sides** to make them active also. The Cap option draws ends on your walls.

4. Pick **Width**.

5. Pick **0 1/8"** and press ⎡ENTER⎤.

6. Press the ⎡S⎤ key, and set your snap to **0 1/2"**, pressing ⎡ENTER⎤ for both the X and Y directions.

7. Press the ⎡~⎤ key to reference a corner.

8. Object snap to the upper-left corner of the concrete outline, as shown in Figure 12.5.

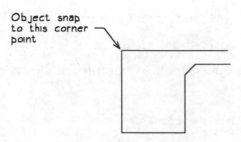

Figure 12.5: Object snap here.

9. Using the X and Y coordinate readout, move your cursor up to measure **0"** in the X direction, and **2"** in the Y direction.

10. Pick to start the stud, as in step 1, Figure 12.6.

11. Object snap back to the corner of the concrete, as shown as step 2, Figure 12.6

12. Pick to the right side for the other side of your wall, as in step 3, Figure 12.6.

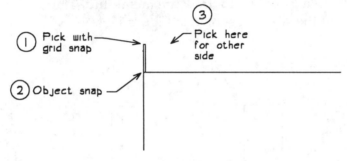

Figure 12.6: Beginning to draw the stud.

13. Measure **3 1/2"** in the X direction, and pick, as in step 1, Figure 12.7.

14. Pick above for the other side of the wall, as in step 2, Figure 12.7.

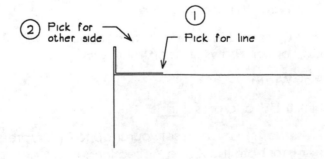

Figure 12.7: Drawing the stud.

15. Measure and pick the last side of the stud (2" in the Y direction), and pick to the left for the other side, as shown as steps 1 and 2 in Figure 12.8.

16. Press mouse button 3 to quit drawing the line. Notice that the ends of the stud have caps, as in Figure 12.8

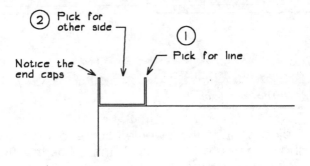

Figure 12.8: Finishing the stud.

Drawing the walls

You'll use the walls function to draw the dry wall, too.

1. Pick the **Width** option in the Architect menu, or press the ⊟ key twice.

2. Pick **0 1/4"** and **0 1/8"**. Notice that the two add together to 5/8".

3. Press ENTER .

4. Object snap to the upper-left corner of the concrete footing again, as step 1 in Figure 12.9.

5. With Orthomode still on, pick as shown in Step 2, Figure 12.9, to create the vertical wall length.

6. Pick to the left for the other side of the wall.

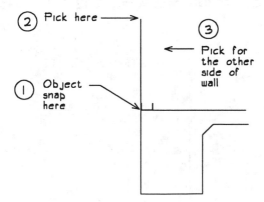

Figure 12.9: Steps for drawing the drywall.

7.   Pick the **Copy** tool, as in Figure 12.10, or press ⓒ for copy.

Pick the Copy tool

Figure 12.10: The Copy tool.

8.   Object snap to the lower-left corner of the dry wall, as shown in Figure 12.11, step 1. This will be the "from" point for your copy distance.

9.   Object snap to the lower-right side of the stud, as in step 2, Figure 12.11. This is the "to" point.

10. Pick **Group** to make it active.

11. Pick the wall, as shown as step 3 in Figure 12.11.

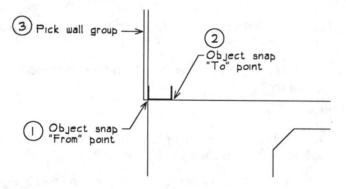

③ Pick wall group ⟶

② Object snap "To" point

① Object snap "From" point

Figure 12.11: Steps for copying the wall.

12. The copy is made, as in Figure 12.12.

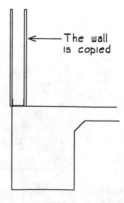

⟵ The wall is copied

Figure 12.12: The wall is copied.

13. Press SHIFT F to file your drawing.

Creating the insulation

The insulation is actually a *linetype* in DataCAD.

1. Press the ▤ key to turn OFF walls.

2. Pick the **Linetype** tool, shown in Figure 12.13.

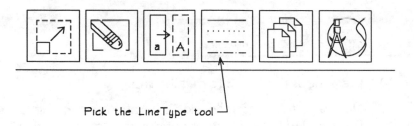

Pick the LineType tool

Figure 12.13: The Linetype tool.

3. Pick the **Insul** linetype. You might have to pick **ScrlFwrd** to find it.

4. You'll have to adjust the spacing so that the line comes out the correct thickness. However, the spacing is a linear measure of the line, as shown in Figure 12.14. Notice that the spacing is one half the width. Divide the width by two for the spacing value.

5. Pick **Spacing**.

6. Pick **1 1/2"** and **0 1/4"** to equal 1 3/4". (You might want the insulation a little narrower than the full stud width. If so, use a value of **1 1/2"** or **1 5/8"** for the spacing.)

7. Press ENTER .

8. Object snap to the middle of the stud, as shown in Figure 12.14.

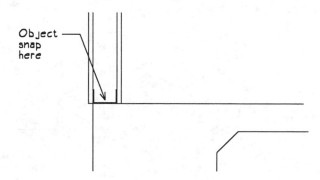

Object snap here

Figure 12.14: Object snap here.

9. Draw the line out as long as your walls, as in Figure 12.15, and pick.

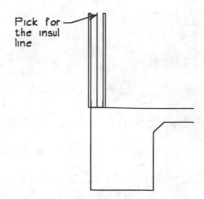

Figure 12.15: Draw this insulation line.

10. Press mouse button 3 to quit the line.

11. Notice that the insulation line dips into the stud a little. Use the **[W]** button in the control panel, and pick two points to zoom into this area, as shown in Figure 12.16.

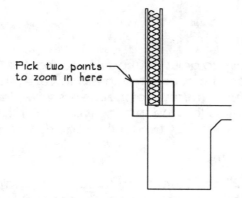

Figure 12.16: Zoom into this area.

12. Press mouse button 3 to exit the Window In menu.

13. The reason the line dips like this is because the line pattern is created so that it turns back on itself, as shown in Figure 12.17.

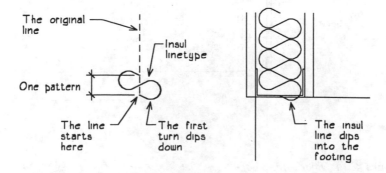

Figure 12.17: How the insul linetype is designed.

14. Pick the **Move** tool, indicated in Figure 12.18. Or press Ⓜ to go to the Move menu, to move the insulation line.

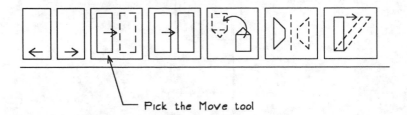

Pick the Move tool

Figure 12.18: The Move tool.

15. Press Ⓧ to turn off grid snap for now. Leave Orthomode on.

16. Pick near the end of the line for the from point of the move, as shown as step 1 in Figure 12.19. Don't object snap, because this isn't really the end of the line.

17. Pick near the middle of the stud, as indicated in Figure 12.19, step 2. Don't object snap, since it might make a crooked move distance.

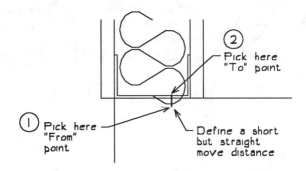

② Pick here "To" point

① Pick here "From" point

Define a short but straight move distance

Figure 12.19: Pick the move distance.

18. Pick **Entity** to make it active.

19. Now pick the middle of the insulation line, as shown in step 12.20. (Remember, the system thinks this is a straight line, so you have to pick the middle, where a straight line would be.) The line will move.

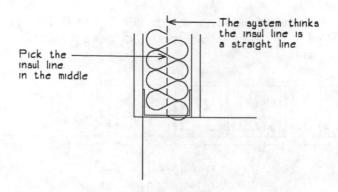

Figure 12.20: Picking the insulation line.

20. Press [PG UP] to zoom back out of your detail.

Draw the ground lines

1. Press [X] to turn on grid snap again.

2. Press [Q] many times to scroll through the linetype list until the message reads: *linetype is Solid.* [Q] is the quick key to change linetypes! [SHIFT] [Q] scrolls you through the list backwards.

3. Using the increment snap, pick to draw the ground lines, shown in Figure 12.21. Make sure the ground line on the left side of the footing is 6" long. (You'll use this line later to mirror your footing detail.)

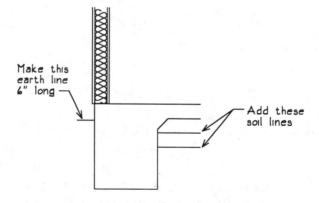

Figure 12.21: Draw these ground lines.

Creating the section line

You can draw the section line. Later, you can add it to your symbol library to use it over and over. The section lines you use in your office might look different, but you can use these directions as a guide and create your own.

1. Turn off orthomode by pressing [O].

2. Draw a line at angle across the part of the footing and ground lines, shown in Figure 12.22.

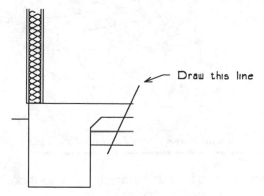

Draw this line

Figure 12.22: Draw a line for the section line.

3. Draw the little zigzag line, as shown in Figure 12.23.

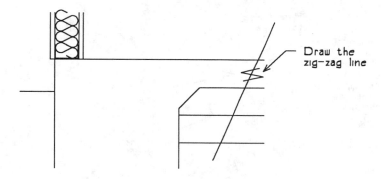

Draw the
zig-zag line

Figure 12.23: Add the zigzag.

4. Pick the **Erase** tool, shown in Figure 12.24, or use the fast key and press ⒠.

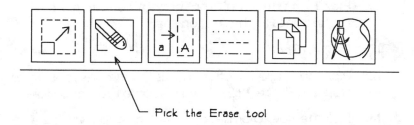

Pick the Erase tool

Figure 12.24: The Erase tool.

5. Pick **Partial**.

6. Pick the angle line to erase a gap out of, as shown as step 1, then object snap to the intersection of the zig-zag lines, as shown in step 2 and 3 in Figure 12.25.

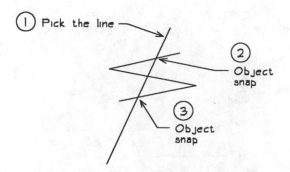

Figure 12.25: Steps to erase part of the section line.

7.   If you wish to further clean up your section line, press
      [ALT] [J] to go to 2 Ln Trim (Join).

8.   Pick the lines to trim up, as shown as steps 1, 2, 3 and 4
      in Figure 12.26. Remember to pick the lines on the
      sides you want to keep.

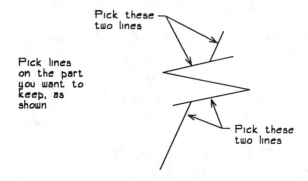

Figure 12.26: Steps to trim lines.

9.   Press mouse button 3 once, and you'll be in the
      Cleanup menu.

10.   Pick **1 LnTrim**. You'll use this feature to trim the
      ground lines to the section line.

11.   Pick **Entity**.

12.   Pick the angled section line as the trim line, shown as
      step 1 in Figure 12.27. It will become gray and dashed.

13.   Pick the side to erase, as shown as step 2 in Figure
      12.27.

14.   Make sure the **Entity** selection mode is active.

15.   Pick the two lines to trim, as shown as step 3 in Figure
      12.27.

16.   Press [SHIFT] [F] to file your drawing.

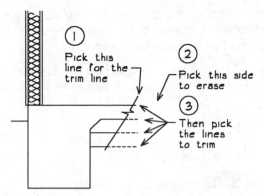

Figure 12.27: Steps to clean up the ground lines.

Creating the hatch boundary

Texture patterns, called *crosshatching*, are created in Data-CAD using the Hatch option. Before you create your hatch, you must first define a hatch *boundary*. You can think of the boundary as a fence that contains your hatch.

1. Press ⌨Tab to go to the **Hatch** layer.

2. Press ⌨H to go to the Hatch option, found in the Utility menu.

3. Make sure the **Assoc** option is active. This option makes the hatch a single entity, which can be modified by changing the scale, or pattern, or by being stretched.

4. Pick the **Boundary** option.

5. Using Object snap, define the boundary for the concrete, as shown in Figure 12.28. You might want to turn off Orthomode by pressing the ⌨O key.

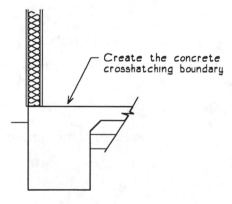

Figure 12.28: Define the hatch boundary.

Boundary works like the Fence option. After a few picks, the **Backup** option appears. If you make a mistake creating the boundary, you can pick Backup and define the corner of the fence again. Pressing mouse button 3 closes the boundary.

6. When the last point is defined for the boundary, press mouse button 3 to close and return to the main Hatch menu.

7. Pick the **Pattern** option.

8. Pick the **Concrete** option.

9. Pick the **Scale** option.

10. Type in **20** and press `ENTER` .

11. Pick **Begin**. Your drawing should look like Figure 12.29.

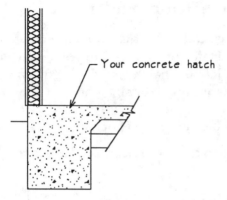

Figure 12.29: The hatch is created.

To adjust your associated hatch

If you want the hatch pattern larger or smaller in the associated hatch, you can edit it. (If it were not associated, you would have to create it all over again.) You can try the following steps.

1. Pick the **Entity** option to make it active.

2. Pick the hatch, as in Figure 12.30. It will become gray and dashed.

3. Pick the **Scale** option.

4. Type in **30** to enlarge the scale of the pattern. Press `ENTER` .

5. Pick **Begin**.

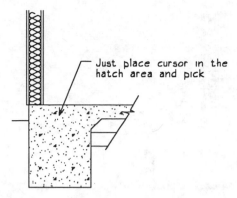

Figure 12.30: Pick the hatch to make it active for editing.

6. The scale of the pattern will change, as in Figure 12.31.

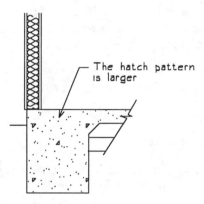

Figure 12.31: The hatch scale is modified.

Note: *This detail shows entire areas, such as the concrete footing, being filled in with hatch textures. However, you might wish to only "spot" fill areas, in order to make plotting faster, and for the appeal of the detail. To do this, just pick small areas for the boundaries. You might, for example, create a few triangle-shaped boundaries in the corners of the footing to show the concrete texture. Use this same techniques later to show a "spot" of the earth texture, etc.*

Creating the sand hatch

You can use the line hatch pattern for sand.

1. Press **H** to start a new hatch group.

2. Pick **Boundary**.

3. Define a boundary for the sand, using object snap, as shown in Figure 12.32. Press mouse button 3 to close the boundary

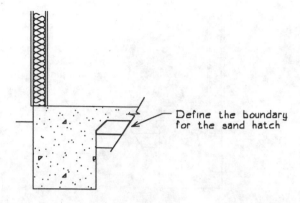

Figure 12.32: Define the hatch boundary.

4. Pick **Pattern**.

5. Pick **ScrlFwrd** until you see the **Line** pattern. As you highlight the Line pattern name, you'll notice that the pattern has the wrong angle. You'll change this angle next.

6. Pick **Line** to make it the current pattern.

7. Pick **Angle**.

8. Pick **90** and press [ENTER] .

9. Pick **Scale** and check that it is **30**, which is about right for the line pattern. Press [ENTER] .

10. Pick **Begin**. Your drawing should look like Figure 12.33.

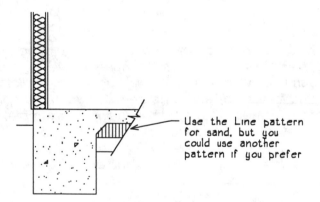

Figure 12.33: The sand hatch is created.

Creating the gravel hatch

There isn't a "gravel" hatch, but some people use the honey-comb pattern. (You could also draw a few small circles or ellipses using the Curves menu.)

1. Press [H] to begin a new hatch group.

2. Pick **Boundary**.

3. Define the hatch boundary shown in Figure 12.34. Press mouse button 3 to close the boundary.

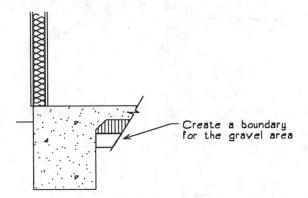

Create a boundary for the gravel area

Figure 12.34: Define the hatch boundary.

4. Pick the **Pattern** option.

5. Pick **ScrlFwrd** until you see the Honey option.

6. Pick **Honey** to make it the current pattern.

7. Pick **Scale**.

8. You might want to try a **20** scale for this pattern. Press `ENTER` .

9. Pick **Begin**. Your drawing should look like Figure 12.35.

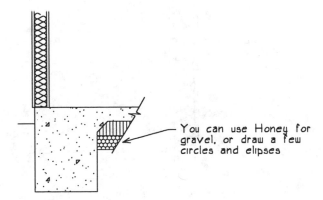

You can use Honey for gravel, or draw a few circles and elipses

Figure 12.35: Your drawing should look like this.

The drywall hatch

You'll use the cement pattern for the drywall.

1. Press `H` to begin a new hatch group.

2. Pick **Boundary**.

3. Define the hatch boundary shown in Figure 12.36. Press mouse button 3 to close the boundary.

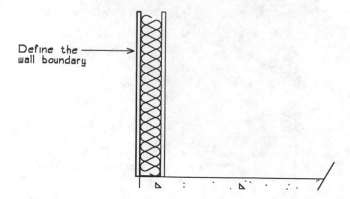

Figure 12.36: Define the hatch boundary.

4. Pick the **Pattern** option.

5. Pick **ScrlFwrd** until you see the Cement option.

6. Pick **Cement** to make it the current pattern.

7. Pick **Scale**.

8. **10** seems to work well for drywall. Press [ENTER].

9. Pick **Angle** and change it back to **0**. Press [ENTER].

10. Pick **Begin**. Your drawing should look like Figure 12.37.

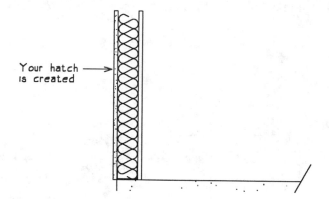

Figure 12.37: You drawing should look like this.

11. Copy the hatch pattern to the other wall, using the fast key. Press [C] for copy.

12. Object snap the "from" point, as shown in Figure 12.38.

13. Object snap the "to" point, as in Figure 12.38.

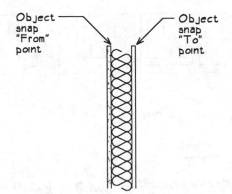

Figure 12.38: Object snap the from and to points.

14. Make sure **Entity** is active.

15. Check to turn OFF **LyrSrch**, to make picking the hatch easier. This way, you can't pick the wall by mistake, because it's on another layer.

16. Pick the hatch. It will copy to the other side, as in Figure 12.39.

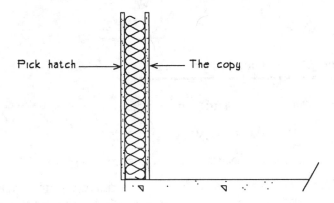

Figure 12.39: Copy the hatch.

17. Press [SHIFT] [F] to file your drawing.

Mirroring the detail

Your detail is ready to mirror to the other side.

1. Pick the **Mirror** tool, as shown in Figure 12.40.

2. Object snap to the midpoint of the 6" line, as step 1, shown in Figure 12.41. This will be the start point of the reflection line.

3. Press [O] to turn ON orthomode.

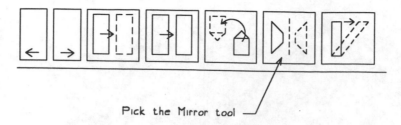

Pick the Mirror tool

Figure 12.40: The Mirror tool.

4.   Move the cursor up and pick for a vertical reflection line, as shown in Figure 12.41.

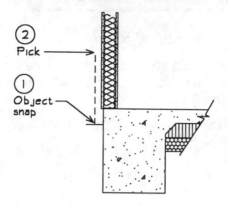

② Pick

① Object snap

Figure 12.41: Define a reflection line.

5.   Make sure **AndCopy** is active.

6.   Make **Area** active.

7.   **LyrSrch** needs to be active also, so pick it.

8.   Indicate an area around the entire detail, leaving an end of the 6" line out so that it's not mirrored also, as in Figure 12.42.

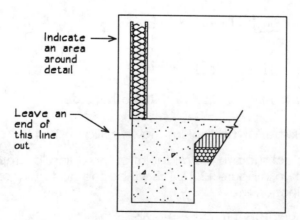

Indicate an area around detail

Leave an end of this line out

Figure 12.42: Indicate a mirror area.

9.   The copy is mirrored, as in Figure 12.43.

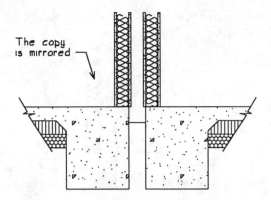

Figure 12.43: The second footing is mirrored.

10. Press [SHIFT] [F] to file your drawing.

Creating the earth hatch

1. Press [H] to go to Hatch.

2. Pick **Boundary**.

3. Define a boundary for the earth hatch, as shown in Figure 12.44. You'll want to object snap as applicable. Press mouse button 3 to close the boundary. (Remember, you don't have to make this boundary large enough to fill in the entire area. You could make a few small boundaries for a spot effect.)

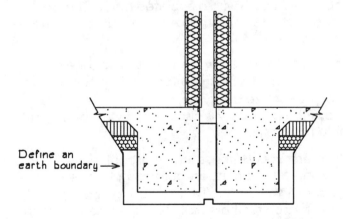

Figure 12.44: Define the hatch boundary.

4. Pick **Pattern**.

5. Pick **ScrlFwrd** until you see Earth.

6. Pick **Earth** to make it the current pattern.

7. Pick **Scale**.

8. Type in **90** and press [ENTER] . If this scale is too small for your needs, you can edit the hatch later.

9. Pick **Begin**. Your drawing should now look similar to Figure 12.45.

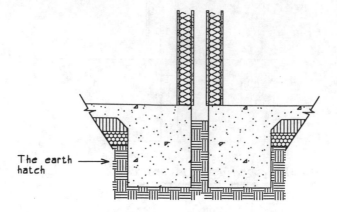

The earth hatch →

Figure 12.45: Your drawing should look similar to this.

10. Press SHIFT F to file your drawing.

Final hints on hatching

Here are a few tips to help you hatch in the future.

- You can use the **[I]** button in the control panel to identify an existing *associated* hatch. When you pick **SetAll**, it changes your hatch settings to match!

- You can use **Stretch** with associated hatch. The boundary will stretch larger or smaller and readjust the texture automatically.

- There is an option to show the boundary outline of your hatch in **Hatch, HatchTyp**. The boundary outline can then be edited like a Polyline, using the **POLYLINE** Macro. If the boundary is displayed, it will plot, so you'll want to turn it off again.

- If you do edit your Hatch, such as changing the **Scale** or turning on/off the boundary outline, make sure you use **[I]** to *Identify* the existing hatch, picking **SetAll** first, *then* edit. The reason for this is that the current settings in the hatch menu take effect during an edit. So, if you had *Line* as the current pattern, but wanted to change the scale of your existing *Earth hatch*, the Earth pattern would change to the *Line* if you hadn't updated your settings first!

Centerlines and property lines

1. Tab to the Dims layer.

2. Pick the **LineType** tool, shown in Figure 12.46.

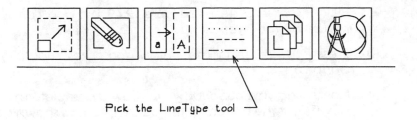

Pick the LineType tool ⟍

Figure 12.46: The LineType tool.

3. Pick **Centerline**.

4. Pick **Spacing**.

5. Type in **.6** for the pattern spacing, and press ⟦ENTER⟧ .

6. Draw one grid line, as in Figure 12.47. Use Orthomode.

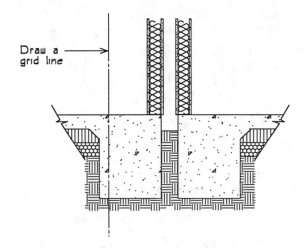

Draw a — grid line

Figure 12.47: Draw the grid line.

7. Pick the **Propline** linetype.

8. Object snap to the midpoint of the earth line shown in Figure 12.48.

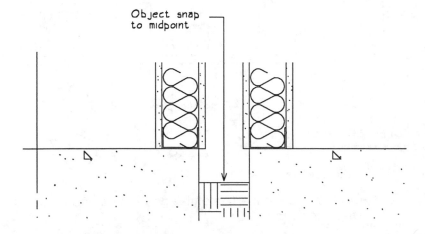

Object snap to midpoint

Figure 12.48: Object snap here.

9. Pick as shown as step 1 in Figure 12.49, but *don't press mouse button 3 yet.*

10. Press ⟨ to erase this line, but *still don't press mouse button 3.*

11. Now, bring your cursor down to draw a complete line, down past the bottom of the earth hatch, as shown as step 2 in Figure 12.49, and pick. Your new line is still in the center of the two footings! This is a good trick for many circumstances.

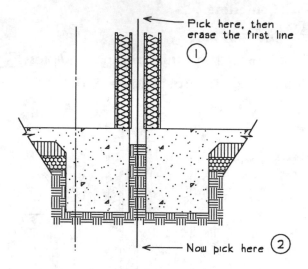

Figure 12.49: Drawing the property line.

12. Press mouse button 3 to quit the line.

13. Pick the **Solid** from the Linetype menu to return the current linetype to solid.

Making the grid line bubble

1. Pick the **Curves** tool, as in Figure 12.50.

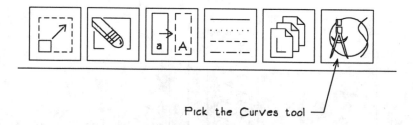

Figure 12.50: The Curves tool.

2. Pick **DiaCir**.

3. Object snap to the top of the grid line, as shown as step 1 in Figure 12.51.

4. As you move your cursor, you'll see that the circle is attached. Orthomode should be ON so that you can draw the circle straight (O = Orthomode On/Off).

5. Pick to draw a circle about 4" in diameter. You can turn on grid snap to make this accurate, but you don't have to (X = grid snap on and off). This circle is shown in Figure 12.51.

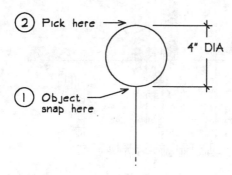

Figure 12.51: Draw this circle.

6. Use the **Text** option (ALT T) to create the GL text inside the bubble, as shown in Figure 12.52.

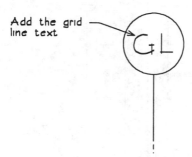

Figure 12.52: Add the grid line text.

7. Pick the **Mirror** tool, shown in Figure 12.53.

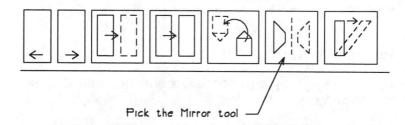

Figure 12.53: The Mirror tool.

8. Use the property line as the reflection line by object snapping to it and drawing a vertical line, as shown as step 1 in Figure 12.54.

9. Mirror the a copy of the grid line using **Entity**. Mirror copies of the text and bubble using **Area**. See step 2 in Figure 12.54.

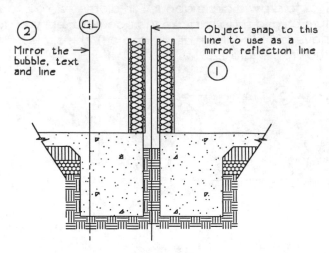

Figure 12.54: Mirroring the grid line.

10. Your drawing should now look like Figure 12.55.

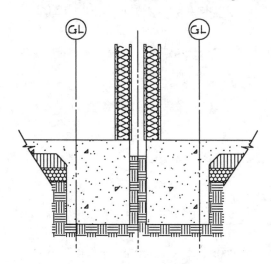

Figure 12.55: Your drawing should now look like this.

The dimensions

1. Press `ALT` `D` to go to the Dimensions menu. Check that **Assoc** is *off*.

2. Object snap to the lower corner of the first footing, as shown in step 1, Figure 12.56.

3. Object snap to the end of the property line, shown as step 2 in Figure 12.56.

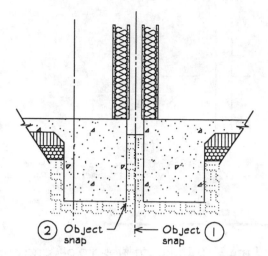

Figure 12.56: Object snap here.

4. Pick to place the dimension line.

5. Press ⎡ENTER⎤ to accept the **3"** dimension.

6. Because the space is so small for the dimension, the system won't automatically place the text. Instead, a small box appears on your cursor, which represents the text. Put the small box in the dimension and pick to place it, as in Figure 12.57.

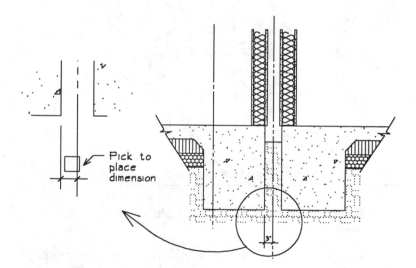

Figure 12.57: Place the dimension text.

7. Follow the steps in Figure 12.58 to add the second 3" dimension. (Don't pick Strnglin, as the Line2 extension line wouldn't be drawn on the footing corner.)

8. To create the grid line dimensions, which have no extension lines, pick **DimStyl**.

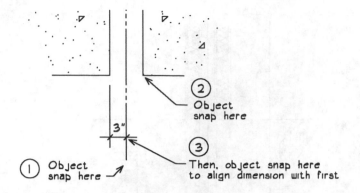

Figure 12.58: Creating the second dimension.

9. Turn off **Line 2**, so that *both* lines are off, and press mouse button 3 to return to the Dimension Linear menu.

10. Object snap to the first grid line, then object snap to the inside wall, for the face of stud dimension, as in step 1 and 2, Figure 12.59.

11. Pick to place the dimension, as in step 3, Figure 12.59.

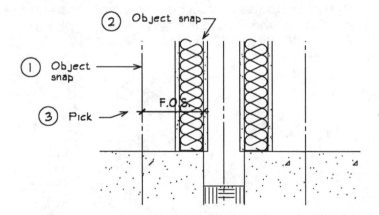

Figure 12.59: Creating the grid line dimension.

12. Type in **F.O.S.** for the Face Of Stud notation, and press `ENTER` .

13. The text will appear in the wall. You'll move it later.

14. Pick **Strnglin** and continue the dimension string, repeating the process for the property line, and other wall and grid line, as in Figure 12.60. To create a blank dimension, press the `SPACE` when the text comes up in the message area.

15. Your detail should look like Figure 12.60.

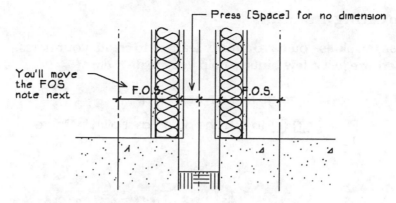

Figure 12.60: Your dimensions should look like this.

16. Pick the **Move** tool, shown in Figure 12.61. Or, press Ⓜ to go to the Move menu.

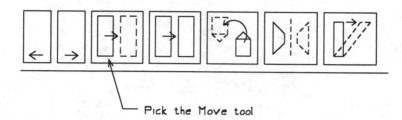

Figure 12.61: The Move tool.

17. Pick **Drag**.

18. Turn OFF **LyrSrch** to make picking the text of your dimension easier.

19. Using **Entity**, pick one of the F.O.S. text.

20. Pick a handle point, then drag the text box out of the wall, still remaining on the dimension line. *Orthomode on* helps you move the text in a straight line.

21. Repeat to the other F.O.S. text. Your dimensions should now look like Figure 12.62.

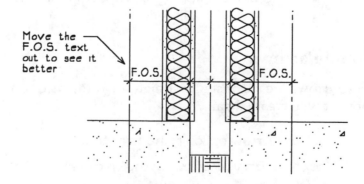

Figure 12.62: Move the dimension text so it can be read.

Creating notation

Use the skills you have already learned to create your notes.
Here are just a few hints to help you create them.

1. Press [Tab] to go to the **Notes** layer.

2. Press [ALT] [T] to add the notes, as shown in Figure
    12.63.

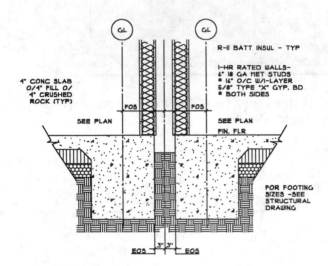

GL   GL

R-II BATT INSUL - TYP

I-HR RATED WALLS-
6" 18 GA MET STUDS
@ 16" O/C W/I-LAYER
5/8" TYPE "X" GYP. BD
@ BOTH SIDES

4" CONC SLAB
O/4" FILL O/
4" CRUSHED
ROCK (TYP)

FOS   FOS

SEE PLAN   SEE PLAN
                  FIN. FLR

FOR FOOTING
SIZES -SEE
STRUCTURAL
DRAWING

EOS   3" 3"   EOS

Figure 12.63: Add these notes.

3. If you've made a note and wish to move it, you can
    use the **Move** tool or press [M] , pick the **Drag** option,
    and use **Group** to pick the note. The entire paragraph
    is a group. Then move the text to the new location,
    turning off Orthomode if needed, by pressing [O] .

4. To make notes inline with each other, press [ENTER] a
    couple of times once you've completed the first note.
    Now type the next one. They'll line up exactly. The only
    thing is, you need to remember they're a group.

5. If you've already typed a note and wish to line up
    another note to it, you can object snap to the start of
    the first note. Then press [ENTER] a few times and start
    typing!

Double arrows

These arrows are surprisingly straightforward, once you
know how to create them.

1. Pick the **Arrow** option in the Text menu.

2. Pick to begin your arrow, as shown as step 1 in Figure
    12.64.

3. Press [O] to turn ON orthomode.

4. Create a straight arrow, as shown as step 2 in Figure 12.64. Press mouse button 3 to quit and the arrow will be made.

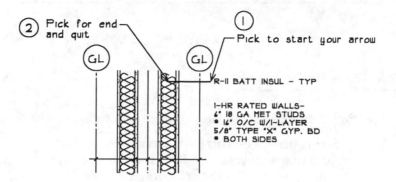

Figure 12.64: Create this arrow.

5. Now object snap to the point of this arrow to start the second arrow, as in step 1 in Figure 12.65.

6. Pick to define the end, and press mouse button 3 to create the arrow head, as in step 2 in Figure 12.65.

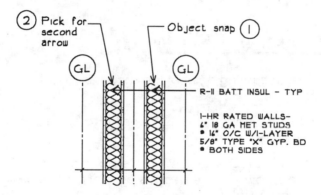

Figure 12.65: Creating the double arrow.

7. Create the second set of double arrows using the same technique.

Curved arrows

This technique uses a combination of an arc and an arrow.

1. Pick the **Curves** tool, shown in Figure 12.66. (The quick key is [ALT] [A] for Arcs.)

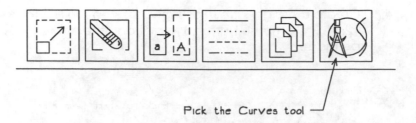

Pick the Curves tool ─

Figure 12.66: The Curves tool.

2.   Pick the **3PtArc** option.

3.   The 3 Pt Arc option allows you to pick a start point and an end point for your arc. Then the curve of the arc moves dynamically with your cursor. Figure 12.67 illustrates how this feature works.

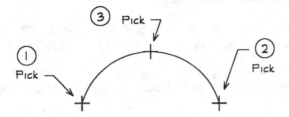

Figure 12.67: How a 3 point arc is created.

4.   Pick the beginning point of the arc, as in step 1 in Figure 12.68.

5.   If you have Orthomode ON, press ☐O to turn it OFF to make picking easier.

6.   Pick near the F.O.S. dimension, step 2 in Figure 12.68. This gap (shown where step 2 is pointing) will be filled with an arrow later.

7.   Pick to place the curve of the arc, as in Step 3, Figure 12.68.

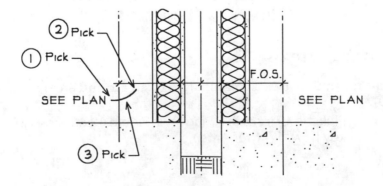

Figure 12.68: Create this arc.

8.   Press [ALT] [T] to go to Text.

9. Pick **Arrow**.

10. Object snap to the end of the arc, then pick on the dimension line, shown as steps 1 and 2 in Figure 12.69.

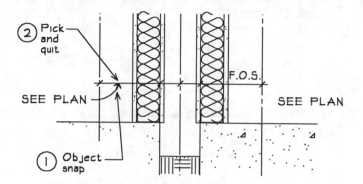

Figure 12.69: Creating the arrow on the arc.

11. Press mouse button 3 to create the arrowhead.

12. Pick the **Copy** tool, as shown in Figure 12.70, to copy the curved arrow. Or, press Ⓒ to go to Copy.

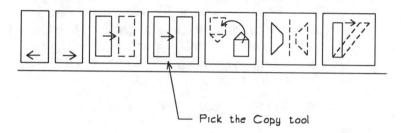

Figure 12.70: The Copy tool.

13. Pick "from" and "to" points, as shown in Figure 12.71, to define the copy distance. Orthomode (press Ⓞ) helps to make this distance straight.

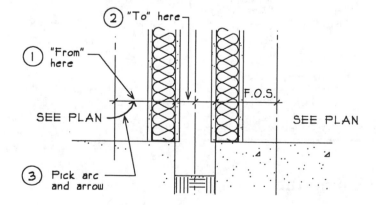

Figure 12.71: Copying the note curved arrow.

14. Using **Group**, pick the arc and the arrow to copy, as shown by Figure 12.71.

15. Now connect the second curved arrow to the original note with a straight line, shown in Figure 12.72. Use object snap!

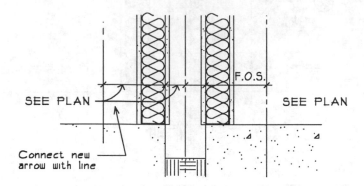

Figure 12.72: Connect with a line.

16. Press ⌷SHIFT⌷ ⌷F⌷ to file your drawing.

17. **Mirror** these arrows to the other side (pick **Mirror** tool), using the property line to define the reflection line (object snap and create vertical line). Use **Group** to select the line, arcs, and arrows to mirror. (Or use **Area** very carefully, making sure not to select the tic marks of the dimensions.)

18. Your drawing should look like Figure 12.73.

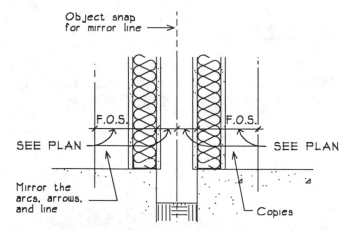

Figure 12.73: Finish your drawing.

Finishing the detail

1. Use **Text** (⌷ALT⌷ ⌷T⌷) to create the **PL** text as separate **P** and **L** text, then **Move** them (⌷M⌷ to move), **Dragging** them in place to overlap on the property line.

You might want to make them a larger size, such as **2 1/2"** or **3"**.

2. Add the rest of the arrows ([ALT] [T] , **Arrows**).

3. **Move**, **Drag**, by **Area**, with **LyrSrch** on, and move the entire detail so that it's centered in the detail box.

4. Use **Change** (pick Change tool), **Text**, **Contents**, and edit the detail title to: **PROPERTY LINE FOOTING**.

5. Your drawing should now look like Figure 12.74.

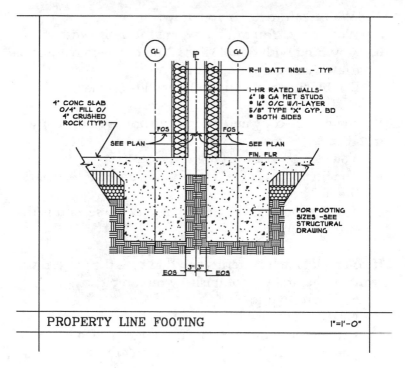

PROPERTY LINE FOOTING   1"=1'-0"

Figure 12.74: Finish your drawing.

6. Press [SHIFT] [F] to file your drawing.

7. You can make a **Pictogram** if you'd like. Do you remember the steps?

8. To quit DataCAD, press [ALT] [Q] , and answer **Yes** to file your drawing before you leave.

DataCAD exercise 11

Please complete the following exercise by reading each question carefully, then circling the letter that corresponds to the correct answer.

1. Before creating the hatch in your drawing, you must:
   a. Create a boundary.
   b. Notate it.
   c. Delete any existing boundaries.

2. The Walls feature helps you draw:
   a. Walls only. You can't draw anything else with it.
   b. Anything with double lines. You can even have ends drawn using Cap.
   c. Double line, but you can't put ends on them.

3. When you use copy and define two points as the copy distance:
   a. You can never invert the distance.
   b. The first point is the "from" point, and the second is the "to" point.
   c. The first point is the "to" point, and the second is the "from" point.

4. If you pick Hatch Patterns, and don't see the pattern you want on the first part of the list, you can pick:
   a. **ScrlFwrd** to find it.
   b. **NextPage** to find it.
   c. **Exit**, because there is only one page of each list, and if you don't see it the first time, it isn't there.

5. When you use a linetype, such as Insul line, the system sees it as:
   a. A solid line, so you must pick it in the middle.
   b. Many pieces of lines, such as arcs in the Insul linetype. So you can pick it anywhere.
   c. One size. You can't change the spacing.

6. When you use create an associated hatch pattern, it is:
   a. A group of many entities.
   b. Many entities, but not a group.
   c. A single entity.

7. If you wish to edit an associated hatch, you must:
   a. Use the **Hatch** option.
   b. Delete it first and create it all over again.
   c. Use the **Change** option.

8. To quickly update your Hatch settings to match an existing hatch:
    a. It can be associated or unassociated. Use **[I]** Identify and **SetAll** options.
    b. The hatch must be associated. You can use **[I]** Identify and **SetAll**.
    c. The hatch must be associated. You can use **[I]** Identify and **Update**.

9. When you create Hatch, you need to set the:
    a. **Scale** option in the Hatch menu to a reasonable size for your scale drawing. You only need to do this once, since all the patterns are based on the same scale factor.
    b. Plotter menu **Scale** first. This way, the hatch will automatically scale to the final size of the drawing.
    c. **Scale** option in the Hatch menu to a reasonable size for your scale drawing. You'll probably need to do this several times, since all patterns are different.

10. To quickly erase the last line you drew, you can:
    a. Use the Erase menu only. There is no quick way to erase.
    b. Press ⟨ to undo last entity.
    c. Press ⟩ to undo the last entity.

11. To turn off the grid snap, press the:
    a. SHIFT X keys.
    b. G key.
    c. X key.

12. If you create a dimension so small that the text won't fit:
    a. A text box is attached to your cursor, allowing you to place it.
    b. You can't make the dimension. It must be bigger.
    c. The text comes in squished to fit.

13. When you turn off a dimension extension line:
    a. It stays off for one dimension only, then turns back on.
    b. You can only make one dimension.
    c. It stays off until you turn it back on, so you have to be careful how you create your dimensions.

14. When you create a 3 Point Arc (3PtArc), the:
    a. 3 points are picked, and then a circle is drawn through the points.
    b. First pick is the start point; the second pick is the end point. Your third pick is to define the size of the arc.
    c. First pick is the start point, the second pick is a point on the curve, and the third pick is the end of the arc.

Review Questions

15. To permanently save your drawing file, you:
    a. Press [SHIFT] [F] every half-hour or before a major change in your drawing.
    b. Let the Autosave feature do it for you.
    c. Quit DataCAD then pick the Abort option.

16. Checking the size of your drawing is accomplished using the:
    a. File I/O menu, **FileSize** option.
    b. Directory menu.
    c. Display menu, **FileSize** option.

17. Before changing the color of a symbol, you must:
    a. File your drawing.
    b. Explode the symbol.
    c. Use the Change menu and pick a new color.

18. The two correct ways to explode a symbol are by using the:
    a. **Explode** option found in the 3D Edit menu and the **SymExp** in the macro menu.
    b. **Explode** option found in the Dimension menu and the **Explode** option in the Template menu.
    c. **SymExp** in the macro menu and the **Explode** option found in the Template menu.

19. To create a series of chained dimensions, you pick the:
    a. **Chain** option.
    b. **StrngLin** option.
    c. **Series** option.

20. To make your text appear skinnier, you can adjust the:
    a. **Factor** option.
    b. **Justify** option.
    c. **Aspect** option.

21. If you want to italicize your text or give it a back stroke, you can use the:
    a. **Slant** option.
    b. **Italics** option.
    c. **Angle** option.

22. If the text you're typing in appears at the message area of the screen, but you wish it to appear on your drawing as you type, you should pick the:
    a. **OnScreen** option.
    b. **Dynamic** option.
    c. **On Drwng** option.

23. If you need to turn your drawing 90-degrees to plot it, you can use the:
    a. Rotate menu and rotate your entire drawing before using the Plotter menu.
    b. Plotter menu, then pick **Rotate**.
    c. Rotate feature in the File I/O menu.

24. If you want your plotter to make pen changes, you must have active:
    a. **ClrPlot**.
    b. **UsePens**.
    c. **Multipen**.

Creating templates and symbols

Templates and symbols

You've used symbols, and you already know that symbols are gathered into templates. In this chapter, you'll create a template for your footing details. You'll save the detail you just created into the template as a symbol, and then you'll use the symbol in your detail sheet.

Here are some of the things you'll learn in this chapter:

- Creating new template pathnames.
- Starting a new template.
- Saving a symbol to the template.
- Adding the new symbol to another drawing.
- Unassociating crosshatching.
- Scaling your details.
- Exploding associated dimensions.

Creating symbols

Making symbols from items in your drawing is a very important skill. It allows you to share areas of your drawing with other drawings easily, such as lighting symbols, plumbing symbols, or even entire bath areas that might be repeated throughout a condo development.

To create symbols, you have to:

- Create the drawing that contains your symbols, and have the drawing displayed on the screen. (One drawing can have several symbols in it. Or it can be a drawing, such as a floor plan, that contains items you'd like to make into symbols.)

- Prepare the items that will become the symbol, for use over and over again. This might mean changing the size so that they're easily used, or putting in text that's easily edited.

- Create your new template, or call up an existing template to use.

- Add your symbols to the template.

Display the detail drawing

1. Start DataCAD.

2. Call up the drawing that contains the detail you just created in Chapter 12, **ftgdet**, by picking the name from the list. The drawing will be displayed on your screen, as in Figure 13.1.

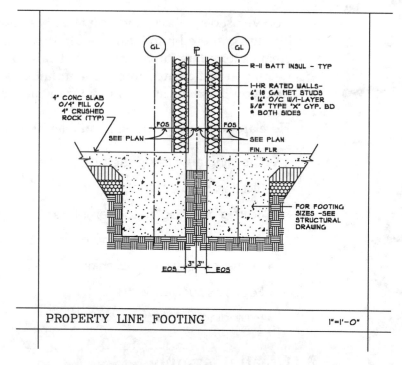

Figure 13.1: The detail.

Preparing the detail to make into a symbol

The detail will be scaled to 1"=1'-0" before making it into a symbol using the Enlarge feature. You need to know that changing the size of your detail can effect items in your drawing, such as associated dimensions and hatching.

Associated dimensions will reflect *any* size change, such as stretching or enlarging. For example, an 1'-0" dimension would be 1" after being scaled. Steps to "unassociate" dimensions are shown in this chapter.

Associated hatching will *not* reflect a size change. In other words, the hatch scale size remains the same, although the detail is greatly reduced. (You'd get a little detail with big-sized hatch.) There isn't a simple way to scale all of the different hatch patterns in your drawing at one time, or to "unassociate" hatch either. But a workaround that solves this problem is shown in this chapter.

Exploding dimensions

To unassociate your dimensions, you'll *explode* them (the name of the option is Explode). Even though you didn't use associated dimensions, it is very important to know these steps.

1. Press ⟦ALT⟧ ⟦D⟧ to go to Dimensions, Linear.

2. Pick **Explode**.

3. Make **Area** and **LyrSrch** active.

4. Indicate an area around the entire detail, as in Figure 13.2.

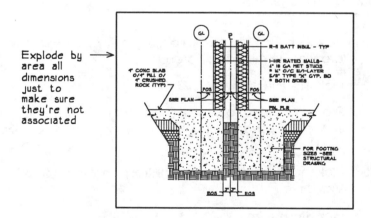

Figure 13.2: Exploding the dimensions.

5. Any associated dimension would now be unassociated and ready for scaling.

Unassociating hatching

As mentioned earlier, there's no option for exploding hatch. But there is a clever way to work around this problem. You'll use the *SaveImage* feature in the 3D Viewer, creating an image of the hatch and saving it to another layer. Using this option also offers an advantage. You'll still have the original associated hatch (for later editing or changing into another detail) and a copy of the hatch, unassociated, on a second layer.

1. To check that the hatching is associated, pick the **[I]** button in the control panel to go to Identify.

2. Pick a line of one of the hatches. The entire hatch will become gray and dashed, and should be identified as a PolyLine (see F1 option, which lists the entity type). The Polyline item type is displayed for associated hatch, because the hatch is controlled by a polyline boundary.

3. Pick the **Layers** tool, as shown in Figure 13.3, or press ⌨L.

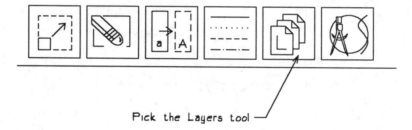

Pick the Layers tool

Figure 13.3: The Layers tool.

4. Pick **ActvOnly** to quickly display only one layer in your drawing, in this case, Hatch.

5. Pick the **Hatch** layer.

6. Press mouse button 3 to exit the ActiveOnly menu, but stay in the Layers menu. Your drawing should now look like Figure 13.4.

7. Pick the **[V]** button in the control panel to go to 3D Viewer.

8. Pick **SavImage**.

9. Pick **NewLayer**.

10. Type in the name of your new layer: **EXHatch** and press ENTER .

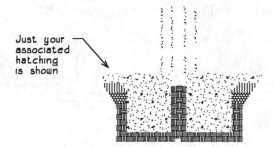

Just your
associated
hatching
is shown

Figure 13.4: Only the hatching is shown.

11.   Pick **On** to leave the new layer on (displayed).

12.   Press mouse button 3 to exit the 3DViewer. You'll return to the Layers menu.

13.   Pick the **On/Off** option to turn on your layers.

14.   Pick all of the layers to turn on, except the original Hatch layer, which still holds the *associated* hatch, which you need to pick to turn OFF. You should have active: **Box**, **Detail**, **Dims**, **Notes**, and **EXHatch**.

15.   Press mouse button 3 to exit.

16.   Now pick the **[I]** button in the control panel to go to Identify again.

17.   Pick on of the hatch items, like a line in the earth hatch.

18.   Only the line you picked will become gray and dashed, and it will de identified as a line. It's no longer an associated hatch!

19.   Press [SHIFT] [F] to file your drawing. Your symbol is ready to scale.

Scaling the detail

As before, you'll use the *Enlarge* menu to scale your detail. You'll save your drawing file one more time, then, once you reduce the size of your drawing, you won't file it again. You'll go directly to the template menu and create a symbol from it.

At this point, you'll discover that creating the symbol removes the detail from the drawing. So, once the detail is in the template, you'll abort the empty drawing file (you wouldn't want to file the empty drawing). This way, you'll still have a full size detail drawing file, which you can use to make changes and to create other "look alike" details.

1.   Press [SHIFT] [F] to file your drawing one more (and last) time.

2.   Pick the **Enlarge** tool, as in Figure 13.5.

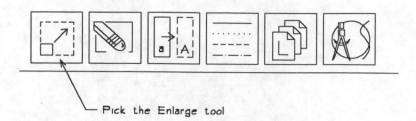

Pick the Enlarge tool

Figure 13.5: The Enlarge tool.

3.   Pick anywhere near the center of the detail, as in Figure 13.6, for the *center of enlargement.*

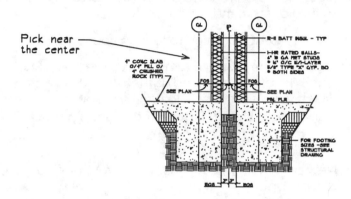

Pick near the center

Figure 13.6: Pick near the center.

4.   Notice that the current enlargement scale (shown in the message area) is **12**. This was the last setting you used when you scaled the border to the 1"=12" value (1"=1'-0").

5.   If the scale isn't 12 because you've changed it at some point, don't worry. Use the **Enlrgmnt** option, and **SetAll** to **12**.

6.   Pick the **Invert** option. This will change the scale to the reduction factor appropriate for 1"=12", which will be .08333333.

7.   Make sure **LyrSrch** and **Area** is active.

8.   Indicate a box around the entire detail, including the box. (Although the box won't become part of your symbol, you'll use it to define the symbols origin point later.) This is shown in Figure 13.7.

9.   The detail will be reduced. Pick the **[R]** button in the control panel to recalculate the view extents.

10.   Press mouse button 3 to exit.

11.   *DON'T* file your drawing!

Pick around
the entire
detail and
box

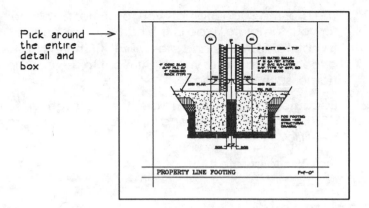

Figure 13.7: Select the entire detail and box.

The template directory

When you used the sofa symbol, you had to go to the directory path that held these templates, in this case, *dcad6\tpl\furn*. You did this by using the NewPath option.

When you create your new template, you'll want it in a correct path that will allow you to quickly access detail symbols. A recommendation, then, is to create a path called *dcad6\tpl\details*. This is very easy to do.

1. Press **T** to go to the Template menu. The templates in the current directory are listed.

2. Pick the **New Path** option.

3. Check the current directory pathname. It might be set to something like *tpl\plumb* or *\dcad6\tpl\plumb*. (These are the same pathname, but the latter is displaying the *entire* path.) Or, it might just say *tpl*, which means that the path is set to the main *\dcad6\tpl* directory, and the subdirectories are listed to choose from.

4. Type in the new directory path for your detail templates: **tpl\details** and press ENTER .

5. A *Yes/No* menu will probably appear, asking if you want to create this new directory. (If you don't get the Yes/No menu, the directory has already been created before.) Pick **Yes** to create it, or press Y .

Creating the new template

Once the directory has been set up, just type in a new name for your template.

1. The user message prompts you to: *"Enter file name:"* for your template. Type in the name for your new template: **footing1** and press ENTER . (If there's already a footing1 template, you might want to use another name, such as *footing2*.)

2. Because this is a new template, the message will say: *"file 'c:\dcad6\tpl\footing1.tpl' does not exist. Create new file?"*

3. Pick **Yes** to create it.

Template fields

Next you'll be prompted to add any additional fields to the template form. "Fields" are the information areas that are attached to each of your symbols. This information can be extracted for schedules. For example, if you used 24 outlet symbols in your floor plan electrical layout, you could easily extract how many were used and how much the total cost is, with tax!

This information (and tax table) can be modified at any time. The symbol information is saved when the symbol is created, and can be edited later. The reports forms are created with simple text files that then can be used with DataCAD, and several are included.

Fields 1 through 6 are already defined. They are:

1. Item name
2. Manufacturer
3. Model number
4. Remark 1
5. Remark 2
6. Cost

Of course, this type of schedule report doesn't work well with a detail sheet. And a report only works with symbols that are not exploded. All your details will be exploded; they must be exploded so you can edit them.

For now, then, you'll only worry about the Item Name part of the report. Since you won't be customizing reports yet, you can quit out of the new fields mode.

1. Press mouse button 3 to quit defining fields.

2. Your new template will appear, as shown in Fig. 13.8.

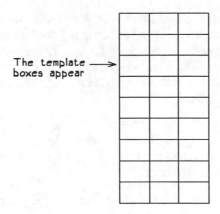

The template →
boxes appear

Figure 13.8: The template boxes appear.

Adjusting the number of template boxes

You can easily define the number of boxes that appear in the template by adjusting the X number of boxes (columns across the X direction), and the Y number of boxes (rows in the Y direction). The default is 3 boxes in the X and 9 in the Y.

1. Pick the **Dvisions** option.

2. Type in: **2** for the X division, and press [ENTER] .

3. Type in: **5** for the Y division, and press [ENTER] .

4. Ten boxes will now be displayed, as in Figure 13.9.

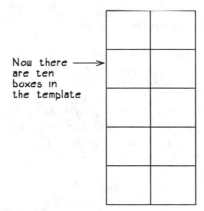

Now there →
are ten
boxes in
the template

Figure 13.9: Now ten boxes are in your template.

Adding a symbol to your new template

Now you're ready to add the detail to your template.

1. Pick the **SaveSymb** option in the Template menu.

2. Make sure **AutoPath** is active.

3. Check the name of the directory path for your symbols. It should be **sym\footing1**. The *Autopath* option creates this directory path for you automatically. Your individual symbol file will be stored in the *SYM* (symbol) directory, under the name that matches your template file, *FOOTING 1*.

4. The message says *"Save to which symbol file:."* Type in the name of your new symbol: **propftg1** (for property line footing), and press ENTER . The file will be created with a *.sm3* extension.

5. Again, look to see that the **Area** and **LyrSrch** options are active.

6. Object snap to two corners of the detail box, as in Figure 13.10 to indicate a rectangle around the entire scaled detail. Object snapping will automatically exclude the detail box itself.

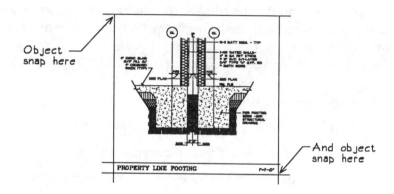

Object snap here

And object snap here

PROPERTY LINE FOOTING

Figure 13.10: Object snap to these corners.

7. Your detail will become dashed. Make a visual check that all pieces of your detail are included, and that the detail box is NOT dashed.

8. If you missed part of your detail, or if the box became dashed because of a selection error, press mouse button 3 and start over. This time, modify your area box to include only the correct items.

9. The message says *"Enter reference point for your symbol."* This will be the lower-left corner of your detail box. Object snap to this point, as shown in Figure 13.11. This point will be the handle point you'll use to place your detail symbol whenever you use it in your detail sheets.

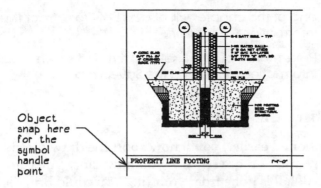

Object snap here for the symbol handle point

Figure 13.11: Object snap here for your symbol handle.

10. The detail will disappear from your drawing and reappear in the first template box, as in Figure 13.12.

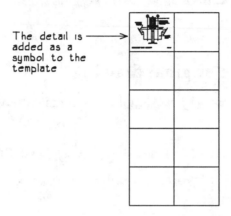

The detail is added as a symbol to the template

Figure 13.12: The detail appears in the template box.

11. Next, you're asked to enter the *"item name"* for the symbol. This is the name that appears when you hold your cursor on the template box where the detail is. You'll notice if you move your cursor to the box right now, only the path and the symbol file name is displayed: *sym\footing1\propftg1.sm3.*

12. Type in: **Property Line Footing** and press ENTER . You can use spaces. The character limit is 32.

Note: *Always press ENTER after typing in the item name (as opposed to pressing mouse button 3). Otherwise, the item name won't be accepted, and only the pathname will appear when you hold the cursor over the template box.*

---

13. Now you're prompted to enter a *"manufacturer"* for your symbol. If you were saving an electrical outlet, for example, or a fluorescent light, you might enter the vender's name here. You would continue to go through the list, adding the cost, etc. A section at the

end of this chapter will discuss how to extract this information for a report.

14.   Press mouse button 3 several times to exit the report information mode and the SaveSymb menu.

Aborting the drawing

As mentioned earlier, you'll now abort the drawing file. This probably makes more sense to you now, since you can see that the detail is gone from your file. You could bring it back in using the symbol, but the symbol would come in on one layer and as one group, which makes editing very hard.

1.   Press ALT N to go to a new drawing.

2.   Pick the **Abort** option. *Don't skip this step!*

3.   Pick **Yes**.

Checking the original drawing

To check that your original detail drawing is still intact, you can pull it up.

1.   Pick the **FTGDET1** drawing name from the list.

2.   It will be displayed. Your detail should look like Figure 13.13.

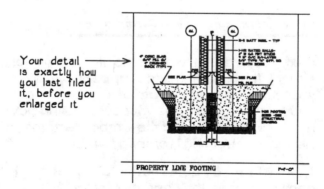

Figure 13.13: Your detail is okay.

3.   Press ALT N to go to a new drawing again.

4.   Pick **Yes** to exit and save. Or you can pick **Abort, Yes,** since no changes were made.

Adding the detail to your detail sheet

Now you'll set up a detail sheet, using the default you created in chapter 11. Then you'll add the detail you just made.

1. At the opening DataCAD screen, pick the **Default** option.

2. Pick the **DETSHEET** default.

3. Type in the new name for your drawing: **cond-dt1**, which could indicate that this is the first detail sheet for a condominium project you're working on, and press ENTER .

4. The detail sheet will be displayed, as in Figure 13.14.

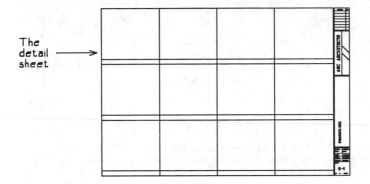

Figure 13.14: The detail sheet.

5. The 3x4 divisions should be displayed, and the Details layer should be active.

6. Press T to go to Templates.

7. Pick the template you created earlier: **Footing1**.

8. The template with your detail will be displayed, as in Figure 13.15.

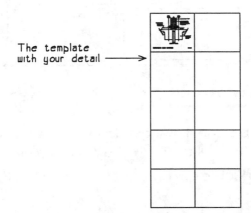

Figure 13.15: Your template is displayed.

9. Pick the **Explode** option to make it active. This way, your detail symbol will be exploded and you can edit it. (Remember, if you forget to explode the detail, you could use the **Macro, SymExp**.)

10. Pick the detail in the template: **Property Line Footing**.

11. Object snap to place the detail into what would normally be the number one spot on the detail sheet. Since offices differ in there numbering sequence, the object snap point shown in Figure 13.16 is meant to be a guideline.

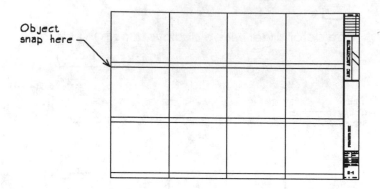

Figure 13.16: You could object snap here for your symbol.

12. The detail will appear, centered in the detail box.

13. Press [SHIFT] [F] to file your drawing.

14. Your drawing will look like Figure 13.17.

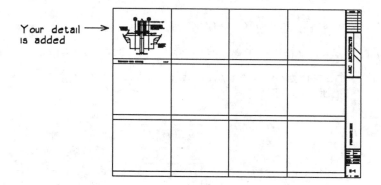

Figure 13.17: The detail is added.

15. You can plot the drawing by following the steps in chapter 7, "Plotting and Printing your Drawing."

17. Press [ALT] [Q] to quit DataCAD, and pick **Yes** to save.

Creating symbol reports

You might want to extract a *symbol report* from a drawing in which you've used many symbols. This drawing might be an electrical layout, for example. For report extraction, the symbols CANNOT be exploded.

Use your own drawing, or create a test drawing, and follow these steps.

1. Call up the drawing that contains the symbols. If you don't have one, pick the **Default** option, pick the **PLAN_1-4** default, and name this new drawing: **reports**, then press ⌨️ENTER .

2. If this is a new drawing, you must add some symbols to your drawing before you can run a report.

3. Press ⌨️T to go to Template.

4. Bring up the template that your symbols are in. The template must be displayed to extract a report.

   For example, to retrieve an electrical template, pick **NewPath**. Pick the ".." option, and then pick **ELEC** to set your path to **tpl\elec**. Press ⌨️ENTER . Pick the appropriate template, such as **RCPTCL** (receptacles).

5. If you're creating a test drawing, make sure **Explode** is NOT on (exploded symbols don't contain report information), then pick the symbols to add, adding ten or so to the drawing.

   For example, you can add 5 or 6 **Triplex Recep Outlets,** some **Duplex Recep Outlets**, and a number of **Trip Rec Split Wired** symbols. You'll want a good variety. Your drawing might look like Figure 13.18.

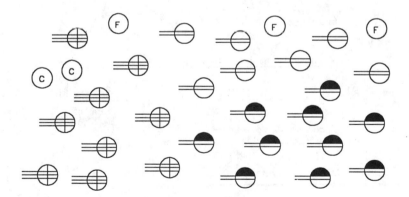

Figure 13.18: Electrical outlets have been added.

6. Once many symbols have been added, pick the **Reports** option.

7. The available reports will be listed as options. (The pathname for report form files is *DCAD6\FRM*.)

8. Pick the report called **DCADCOST**.

9. The report will be displayed on your screen. Notice how each box contains certain information, and some might not contain any at all.

You can edit this information, just as you edited the name of a symbol in chapter 4. For example, you might want to change the cost and vendor of the items you're running the report for.

10. Press the ⌨ENTER to continue.

11. Next, you're given some options for the destination of the report. Pick the **ToDrwing** option.

12. A Text menu is displayed. Pick **FontName**.

13. It's important to pick a font that's monospaced so that the columns of your report line up. Pick **Orig**. You might have to pick **ScrlFwrd** to find this font.

14. Pick **Aspect**. You'll probably want the aspect adjusted to **1.2**, then press ⌨ENTER.

15. Drag the cursor out on your screen. Notice that the cursor has changed to represent the current text size of your report. If you want the text bigger, pick the **Size** option and adjust it now. You could, for example, make the text 2' or 3' tall to see better.

16. Pick a place for your report on your drawing. Keep in mind that your pick will indicate the upper-left-hand corner of the report, as in Figure 13.19. The report will be added to your drawing as regular text.

```
            Example of the DCADCOST report

  ┌─  This is the
  │   placement point
  │
  │
  ▼
 Title,
 Item Name  Manufact  Model No  Remark 1  Remark 2   Qty. Unit Cost  Total Cost
 Dup Rec.  │        │        │        │        │      10 │  0.00  │   0.00
 Triplex R │        │        │        │        │       5 │  0.00  │   0.00
 Duplex Re │        │        │        │        │       7 │  0.00  │   0.00
 Clock Han │        │        │        │        │       2 │  0.00  │   0.00
 Fan Hange │        │        │        │        │       3 │  0.00  │   0.00
                                  TOTAL ITEMS:   31
                                              TOTAL COST:        0.00
                           You'll want to edit ─┘    Tax (4%):
                           the symbol fields        GRAND TOTAL:   0.00
```

Figure 13.19: Placing the report.

17. Press mouse button 3 to quit back to the Template menu.

Changing report information

This will be a good review, since you already edited an item name in chapter 4. Now you might want to change the "Cost" and "Manufacturer" fields to fit your need. The tax field, however, must be changed in the text file, which appears in the *\dcad6\frm* directory as *dcadcost.frm*. (If you edit this file, make a copy of it first in case you make a mistake.)

1. Pick the **EditFlds** option from the Template menu.

2. Pick the template box that contains the symbol you want to edit, such as the **Triplex Recep Outlet** in the RCPTCL template.

3. Pick the first **Manufact** option on the list.

4. Type in a vendor's name, such as: **AV Const Sup** and press [ENTER] .

5. Pick the **Cost** option.

6. Type in a new cost for this symbol, such as: **1.39** and press [ENTER] .

7. Pick the first **Model Nu** option on the list.

8. Type in a number for the outlet. For example, type in: **A013-2** and press [ENTER] .

9. The remark fields can be used for color and model description. Pick **Remark 1**.

10. Type in a color for the outlet. For example, type in: **Ivory** and press [ENTER] .

11. Pick **Remark 2**.

12. Type in a description of the model type, such as: **Designer** and press [ENTER] .

13. Press mouse button 3 to return to the **EditFields** menu.

14. Pick the next symbol you want to edit.

15. Follow this same procedure to edit all of the fields you wish to use in your report.

16. When you're done, press mouse button 3 to exit back to the Templates menu.

17. Pick the **Reports** option again, and pick **DCADCOST**.

18. Now the fields will display the changes made in the previous steps.

19. Press [ENTER] to continue.

20. Pick **ToDrwing**, move your cursor into the drawing area, and pick. The new report will be created and the changes you've made will appear, as in Figure 13.20.

Creating templates and symbols

```
Title
Item Name  Manufact  Model No  Remark 1   Remark 2   Qty. Unit Cost  Total Cost
------------------------------------------------------------------------------
Dup Rec. | AU Const| A113-1  | Ivory    | Designer|    10|    1.63|      16.30
Triplex R| AU Const| A115-3  | Ivory    | Designer|     9|    1.49|      13.41
Duplex Re| AU Const| A115-2  | Ivory    | Designer|     7|    1.39|       9.73
Clock Han| Fans Inc| 93445   | White    | Grade 2 |     2|    2.15|       4.30
Fan Hange| Fans Inc| 83525   | White    | Grade 2 |     3|    2.75|       8.25
                                    TOTAL ITEMS:      31
                                                        TOTAL COST:     51.99
                                                         Tax (4%):       2.08
                                                      GRAND TOTAL:      54.07
```

Figure 13.20: The changed report.

A hint for better-looking reports

The *Factor* (line spacing factor) option doesn't work when generating the text for the report in your drawing. Until it does, create the text in the report a larger than needed (try twice the size as necessary). Then, once the report is created, use **Change**, **Text**, **Size** to change the text to a smaller size. You can use **Group** to select it. Now the text lines will be nicely spaced, as in Figure 13.21.

Using the ORIG font, and new text size

```
Title
Item Name  Manufact  Model No  Remark 1   Remark 2   Qty. Unit Cost  Total Cost
------------------------------------------------------------------------------
Dup Rec. | AU Const| A113-1  | Ivory    | Designer|    10|    1.63|      16.30
Triplex R| AU Const| A115-3  | Ivory    | Designer|     9|    1.49|      13.41
Duplex Re| AU Const| A115-2  | Ivory    | Designer|     7|    1.39|       9.73
Clock Han| Fans Inc| 93445   | White    | Grade 2 |     2|    2.15|       4.30
Fan Hange| Fans Inc| 83525   | White    | Grade 2 |     3|    2.75|       8.25
------------------------------------------------------------------------------
                                    TOTAL ITEMS:      31
                                                        TOTAL COST:     51.99
                                                         Tax (4%):       2.08
                                                      GRAND TOTAL:      54.07
```

Figure 13.21: A better looking report.

Quitting DataCAD

After you've played with the reports, you might want to abort the drawing, either because it was a test or because you've messed up a good drawing.

1. Press [ALT] [N] to go to a new drawing.

2. If you don't want to save any of your changes, pick **Abort**.

3. Now pick **Yes**, or press [Y].

DataCAD exercise 12

Please complete the following exercise by reading each question carefully, then circling the letter that corresponds to the correct answer.

1. A "template" is a:
   a. Series of boxes that will hold your symbols.
   b. Special directory for your forms.
   c. Report form.

2. When you make a template, you:
   a. Shouldn't put it in any special directory.
   b. Should put it in the TPL directory and a proper subdirectory by defining a pathname.
   c. Should put it in the SYM directory by using the **AutoPath** option.

3. When you make a symbol, you:
   a. Should put it in the TPL directory by defining a pathname.
   b. Should put it in the SYM directory and a subdirectory matching the template name by using the **AutoPath** option.
   c. Don't have to worry about directories at all.

4. When using the **AutoPath** option, you:
   a. Should still check that the symbol path is correct before saving your symbols.
   b. Can only save 10 symbols to a template.
   c. Shouldn't pay attention to the pathname. It doesn't make a difference where your symbols go.

5. When you create a symbol that is on more than one layer, you should make sure:
   a. **LyrSnap** is active in the Object Snap menu.
   b. All but one layer is turned off.
   c. **LyrSrch** is active in the Save Symbol menu.

6. If you enter the Template menu to pick a new template file, no template is active, and no template names are displayed in the menu area, you should:
   a. Call someone for help.
   b. Simply check the current pathname by picking **New Path**.
   c. Do nothing. All of your templates have been deleted.

7. When you have a template active, and you want to change to another template, you use the:
   a. **New File** option in the Template menu.
   b. **New Template** option in the Template menu.
   c. Template menu. The template names are automatically displayed.

8. Template fields are:
   a. Information areas for reports that you're able to attain from the symbols in your drawing.
   b. An area in your drawing used in landscaping.
   c. Information that cannot be added to your drawing, but can be extracted by using the Reports option.

9. You can output a report in three ways. They are:
   a. To drawing, to plotter, and to printer.
   b. To drawing, to file, and to printer.
   c. To file, to printer, and to plotter.

10. In order to create a name for your symbol that can be read when you move your cursor to the symbol box in the Template, you:
    a. Define an "item name" for your symbol after adding it to the template. This name can be changed later if you wish.
    b. Have to give the symbol a name that you want before adding it to template. This name cannot be modified.
    c. Define an "item name" for your symbol after adding it to the template. This name cannot be changed once you define it.

11. To reduce your detail, you use the:
    a. Reduce menu.
    b. Scale menu.
    c. Enlarge menu.

12. When creating a detail that will be scaled with the Enlarge menu, any associated hatch:
    a. Should be added after you scale your detail, because it cannot be easily scaled.
    b. Reduces perfectly, using the **AsscHtch** option in the Enlarge menu, and can be added before you scale your detail.
    c. Must be unassociated before reducing.

13. Associated dimensions should always be:
   a. Created after you scale your detail.
   b. Exploded before reducing the size of your detail. Otherwise, the dimensions will change to the new line sizes.
   c. Reduced along with the rest of your detail, without having to explode them, by using the **AsscDims** option in the Enlarge menu.

14. A good way to unassociate hatching in your drawing is to use the:
   a. **UnAssc** option in the Hatch menu.
   b. **Explode** option in the Hatch menu.
   c. **SavImage** option in the 3D Viewer menu.

15. After scaling your detail and adding it to your template, it is wise not to:
   a. Save your file again.
   b. Add any more symbols to the template until you've saved your file.
   c. Save the template.

16. The quick key to go to the Hatch menu, is:
   a. [H] .
   b. [T] .
   c. [ALT] [H] .

17. The quick key to go to the Template menu, is:
   a. [S] .
   b. [ALT] [T] .
   c. [T] .

18. To use a report, the:
   a. Template with the symbols must be shown, and the symbols in your drawing can be exploded or not.
   b. Template with the symbols must be shown, and the symbols in your drawing must not be exploded.
   c. Symbols must not be exploded, but you don't need to have the template displayed.

CHAPTER 14

Modeling walls, openings and roofs

Modeling

You already know that when you draw with DataCAD, you can define a Z-height, and that your drawing can be viewed in 3D. However, the tops of your walls are flat. Now you'll learn how to create modeled walls that can have peaks, like a rake-wall for a gabled roof, and you can add framed windows into the walls.

Here are some of the things you'll learn in this chapter:

- Creating a horizontal slab for a floor.

- Drawing vertical slabs for walls.

- Defining window and door slabs.

- Processing the window and door slabs into voids, which become holes in your walls.

- Using the Roof It macro to create a gable and hip roof.

- Stretching the wall slab to meet the gable roof.

- Using an edit plane to change your working coordinates.

- Using the 3D Edit menu commands to move, copy, and manipulate your entities in 3D.

Working in 3D

Although the items you've drawn in DataCAD are 3D, they're simple 3D entities. You've probably noticed by now that walls are actually *two lines* drawn together, and are represented as two parallel planes when you view them in 3D. They're simple entities because they can't be manipulated into complex shapes, such putting a hole or an archway into the wall. You've been restricted to drawing *planar* to the plan, or ortho, view. Also, all of your drawing entities have been *flat* on the top and bottom. For instance, walls have flat tops as compared to cathedral peaks.

Modeling allows you to create entities that are convoluted or complex. What this means is that you're no longer restricted to having your walls flat on the top and bottom, and you can create curved, three-dimensional items. Walls will be drawn as slabs, and you can manipulate these slabs to create cathedral ceilings or archways. You'll punch holes in the modeled walls so that you can see inside the building. If you were going to use a rendering package, such as RenderStar, you could give the windows added to these holes a transparent quality in order to see into a room, or for a special effect. Figure 14.1 shows the model you'll create in this chapter.

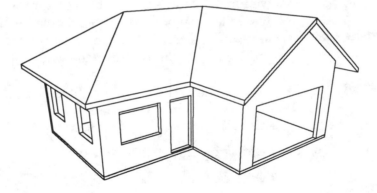

Figure 14.1: The model project.

Creating a new drawing

To start this model, you'll use a new drawing without using a default drawing. Follow these steps to set up your drawing:

1. Start DataCAD.

2. Type in the new name for your drawing: **model1** and press ENTER .

Setting up your drawing

Because you did not use a default drawing, you must define your layers and perform the other steps needed to set up your drawing file. These settings are listed along with reminders on how to accomplish them.

1. Set your grid Snap to **6"** (press S to set snap).

2. Define **5** layers, (Press ⬜L⬜ , use **NewLayer**, enter **4.**)

3. **Name** the layers, and assign colors, as shown (press ⬜K⬜ to change colors):

   Floor (Light Cyan)
   Walls (White)
   Roof (Light Red)
   Windows (Yellow)
   Doors (Brown)

4. In the **Settings** menu, make sure the following is set:

   Show Z
   SaveDlay = 30

5. Also in **Settings**, use **EditDeflts, Scales, LoadFile**, and load the **SMALL** file you created earlier.

6. If you're using a Display list, in the **Display** menu, set the **DispList, Windows** to **4** and the **RgenWarn** to OFF.

7. In the **Object Snap** menu (press ⬜SHIFT⬜ ⬜X⬜), make sure **Fast3D** is OFF and the following is active:

   End Pt 2
   Mid Pt 3
   Center
   Intsect
   LyrSnap

8. Go to **DataCAD 3D** menu (press ⬜J⬜), and in the *3D Settings* menu, make sure **QuickSrch** is OFF and the following is active:

   Dynamic
   MeshGrd
   MeshPnt

9. Press ⬜SHIFT⬜ ⬜F⬜ to File your drawing.

The two modeler menus

Like the 2D side of DataCAD, there are two menus for 3D modeling. They are the *3D Edit* menu and *3D Entity* menus. The 3D Edit menu is shown in Figure 14.2. Although most of

Modeling walls, openings and roofs

these options are named the same as in the regular Edit menu, they *only* work with 3D modeled entities. For instance, the Erase menu will only erase modeled entities, and it will ignore regular 2D items.

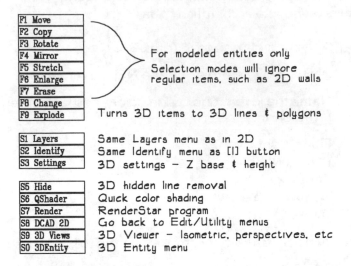

F1	Move	
F2	Copy	
F3	Rotate	
F4	Mirror	For modeled entities only
F5	Stretch	Selection modes will ignore
F6	Enlarge	regular items, such as 2D walls
F7	Erase	
F8	Change	
F9	Explode	Turns 3D items to 3D lines & polygons

S1	Layers	Same Layers menu as in 2D
S2	Identify	Same Identify menu as [I] button
S3	Settings	3D settings — Z base & height

S5	Hide	3D hidden line removal
S6	QShader	Quick color shading
S7	Render	RenderStar program
S8	DCAD 2D	Go back to Edit/Utility menus
S9	3D Views	3D Viewer — Isometric, perspectives, etc
S0	3DEntity	3D Entity menu

Figure 14.2: The 3D Edit menu.

The 3D Entity menu, shown in Figure 14.3, contains the options that create 3D modeled entities.

F1	3DLine	Simple wired frame line in 3D space
F2	Polygon	Planar surface, no thickness, 36 edges
F3	Blocks	Simple block, 6 faced rectangle
F4	Slab	Planar surface w/thickness, 36 edges

F6	3DArc	Arc in 3D space
F7	VertCyln	3D cylinder standing up
F8	HoriCylr	3D cylinder laying on side
F9	Cone	3D cone shaped surface
F0	TrunCone	3D cone with peak cut off
S1	Sphere	Globe and partial globe shapes
S2	Torus	Doughnut shaped surfaces

S4	Contour	3D interpolated contour curves
S5	MeshSurf	Interpolated 16 point patch, contoured
S6	Rev Surf	Outline revolved about line to create surface
S7	Marker	3D snap point, 3D pause

S9	3D Views	3D views, isometrics, perspectives, etc
S0	3D Edit	3D Edit menu

Figure 14.3: The 3D Entity menu.

To access these menus, you can either pick the **DCAD 3D** option in the 2D **Edit** menu, or simply press the [J] key. [J] accesses the **3D Edit** menu, and [SHIFT] [J] goes to the **3D Entity** menu. Once you enter into the 3D modeling menus, you can use mouse button 3 to switch back and forth between these two menus.

1.   Press [J] to go to the DataCAD 3D modeling menus.

2.   Notice that the message area of your screen indicates that you're in the **3D Edit** menu. Also notice that the **S0** option in the menu is 3D Entity. Because your third mouse button selects S0 for you, try pressing it. You'll go to the **3D Entity** menu.

3.   The quick key to go back to the 2D Edit menu is the 🔡 key. Press the 🔡 key.

4.   Another way to quickly return to 2D is to pick one of the 2D tools in the DCAD icon bar!

Displaying the 3D icon tool bar

As you already know, there's more than one tool bar available with DataCAD, and you can create more because they're user definable (although any customizing must take place in the text file outside of DataCAD). You can turn on another tool bar that's been set up for modeling.

1.   Press mouse button 3 until the Utility menu is displayed.

2.   Pick the **Display** menu.

3.   Pick **Menus**.

4.   Pick the **IconFile** option.

5.   Pick the **DCAD_3D** icon file. The new tool bar will be displayed, as in Figure 14.4.

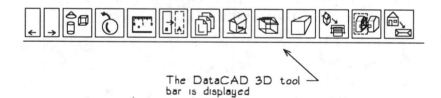

The DataCAD 3D tool
bar is displayed

Figure 14.4: The DCAD 3D tool bar icons are displayed.

6.   Press mouse button 3 until you exit the Settings menu.

7.   Move the cursor over the icons to see what they do. The name of the tools will appear in the message area of the screen.

8.   Pick the **Scroll Forward** tool, pictured in Figure 14.5, to see what other tools are available. You can scroll forward twice.

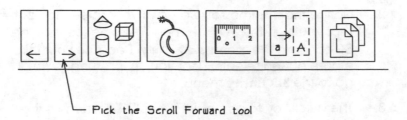

Pick the Scroll Forward tool

Figure 14.5: The Scroll Forward icon.

9. Pick **Scroll Back** until you return to the main bar tools, shown in Figure 14.6.

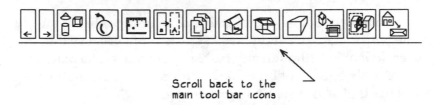

Scroll back to the main tool bar icons

Figure 14.6: Scroll back to these tools.

10. You can see how helpful these tools could be if you customized a bar to show only the ones you need the most in the main set of eleven, so you wouldn't have to scroll forward to find the tool you need. Of course, some of these tools are more easily accessed by a quick key.

11. Anytime you wish to go back to the main tools, follow these steps, but pick the **DCAD** icon set.

Note: The DCAD_3D tool bar will stay active until you change it, even if you go to another drawing.

Creating the floor slab

Your project for this chapter is shown in Figure 14.7. First you'll create a floor "slab" for the model. The *Slab* option is in the 3D Entity menu. You'll use it to create a 4" thick *horizontal* slab for the flooring. This same procedure could be used for ceiling/floors in multistory buildings.

1. Press [Tab] to go to the **Floor** layer.

2. Press [Z].

3. Set the Z-base by typing in: **-.4** and pressing [ENTER].

4. Type in: **0** for the Z-height, and press [ENTER].

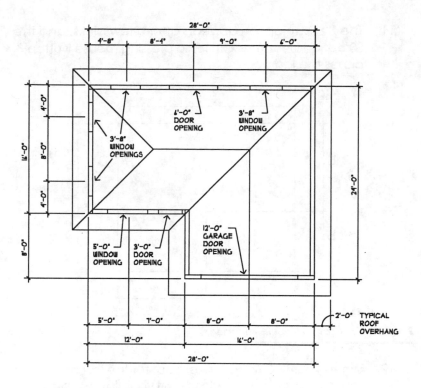

Figure 14.7: Your modeling project.

5. Make sure grid snap is ON (the S is big in SwOTHLUD). If it isn't, press ⌧ until the message says *"Snap is on."*

6. Pick the **3D Entity** tool, as shown in Figure 14.8 (pick the **Scroll** tools if necessary). Or, press ⌈SHIFT⌉ ⌈J⌉ .

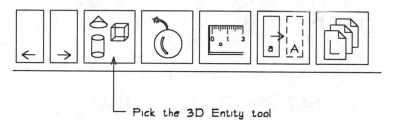

└─ Pick the 3D Entity tool

Figure 14.8: The 3D Entity tool.

7. Pick **Slab**.

8. Pick **Horizntl**.

9. Pick **Bse/Hg**t until it's active.

10. Create the outline of the foundation, as shown in Figure 14.9. You can either grid pick (because your grid is set to 6"), or use relative Cartesian to type in the dimensions. Creating a horizontal slab is similar to the fence or hatch boundary routine. Draw all the sides except for the last one.

11. The **Backup** option appears after a few picks, and the S0 option becomes **Close**, so pressing mouse button 3 closes the last side.

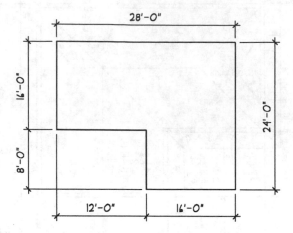

Figure 14.9: Create the slab flooring.

12. When your floor is drawn, except for the last side, press mouse button 3. It will close and your slab will be drawn.

13. Press mouse button 3 again to quit back to the Slab menu.

Drawing the walls

You can use the Slab function to draw your walls, too. This is important, because you can punch holes in slabs and manipulate them into different shapes.

1. Press ⊞Tab to go to the **Walls** layer.

2. Press Z to adjust the Z-base and height.

3. Type in: **0** for the Z-base, and press ENTER .

4. Type in: **9.10** for the Z-height, and press ENTER .

5. Still in the Slab menu, pick **Vertical**.

6. Pick the **Thicknss** option.

7. Change the thickness of your walls (wall width), by typing in: **.6** and pressing ENTER .

8. Make sure the **Bas/Hgt** option is still active.

9. Pick the **Left** option to make it active. This option creates the wall with the "other side" falling on the left side as you draw the wall up vertically (in the positive Y direction). This is illustrated in Figure 14.10. You'll draw the walls counterclockwise, so the wall width will fall to the inside of your building.

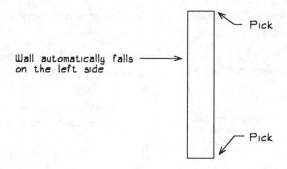

Figure 14.10: The walls automatically fall to one side.

10. Object snap at the first two corners of your floor, as indicated in Figure 14.11. The first wall is created.

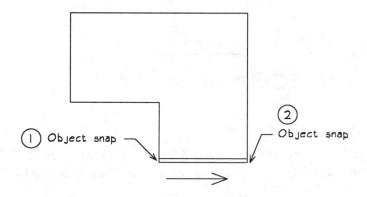

Figure 14.11: Object snap to these corners.

11. Object snap to the next two corners, as in Figure 14.12. Notice how you have to define the walls so that they butt next to each other.

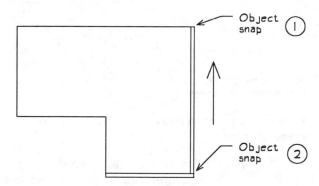

Figure 14.12: Now object snap to these corners.

12. You'll also notice that the corners don't automatically clean to each other, as when using a regular wall. Don't worry about this too much. First of all, a shading or rendering package automatically blends these edges together (such as the Quick Shader or RenderStar). Secondly, there's no way to clean up

these edges because the walls are two separate entities.

13. Follow the steps outlined in Figure 14.13 to complete the walls for your house.

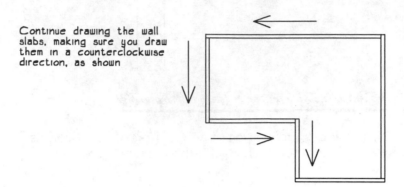

Continue drawing the wall slabs, making sure you draw them in a counterclockwise direction, as shown

Figure 14.13: Create the rest of the walls.

14. Press [SHIFT] [F] to file your drawing.

A quick check in 3D

It's important to keep a visual 3D check on your model. You can monitor your progress as you create your building and get the feel of working in 3D.

1. Pick the **Isometric View** tool, as shown in Figure 14.14.

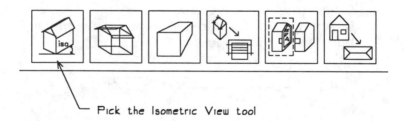

Pick the Isometric View tool

Figure 14.14: The Isometric View tool.

2. Pick the **[R]** button in the control panel to recalculate the view extents.

3. Notice that your house has a flat top so far, as in Figure 14.15. This will change later, once you've added a roof. But for now, you'll put some holes in the walls for windows and doors.

4. Pick the **[Ortho]** button in the control panel to return to the plan view of your drawing.

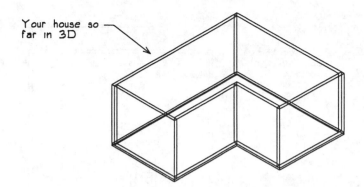

Your house so far in 3D

Figure 14.15: Your model now look like this.

Creating the holes in the walls

To define a hole, you must first create slabs inside your wall, in the size and location you want the hole. Then you'll convert these slabs into *voids*, which are holes.

You'll draw the slabs for your openings at the following Z base and heights:

Doors	Z Base = 2"	Z Height = 6'-8"
Windows	Z Base = 3'-0"	Z Height = 6'-8"
Garage	Z Base = 1/8"	Z Height = 7'-0"

1. Press the ⧈ key to set your Z-base and height for the door openings.

2. Pick **2"** for the Z-base, and press ⧈ENTER .

3. Type in **6.8** for the Z-height, and press ⧈ENTER .

4. Change your snap to 2" by pressing ⧈ , pick **2"** and ⧈ENTER .

5. You should still be in the *Slab, Vertical* menu, and the **Left** option should still be active.

6. Create the door openings for both the front door and rear slider. Use the ⧈ reference key to measure from the corners, and the grid snap to measure your slabs (or you can use relative Cartesian coordinates to type it in). Draw them in the same counterclockwise direction as your walls. See Figure 4.16.

Note: *Opening slabs MUST be created in the same direction as your wall slab! If you forget to do this, the hole won't process properly.*

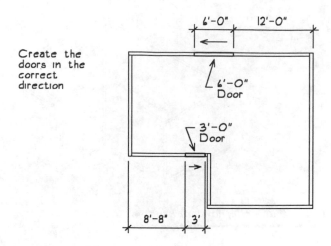

Create the
doors in the
correct
direction

Figure 14.16: Create the door opening slabs.

5. To quickly view the isometric of your model, pick the **Isometric View** tool, shown in Figure 14.17. Are the doors correct?

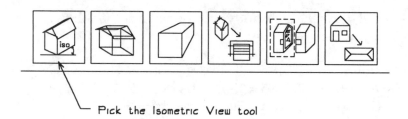

Pick the Isometric View tool

Figure 14.17: The Isometric tool.

6. Pick the **[Ortho]** button in the control panel to return to the plan view of your model.

7. Press $\boxed{Z}$ to change your Z base and height again for the window openings, referencing Figure 14.18.

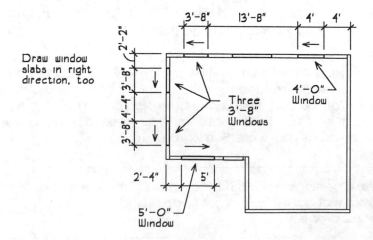

Draw window
slabs in right
direction, too

Three
3'-8"
Windows

4'-0"
Window

5'-0"
Window

Figure 14.18: Create these windows.

8.   Type in: **3** for the Z-base, and press ⌈ENTER⌉ .

9.   Press ⌈ENTER⌉ to keep the Z-height at **6.8**.

10. Create the window slabs, making sure that they are drawn in the same directions as your walls (counter-clockwise). Remember to use the ⌷ key to measure from the corners. See Figure 14.18 for window dimensions.

11. To view your model in isometric, pick the **Isometric View** tool (Figure 14.19). How do the windows look?

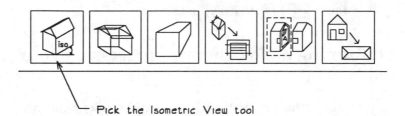

Pick the Isometric View tool

Figure 14.19: The Isometric tool.

12. Pick the **[Ortho]** button in the control panel to return to the plan view.

13. Press the ⌈Z⌉ key to set the size for your garage door.

14. Pick **0.1/8"** for the Z-base, and press ⌈ENTER⌉ .

15. Type in: **7** for the Z-height, and press ⌈ENTER⌉ .

16. Create your garage openings, as in Figure 14.20. Make sure you draw from left to right to follow your wall direction.

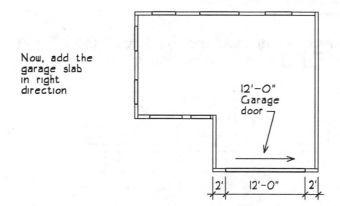

Now, add the garage slab in right direction

12'-0" Garage door

2'   12'-0"   2'

Figure 14.20: Add the garage opening.

17. Pick the **Isometric View** tool, shown in Figure 14.21. Do all the openings look correct? If not, erase them and follow the steps again.

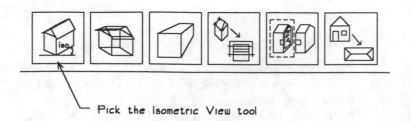

— Pick the Isometric View tool

Figure 14.21: The Isometric tool.

18. Stay in the "iso" view for now.

19. Press SHIFT F to file your drawing.

Performing a hide "before" processing your voids

So you can better understand how a void works, you can quickly perform a *hide* on your model "before and after" you process the openings. Plus, it's fun to see how converting a slab into a void makes it "hide" different!

1. Pick the **Scroll Forward** tool, shown in Figure 14.22.

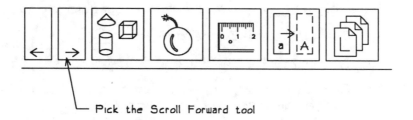

— Pick the Scroll Forward tool

Figure 14.22: The Scroll Forward tool.

2. Pick the **Hide** tool, shown in Figure 14.23. (Or press SHIFT Y to quickly enter the Hide menu.)

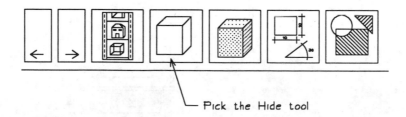

— Pick the Hide tool

Figure 14.23: The Hide tool.

3. Make sure the **SavImag** option is OFF. You won't save this image.

4. Pick **Begin**.

5.   Notice that the walls don't have holes in them yet, as shown in Figure 14.24.

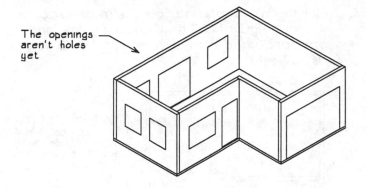

The openings aren't holes yet

Figure 14.24: The openings aren't processed into holes.

6.   Pick the **Scroll Back** tool, shown in Figure 14.25.

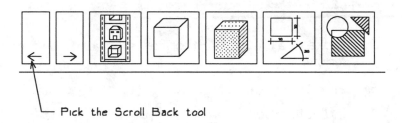

Pick the Scroll Back tool

Figure 14.25: The Scroll Back tool.

7.   Pick the **3D Entity** tool, shown in Figure 14.26. (Or press [SHIFT] [J] to quickly enter the 3D Entity menu.)

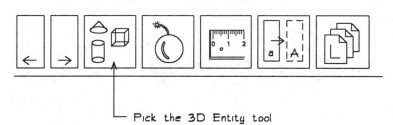

Pick the 3D Entity tool

Figure 14.26: The 3D Entity tool.

Converting slabs into voids

Now you're ready to convert the slabs into voids for your openings.

1.   You could actually perform this operation in your 3D iso view. However, to make things easier, you'll return to your plan view. Pick the **[Ortho]** button in the control panel.

2. Pick **Slabs** in the 3D Entity menu.

3. Pick the **Voids** option.

4. Pick the *Wall* slab to indicate the *master slab*, as shown in Figure 14.27. It will become gray, and it might appear dashed. (Sometimes vertical walls don't show as dashed.)

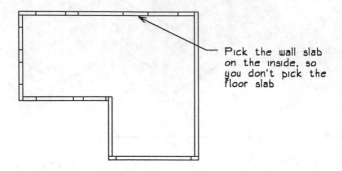

Pick the wall slab on the inside, so you don't pick the floor slab

Figure 14.27: Pick the wall for the master slab.

5. Make sure the **AddVoid** option is active! If it isn't, pick it now.

6. Pick **Area** to make it active.

7. Indicate a box to select all of your window and door openings that are on this wall, as shown in Figure 14.28. They will become gray and dashed also.

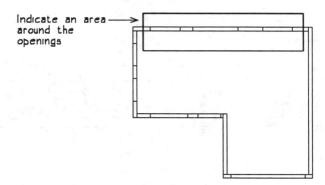

Indicate an area around the openings

Figure 14.28: Select the openings along the wall.

8. Press mouse button 3 once. The slabs will be processed at this point.

9. Check that all slabs are processed correctly. Typically, you'll see a problem, such as creating an opening in the wrong direction, because a "wrong way" void would actually jump to the other side of the wall, as illustrated in Figure 14.29. If you get a problem like this, you must delete the void (use **ErsVoid** in the *Slabs, Voids* menus), and recreate the opening in the correct direction.

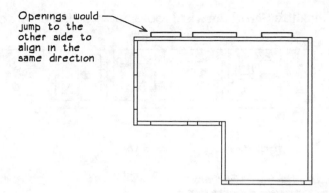

Openings would jump to the other side to align in the same direction

Figure 14.29: A wrong-way void.

10. Pick the next master wall slab (step 1 in Figure 14.30).

11. Using **Area** and **AddVoid**, select the opening slabs along this wall, as shown as step 2 in Figure 14.30.

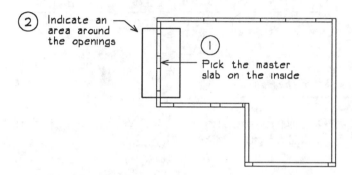

② Indicate an area around the openings

① Pick the master slab on the inside

Figure 14.30: Processing the opening on the next wall.

12. Press mouse button 3 to process these voids. Continue converting the opening slabs into voids, until all walls have been processed.

13. Press [SHIFT] [F] to file your drawing.

Checking the voids with Hide

Now that you have converted the opening slabs into voids, they're holes! Just to check, you can try a hide again.

1 Pick the **Isometric View** tool, shown in Figure 14.31.

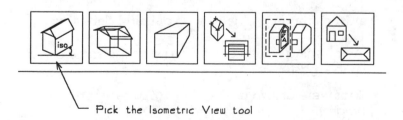

Pick the Isometric View tool

Figure 14.31: The Isometric tool.

2. Pick the **Scroll Forward** tool, shown in Figure 14.32.

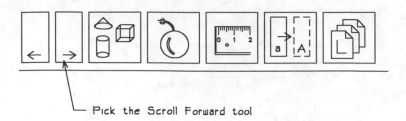

Pick the Scroll Forward tool

Figure 14.32: The Scroll Forward tool.

3. Pick the **Hide** tool, shown in Figure 14.33. (Or press
SHIFT Y to quickly enter the Hide menu.)

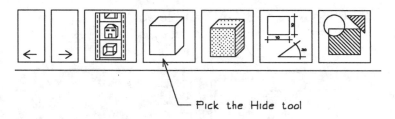

Pick the Hide tool

Figure 14.33: The Hide tool.

4. Did all the openings process? Your drawing should
look like Figure 14.34.

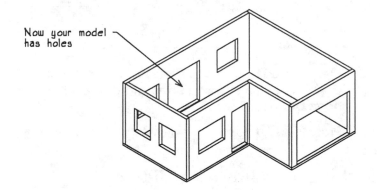

Now your model
has holes

Figure 14.34: You're drawing should look like this.

If your voids don't hide correctly

The most common problems with opening slabs are:

- The opening slabs were not drawn in the *same direction*
as the master slab.

- Slabs were drawn *upside down* (Z base was higher than Z
height).

- Openings were created at the same Z-base or height as the master slab. Boundaries for the opening slab cannot be coincident with any boundary of the master slab.

- Opening slabs touched or crossed over each other.

- Opening slabs were created outside the master slab, or not aligned. They must be completely *inside* and aligned.

- Opening slabs were created with a different thickness. They must be the same thickness to avoid problems.

Drawing the roof

The roof is easy to add because DataCAD has a special macro just for roof development. Before you start drawing the roof, however, you need to add a few sketch lines to your drawing, in order to create an intersection snap point for your roof layout.

1. Press ⌈Tab⌉ to go to your **Roof** layer.

2. Pick the **[Ortho]** button in the control panel to return to the plan view.

3. Using object snap with *Orthomode ON* (⌈O⌉), draw the temporary sketch lines shown in Figure 14.35. Make sure to draw the lines out long enough to make them easy to pick to erase later.

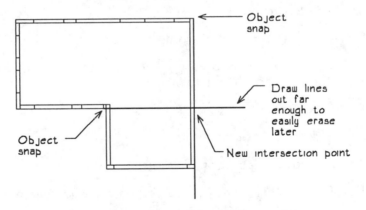

Figure 14.35: Draw these temporary lines.

4. Press ⌈SHIFT⌉ ⌈M⌉ to go to the Macros menu.

5. Pick the **ROOFIT** macro.

Setting up the Roof-It macro

Like most macros, you need to adjust the settings in the menus before you use the Roof-It macro the first time. Then the macro saves these settings (for all drawings) until you change them.

You need to know the *pitch* of your roof and the *top of plate* height, along with the *overhang* measurement. These are shown in Figure 14.36.

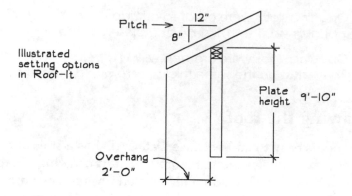

Figure 14.36: The plate, pitch and overhang for model.

1. The first part of the roof you'll create is a Hip roof. Pick **Hip** to make it active.

2. The first option should say **RectRoof**. If it says **PolyRoof**, pick it to change it to **RectRoof**. This allows you to create the roof by picking a rectangular area.

3. Make sure the **Join** option is OFF. This option joins a new roof to an existing roof.

4. Pick **Settings**.

5. Pick **PlatHgt** (plate height).

6. Type in: **9.10** and press ENTER . (Remember to reset your current Z-base back to 0!)

7. Pick **Pitch**.

8. Pick the **8:12** option.

9. Pick **RoofThck** (roof thickness).

10. Type in: **.10** to create a 10"-thick roof, which will look like a fascia, and press ENTER .

11. Pick **Overhng**.

12. Type in **2** and press ENTER to create a 2'-0" overhang.

13. Make sure the option in the *FO* spot says **SoffIncl** (inclined soffit). If it now says **SoffHorz**, pick it to change it to **SoffIncl**.

14. Also make sure the option in the *SI* spot says **FaciaPlb** (plumb, vertical, fascia). If it say **FaciaSqr**, pick it to change it to **FaciaPlb**.

15. Press mouse button 3 to exit the Settings menu and return to the main Roof It menu.

Adding the hip roof

Three points define a roof. The first two define the *lower edge of the eave*, along the top of the plate, and the roof *length*. The last pick defines the *width*. Figure 14.37 shows the order of these picks.

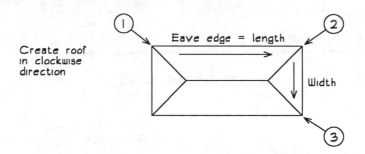

Figure 14.37: The correct pick order for a roof.

Note: *If you pick the roof in the wrong direction, it will be made upside down. This technique doesn't work well for the ridge of your main roof, but this method can come in handy to create a small valley area.*

---

1. Press the Z key and set the Z-base back to **0**, and press ENTER twice. Even though the plate height is calculated from the absolute 0 elevation, it's a good habit to reset the 0 elevation so that you don't make mistakes later.

2. Object snap to the first corner of your house, shown as step 1 in Figure 14.38. This will be the first corner of the length along the eave.

3. Object snap to the second corner, shown as step 2 in Figure 14.38. This second point defined the length along the eave edge.

4. Object snap to the corner on the other side, as shown as step 3 in Figure 14.38. This pick defines the hip end and the width.

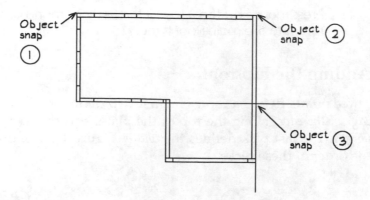

Figure 14.38: Object snap order for the roof of your house.

5. The hip roof section is calculated and drawn, as in Figure 14.39.

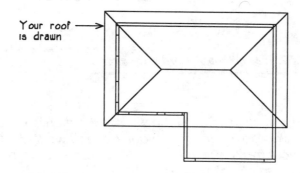

Figure 14.39: The roof is drawn.

Joining a roof section

The next part of your roof is *joined* to the first, and it's a *gable* roof.

1. Pick **Join** to make it active.

2. Pick **Gable**.

3. Pick **Settings**.

4. Pick **EndWall** to turn it OFF. This option automatically models an end wall to fill in the top of your walls, which works great with Gable. However, you'll learn how to add a peak to your wall to fill in this area.

5. Press mouse button 3 to exit back to the main Roof It menu.

6. Object snap to the corner shown as step 1 in Figure 14.40. This point indicates the first corner of the eave edge.

7. Object snap to the second corner, which is shown by step 2 in Figure 14.40. This point defines the length of the eave edge.

8. Object snap to the corner shown as step 3 in Figure 14.40. This point defines width of the gable.

9. Now pick the front edge line of the existing roof plane you want to butt this roof to, shown as step 4 in Figure 14.40. You might have to pick the edge twice, if the first time the pick grabs the fascia instead (you'll get a message that you can't join a roof to this surface, and a chance to try again).

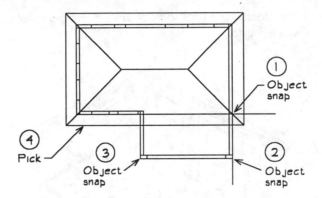

Figure 14.40: Four steps to join a roof to an existing roof.

10. The roof will be drawn, as in Figure 14.41.

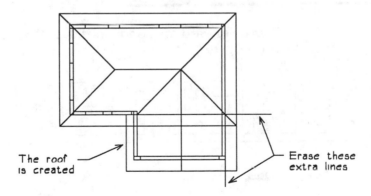

Figure 14.41: The roof is done.

11. Press Ⓔ and erase the extra temporary lines, as noted in Figure 14.41.

12. Press SHIFT Ⓕ to file your drawing.

Checking the model with Quick Shader

You can also use the Quick Shader to see how your model is progressing.

1. Pick the **Isometric View** tool, shown in Figure 14.42. You might have to pick the **Scroll Back** tool to find it.

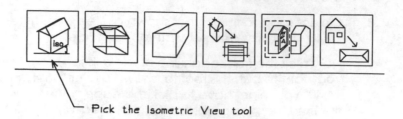

Pick the Isometric View tool

Figure 14.42: The Isometric tool.

2. How does your roof look so far? It should look similar to Figure 14.43.

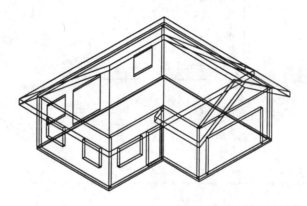

Figure 14.43: Your model should look like this.

3. Pick the **Scroll Forward** tool, and pick the **QShader** tool, shown in Figure 14.44.

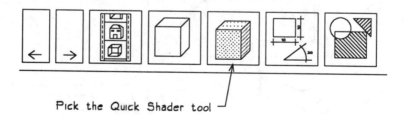

Pick the Quick Shader tool

Figure 14.44: The QShader tool.

4. Pick **LightL** (light source from the left side), **NoEdge**, and **All** to make them active.

5. Pick any other active options to turn them OFF.

6. Pick **Begin**.

7. Notice that there's a hole in the front wall, under the gable roof. You'll fix this next. Your drawing should look similar to Figure 14.45, but shaded in color.

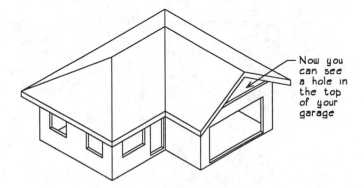

Figure 14.45: Your model should look like this.

Defining a new working plane

So far in your drawing, you have been creating geometry based on viewing from the *ortho*, or plan view. When in this view, the X, Y, and Z coordinates have been very helpful in creating the items in your drawing.

Your *working coordinates* have been based on the ortho plane. You know this as X is across the screen, Y is up and down, and Z is coming out at you. And, up to now, you've drawn in the plan view.

Using an edit plane

Now you're going to draw in another view in order to pull up a peak in your wall to meet the gable roof. You'll do this using the *Edit Plane* feature in DataCAD. When you draw in another plane, it also becomes your view plane, and it's very easy to work with. The X coordinate will still be across the screen, Y is still up and down, and Z still comes out at you. You're just looking at your model from a *new working view*.

1. Pick the **[V]** button in the control panel to go to the 3D Views menu.

2. Pick **EditPlne**. This option allows you to set up a new editing view plane.

3. Pick **Reset**, which returns you to the Ortho view and resets the edit plane.

4. Object snap to the front edge of the garage, as indicated in Figure 4.46.

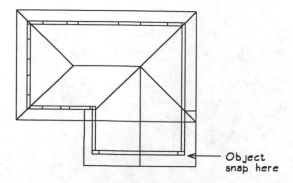

Figure 14.46: Object snap to the front of the garage.

5. Move your cursor, and you'll see an arrow attached to it, and a line indicating an "edit plane" moves along with the arrow.

6. With orthomode ON (press ⊡ until it's on), the working plane will move to 45-degree increments. Move the cursor back into the garage, and pick so that the plane line is flat against the front of the garage and the viewing direction is into the garage, as shown in Figure 14.47.

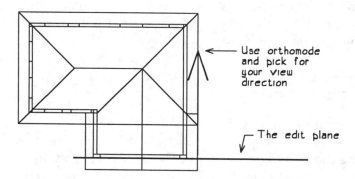

Figure 14.47: Pick with orthomode on for the edit plane.

7. Your view angle will change, and the face of the garage will be flipped parallel to the screen, as in Figure 14.48.

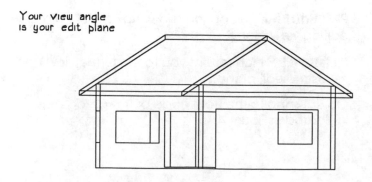

Figure 14.48: Your new edit plane.

8. Press mouse button 3 to exit.

Modifying the wall slab for the gabled roof

You'll use the function called *Partial* to modify the slab into a peaked wall. This option allows you to add, delete, and move vertices (corners) of your slabs.

1. Pick the **3D Entity** tool, shown in Figure 14.49. You might have to pick the **ScrlBack** tool first. (Or press SHIFT J .)

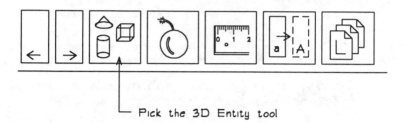

Pick the 3D Entity tool

Figure 14.49: The 3D Entity tool.

2. Pick **Slab**.

3. Pick the **Partial** option.

4. Pick the **AddVrtex** option.

5. Pick (don't object snap) somewhere around the middle of the top line defining the garage wall, as illustrated in Figure 14.50.

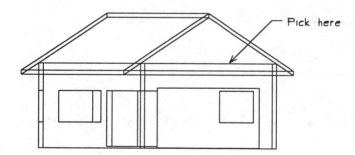

Pick here

Figure 14.50: Pick here.

6. Move your cursor, and you'll see you're dragging a new corner of the wall!

    The new vertex should be on the *front wall* of the garage, not the back wall. (This would be easy to tell because the back wall extends the entire length of the house, while the front wall only is the size of the front of the garage.) Since your work plane is on the front wall, you probably won't have this problem,

Modeling walls, openings and roofs

shown in Figure 14.51. However, if you grab the back wall by accident, press mouse button 3 and try again.

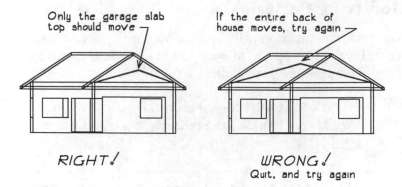

Figure 14.51: Grab the front of the garage, not the back.

7. Once you have the correct slab, move your cursor up to the roof peak and object snap (Figure 14.52).

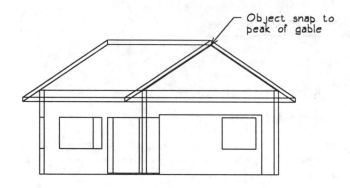

Figure 14.52: Object snap to the gable roof peak.

8. Press mouse button 3 to quit.

9. Press [SHIFT] [F] to file your drawing.

Creating a shaded perspective of your finished house

1. Pick the **Set Perspective** tool, as shown in Figure 14.53. You might have to **Scroll Back** to find it.

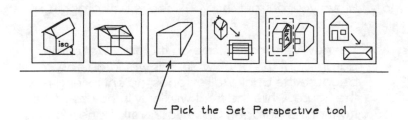

Pick the Set Perspective tool

Figure 14.53: The Set Perspective tool.

2.   To create your perspective view, pick as shown in Figure 14.54.

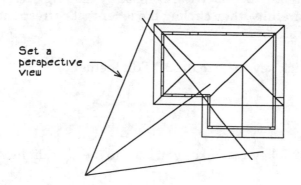

Set a
perspective
view

Figure 14.54: Pick for your perspective.

3.   Pick the **Scroll Forward** tool, and pick the **QShader** tool, shown in Figure 14.55.

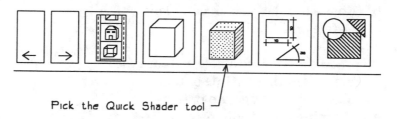

Pick the Quick Shader tool

Figure 14.55: The QShader tool.

4.   Pick **Begin**. Your drawing should look similar to Figure 14.56, but shaded in color.

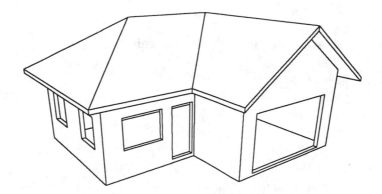

Figure 14.56: Your model should look like this.

Quitting DataCAD

1.   Press `ALT` `Q` to quit DataCAD.

2.   Pick **Yes** to save your drawing, or press `Y` .

DataCAD exercise 13

Please complete the following exercise by reading each question carefully, then circling the letter that corresponds to the correct answer.

1. The quick key to go to the 3D Edit menu is:
   a. ⌊J⌋ .
   b. ⌊V⌋ .
   c. ⌊Y⌋ .

2. The quick key that takes you back to the 2D Edit menu, is:
   a. ⌊S⌋ .
   b. ⌊E⌋ .
   c. ⌊;⌋ .

3. Before a hole can be punched in a slab wall, you must:
   a. Define a slab that will be processed as an opening.
   b. Rotate the slab into an edit plane.
   c. Define an edit plane.

4. To process a slab into a hole, you use the:
   a. **Slab, Partial, AddHole** options.
   b. **Slab, Voids, AddVoid** options.
   c. **Openings, Add** options.

5. The wall slab that will have a hole cut out of it is called the:
   a. Void.
   b. Master slab.
   c. Opening slab.

6. The slab that becomes the hole is called the:
   a. Void.
   b. Master slab.
   c. Window slab.

7. To easily create a roof, you use:
   a. Vertical slabs.
   b. Roof slabs.
   c. Roof-It macro.

8. To define the pitch of your roof, you:
   a. Define a Z-base and height.
   b. Pick a pitch option, such as **4:12**.
   c. Input an angle.

9. In order to draw something in a view other than the Ortho view, you use the:
   a. **Perspective** option.
   b. **EditPlne** option.
   c. **New View** option.

10. In order to add a new corner to a slab, you use:
    a. **Slab, Partial, AddVrtex.**
    b. **Slab, Partial, NewCornr.**
    c. **Corner, AddNew.**

11. To bring in a new tool bar, you pick:
    a. **Settings, Icons, NewFile.**
    b. **Display, Menus, IconFile.**
    c. **Settings, ToolBars, LoadFile.**

12. If you don't see the tool in the tool bar, you might try to:
    a. Scroll forward or back to see if it's there.
    b. Hold the `CTRL` key down to see the other tools.
    c. Turn off the tool bar because the option's not there.

13. Once you set all of the options in a Macro:
    a. They stay set, but only for the drawing you're in.
    b. They change back to the original defaults once you leave the macro.
    c. They stay set until the next time you use it, even in another drawing.

14. When you pick another tool bar to use, such as the 3D tool bar:
    a. It stays set even when you go to another drawing.
    b. The bar only is set for the current drawing.
    c. You can't reset it back for the current drawing.

Modeling windows and doors

Modeled windows and doors

Adding realistic windows and doors to your model enhances it and is easy to do because DataCAD has a special macro for this.

Here are some of the things you'll learn in this chapter:

- Using the AEC_MODL macro.
- Filling in the form for window definition.
- Creating modeled windows.
- Creating modeled doors.
- Using the window options to create a roll-up garage door.
- Extracting a front elevation.
- Adding textures to your front elevation and hidden line perspective.

The AEC_MODL macro

Like the ROOF IT macro, the AEC_MODL macro provides you with additional menus that are specifically designed for the creation of windows and doors.

1. Press [SHIFT] [M] to go to the Macro menu.

2. Pick the **AEC_MODL** macro.

3.   The menu will appear for the macro. The two main choices on this menu are *Doors* and *Windows*. At the bottom of the menu, there are options that you can use to go to *3D Views* and to the *Hide* menu.

Note: *Whenever you're in a macro, pressing a quick key or mouse button 3 will drop you back into regular DataCAD.*

---

4.   The first option you'll use is to create windows. Pick the **Windows** option.

5.   Pick **In Plan** until it's active. This option allows you to define the window in the plan view, as opposed to an elevation view. (You would need to define an *Edit Plane* to use the **In Elev** option.)

6.   In the Window menu, several options are displayed. You could go into each of the options separately, or use the *Window Form* feature, which displays all of the options in a one page format.

7.   Pick **WndwForm**.

8.   Your cursor will be set on the first option, *Sill Hght*. To move your cursor in this screen, press `Tab`. to go backwards, press `SHIFT` `Tab`.

9.   Once making a change, you must press `ENTER` to accept it.

10. The following list is a suggestion for your window set up for your model project. Later, you'll customize these settings for your own models. The resulting window will look like Figure 15.1.

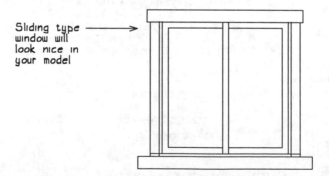

Sliding type window will look nice in your model

Figure 15.1: The settings will create a sliding window.

---

11. Remember to press `ENTER` after every option change. (If you press `Tab` to go to the next option, the change you made will not stay.)

Sill Hght = **3**
Head Hght = **6.8**
Unit Type = press `SPACE` to set **Sliding**

      % open = **0**
    Casing (Outside Trim):
        At Head = press SPACE to set **Yes**
        Width = **.4**
        Thickness = **.1**
        Extension = **.1**
        At Jambs = press SPACE to set **Yes**
        Width = **.4**
        Thickness = **.1**
        At Sill = press SPACE to set **Yes**
        Width = **.4**
        Thickness = **.1**
        Extension = **.4**
    Trim (Inside Trim):
        At Head = press SPACE to set **No**
        At Jamb = press SPACE to set **No**
        At Sill = press SPACE to set **No**
  Head = press SPACE to set **No**
  Jamb = press SPACE to set **Yes**
        Jamb width = **.4**
        Jamb Thk = **.1**
  Sill = press SPACE to set **Yes**
        Sill Thk = **.1**
        In Ext = **.2**
        Out Ext = **.2**
        Side Ext = **.3**
  Sash = press SPACE to set **Yes**
        Sash width = **.2**
        Sash Thk = **.1**
        Offset = **0**
  Muntins = press SPACE to set **Yes**
  Glass = press SPACE to set **Yes**
        Glass Thk = **..1/8**
        Qty Horz = **1**
        Qty Vert = **1**

12. Once you've finished making your changes, remember to press ENTER on the last option you changed.

13. Press ESC to accept all of your changes. *Don't use mouse button 3 to exit this form, or all of your changes will be lost.*

Note: *Even though the windows you're creating don't have muntins, for some reason the program wouldn't create a glass panel without the "Muntins" option set to "Yes."*

Creating the modeled windows

Creating the windows is easy, you just object snap to the openings. It takes three object snaps. The first two define the *length* of the window along the inside of the wall, and the last one defines the *width* of the wall and the outside.

1. Press [Tab] to go to the **Windows** layer.

2. Pick the **[W]** button in the control panel and pick two points to zoom into the area shown in Figure 15.2.

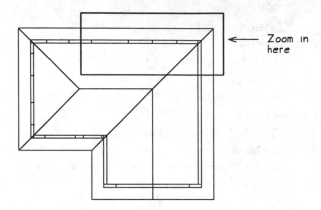

Figure 15.2: Zoom into this area.

3. Press mouse button 3 to return to the Windows menu.

4. Notice the current Z-base setting (displayed in the message area). Since the sill height is caculated from the base, it should be **0**. If it isn't, press the **Z** key and set it now. (The height doesn't matter.)

5. Object snap to the first inside edge of one of your window openings, as in step 1 in Figure 15.3.

6. Object snap to the second edge, as in step 2 in Figure 15.3. This defines the inside and length of the window.

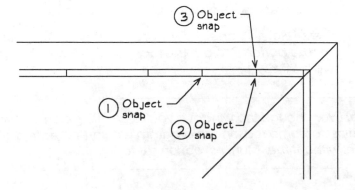

Figure 15.3: The object snaps for your first window.

7.   Then object snap to the outside corner to define the wall width, as in step 3 in Figure 15.3.

8.   The window is created, as in Figure 15.4.

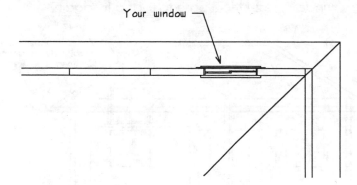

Figure 15.4: The window is drawn.

Saving your settings

You can save the window set up for future use.

1.   Pick **SaveWind**.

2.   Type in a name for your window file, such as: **slid1pne** (slider type window with single pane), and press ⌜ENTER⌟.

Getting a front view of your model

You should check how the first window positioned in your model by viewing the front elevation.

1.   Pick the **[Front]** button in the control panel. You might not see your model at this point because it's off the view window.

2.   Pick the **[R]** button to recalculate the view window. Your model should look like Figure 15.5.

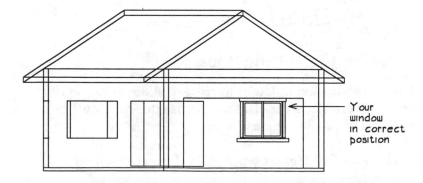

Figure 15.5: The sliding window should look like this.

3. A common mistake that occurs at this point is the window is up in the air too high for the opening. This would be due to an improper Z-base setting, as in Figure 15.6. You would press SHIFT < to delete the window, reset the Z-base to **0**, and try again.

Figure 15.6: The window is too high due to Z-base setting.

4. Pick the **[Ortho]** button in the control panel to continue creating your windows.

5. Follow these same steps, using object snap, to create the rest of your windows, as indicated in Figure 15.7.

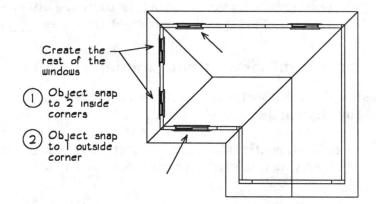

Figure 15.7: Create the rest of the windows.

6. Press SHIFT F to file your drawing.

Creating the sliding door

There is an option in Doors to create a sliding door, but it doesn't have glass panels. You can use the Windows function to create your sliding glass door.

1. Pick **Sill Hght**, change it to **.2** and press ENTER .

2. Object snap to the opening for the rear slider, as shown in Figure 15.8.

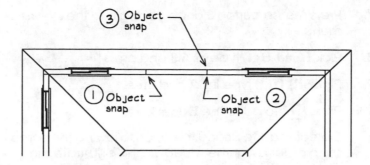

Figure 15.8: Object snap to 3 points for the rear sliding door.

3.   You can pick the **[Back]** button in the control panel to check your process. Your model should look like Figure 15.9. You might have to pick **[R]** to recalculate your view.

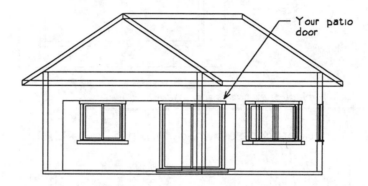

Figure 15.9: The back view of your model.

4.   Pick **[Ortho]** to return to your plan view.

Adding the front door

You'll use the Door feature of this macro to create the front door of your model.

1.   Press mouse button 3 to exit the Windows menu and return to the main AEC Model menu.

2.   Pick the **Doors** option. In this menu, you'll use the options to make your settings, as opposed to using the DoorForm.

3.   Make sure the **In Plan** option is active.

4.   Pick the **UnitType** option.

5.   Pick **Single** to make it active.

6.   Pick the **% open** option, set it to **0** and press [ENTER] . This will result in a door that is closed.

7. Press mouse button 3 once, to return to the Doors menu.

8. Pick **Head Hgt**, type in: **6.8** and press [ENTER] .

9. Pick **Sill Hgt**, type in: **.2** and press [ENTER] .

10. Press [Tab] to go to the **Doors** layer.

11. Object snap to define the door, following the same snap order as for the windows. This is illustrated in Figure 15.10.

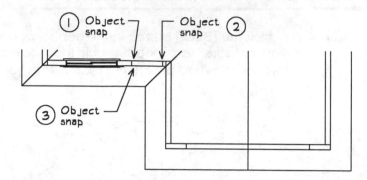

Figure 15.10: Object snap to the front door opening.

12. Your door will be drawn, as shown in Figure 15.11.

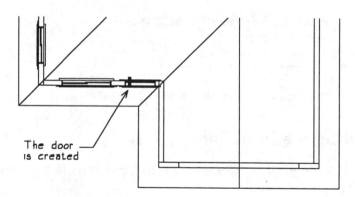

Figure 15.11: The entry door.

13. Press [SHIFT] [F] to file your drawing.

Adding the garage door

There is no option to create a *garage door*. But you can use the capabilities in the Windows menu, adjusting the panes, to create what looks like a roll-up door.

This door will "hide" well and look good in your shaded image. (If you were going to take this model into a rendering package, such as RenderStar, you'd want to change the glass panes to another color so that you could give them an opaque surface quality.)

1. Pick **WndwForm**.

2. Change the **Sill Hght** to **..1/8**.

3. Change **Head Hght** to **7**.

4. Set the **Unit Type** to **Fixed**.

5. Change the **Glass, Qty Vert = 4**, or 5 if you want more panels in your door.

6. Once you've made these changes to the form, press [ENTER] on the last option, then press [ESC] to exit and save your changes.

7. Object snap to the garage door opening, as shown in Figure 15.12.

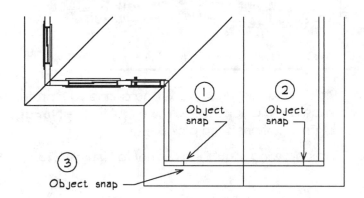

Figure 15.12: The object snaps for your garage door.

8. The garage door will be created, as in Figure 15.13. Pick the **[Front]** button in the control panel to see it.

9. Press [E] to go to Erase (or pick the **Erase** tool), and pick **Entity**. Erase the bottom sills of the garage and the patio door, also shown in Figure 15.13.

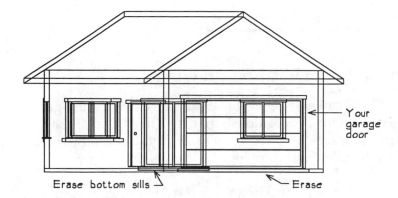

Figure 15.13: Your garage door. Erase these sills.

Creating a shaded imade of your model

Follow these hints to create a perspective shaded image of your model.

1. Use the **Set Perspective** tool to define a perspective of your model, or use the perspective you set up before by picking the **[Persp]** button in the control panel. Your model might look like Figure 15.14.

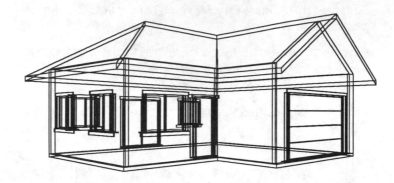

Figure 15.14: Your perspective might look like this.

2. Pick the Quick Shader tool, and define your preferences for a quick shade. You might try the **NoEdge**, **Light L** options, then pick **Begin**.

3. Your drawing should look similar to Figure 15.15.

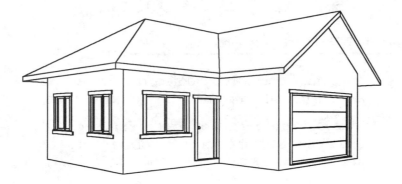

Figure 15.15: The shaded perspective.

Creating an elevation drawing

The model can also be used to extract an elevation image. Use these hints to accomplish that. You'll notice that the hidden line removal becomes slower as you add more modeled entities to your drawing.

1. Pick the **[Front]** button, and **[R]** to recalculate a view window.

2. Use the **Hide** tool, or press [SHIFT] [Y] to go to Hide. Set **SaveImg** to active. Pick **Options**, and set **DelDoubl** to eliminate duplicate lines. Use **Join** so that colinear lines are joined into one line (instead of many fragmented lines), and **BackFace** to ignore the part of the drawing that's behind the elevation to speed up the hide. **Exit** the Options menu and pick **Begin**.

3. Pick **NewLyr** and name it **FrntElev**, pick **On**.

4. Press [L] to go to Layers, pick **ActvOnly**, then pick **FrntElev** to make it the only displayed layer, and **Exit**. Pick **[Ortho]** to return to your plan view, and **[R]**.

5. Press [E] to go to Erase and, using **Entity**, pick the extra lines you don't need for this view, such as the lines where two slabs come together. **Exit** Erase and add any details you wish (such as glass accent lines) or effects you desire.

6. Your drawing should look like Figure 15.16.

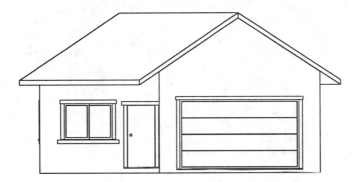

Figure 15.16: The front elevation cleaned up.

7. Press [H] for the Hatch menu to add siding texture, either using **Cement** (Scale = **70** or so) in spots here and there to show stucco, or **Line** (Scale = **192** for 6" panels, **284** for 12" panels) to illustrate wood siding. You can also use other hatching to add shadows or a roof texture.

8. Your drawing might look similar to Figure 15.17.

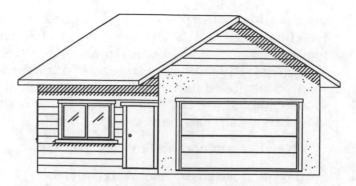

Figure 15.17: A front elevation with hatching.

9. The same effects can be added to a perspective view of the model. For example, Figure 15.18 shows the rear perspective with hatching added.

The back perspective of your model

Figure 15.18: The rear perspective.

DataCAD exercise 14

Please complete the following exercise by reading each question carefully, then circling the letter that corresponds to the correct answer.

1. The quick key that takes you to the DataCAD Macro menu, is:
    a. ⌨ALT ⌨M .
    b. ⌨SHIFT ⌨M .
    c. ⌨M .

2. The macro that facilitates the creation of modeled doors and windows, is called:
    a. DCAD_AEC.
    b. DRS&WNDW.
    c. AEC_MODL.

3. To change the type of window that you want to create, you use the:
    a. **UnitType** option.
    b. **WindwTyp** option.
    c. **Change** option.

4. To define the number of panes in your window, you use the:
    a. **Lites** option.
    b. **Panes** option.
    c. **Qty Vert** option.

5. To create a sliding glass door, you can use:
    a. **Windows**, and define **Sliding** as the type.
    b. **Door**, and set **Slider**.
    c. There is no way to create a sliding glass door.

6. When using the Hide function:
    a. It works fast, no matter how many modeled entities in your drawing.
    b. The windows and doors don't hide.
    c. The more items you add, the slower it will work, so be careful, because a hide can take an hour or more in a very complex building.

7. Macros:
    a. Shouldn't be used very often because they're only for advanced users.
    b. Are a great way to save steps.
    c. Don't come with DataCAD.

8. A roll-up garage door can be created using:
   a. **Windows, Fixed,** and adding as many panes as you want to look like panels.
   b. **Doors, Garage, Roll up,** and adding as many panels as necessary.
   c. **Doors, Paneled,** and adding as many panels as necessary.

9. While using the WndwForm menu, if you make a change to an option, you must press:
   a. [Tab] to save it and go to the next option.
   b. [ENTER] to save it and go to the next option.
   c. [SHIFT] [Tab] to save it and go to the next option.

10. When exiting the WndwForm menu, you can save your changes by pressing:
    a. Mouse button 3 to exit.
    b. [ENTER] to exit.
    c. [ESC] to exit.

11. To define a front view of your drawing, you use the:
    a. **[Front]** button in the control panel.
    b. **[South Elev]** button in the control panel.
    c. **Front** tool in the tool bar.

12. The **[Ortho]** button:
    a. Turns on the orthomode for drawing straight lines.
    b. Returns you to the plan view of your drawing.
    c. Returns you to the last elevation view.

13. After changing all the settings in the **Window Form** of the AEC_MODL, you:
    a. Can save them to a file, using **SaveWind.**
    b. Can't save them, so you should write them down to remember them.
    c. Shouldn't exit the macro until you're done so that you don't lose your settings.

14. When creating a door or window in the AEC_MODL program macro, you:
    a. Are guided through the use of it by the user prompts.
    b. Must remember everything because there are no user prompts.
    c. Must set everything each time you use it, since the settings will not stay.

APPENDIX

Answers to exercises

Chapter 2 - Exercise 1

1.	a	7.	a	13.	a
2.	b	8.	c	14.	c
3.	b	9.	b	15.	b
4.	c	10.	b	16.	a
5.	b	11.	b		
6.	c	12.	c		

Chapter 3 - Exercise 2

1.	b	7.	c	13.	b
2.	a	8.	a	14.	a
3.	c	9.	a		
4.	a	10.	b		
5.	b	11.	a		
6.	c	12.	b		

Chapter 4 - Exercise 3

1.	a	7.	c	13.	b	19.	a
2.	c	8.	b	14.	c	20.	c
3.	b	9.	c	15.	b		
4.	b	10.	a	16.	a		
5.	b	11.	c	17.	a		
6.	a	12.	a	18.	b		

Chapter 5 - Exercise 4

1.	b	7.	b	13.	c
2.	a	8.	a	14.	b
3.	b	9.	b	15.	a
4.	c	10.	c	16.	a
5.	b	11.	b	17.	a
6.	a	12.	a		

Chapter 6 - Exercise 5

1.	a	7.	b	13.	b
2.	a	8.	c	14.	a
3.	c	9.	a	15.	a
4.	b	10.	b	16.	a
5.	b	11.	c		
6.	c	12.	b		

Chapter 7 - Exercise 6

1.	c	7.	a	13.	c
2.	b	8.	a	14.	c
3.	c	9.	c	15.	a
4.	a	10.	c	16.	c
5.	a	11.	a		
6.	c	12.	a		

Chapter 8 - Exercise 7

1.	b	6.	a
2.	b	7.	c
3.	c	8.	c
4.	c	9.	a
5.	b	10.	b

Chapter 9 - Exercise 8

1.	b	7.	b	13.	c
2.	c	8.	a	14.	b
3.	a	9.	a	15.	a
4.	b	10.	b	16.	b
5.	b	11.	c	17.	b
6.	c	12.	c		

Chapter 10 - Exercise 9

1.	a	7.	c	13.	c	19.	b
2.	b	8.	a	14.	a	20.	a
3.	b	9.	b	15.	a		
4.	c	10.	c	16.	c		
5.	a	11.	c	17.	b		
6.	b	12.	b	18.	c		

Chapter 11 - Exercise 10

1.	b	6.	c	11.	a
2.	b	7.	b	12.	a
3.	c	8.	c	13.	b
4.	b	9.	a		
5.	a	10.	c		

Chapter 12 - Exercise 11

1. a	7. a	13. c	19. b
2. b	8. b	14. b	20. c
3. b	9. c	15. a	21. a
4. a	10. b	16. b	22. b
5. a	11. c	17. b	23. b
6. c	12. a	18. c	24. a

Chapter 13 - Exercise 12

1. a	7. a	13. b
2. b	8. a	14. c
3. b	9. b	15. a
4. a	10. a	16. a
5. c	11. c	17. c
6. b	12. c	18. b

Chapter 14 - Exercise 13

1. a	6. a	11. b
2. c	7. c	12. a
3. a	8. b	13. c
4. b	9. b	14. a
5. b	10. a	

Chapter 15 - Exercise 14

1. b	6. c	11. a
2. c	7. b	12. b
3. a	8. a	13. a
4. c	9. b	14. a
5. a	10. c	

Index

Symbols

A

B

C

D

T

About the author

Carol Buehrens is a CAD Course Designer/Training Specialist. Since she became involved with CAD in 1975, she hasn't stopped writing.

Carol began her interest in this highly specialized area as a general machinist, from which she entered the design drafting field, just as computer-aided-drafting was becoming popular. Carol later perused integrating CAD into the architectural design industry.

Companies for which Carol has designed CAD training programs, course curriculum, and training materials for 2D and 3D CAD engineering and architectural systems, include Northrop Corporation - Advanced Systems, Bechtel Corporation, McDonnell Douglas Company, GE/Calma Corporation, Calcomp, ComputerVision Corporation- VersaCAD, CR/CADD, Desktop Productions, and CADKEY Incorporated.

Carol writes magazine and newspaper articles and you can read her monthly contributions in *Key Solutions*, a magazine written for CADKEY and DataCAD software users. She also is the author of children's books and an occasional mystery novel.